James Frehmer

Oct. 1930.

INTERVIEW WITH INDIA

Books by John Frederick Muehl

AMERICAN SAHIB

INTERVIEW WITH INDIA

JOHN FREDERICK MUEHL

Interview with
INDIA

AN *Asia* BOOK

THE JOHN DAY COMPANY   NEW YORK

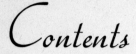Contents

*A glossary of Indian words will
be found at the end of the book*

I N D I A

RAJPUTANA

NAWANAGAR

SUIGAM

ABU

Rann Bursad

MEHSANA

Halvad

Landra · · Viravoli

KATHIAWAR Bhal-Bundawa

ZAINABAD
GUJARAT

DAMAN

BOMBAY

POONA

MAHA-
RASHTRA

Baramoti HYDERABAD
Khed
Chiplun

SANGAMESHWAR

BELGUAM

Kisna R.

KARWAR

HUBLI

KOORNOOL

Binge
Shadur

Kanara Coast

TAMILNAD MADRAS

CALICUT

TANJORE

Trichur · DEVIKOLAM

MADURA

- - - - - AUTHOR'S ROUTE
▲▲▲▲▲ MYSORE FORESTS
////// COMMUNIST AREA

Scale of Miles

0   100   200   300   400   500

M.A.Thomas

INDIAN OCEAN

Cape Comorin

Introductory

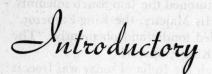

Introductory

[1]

THE Maharaja of Navanagar rose from his chair with a certain elephantine dignity. The meal was over; at any rate he had finished, and so now it was time for the toasts to begin. His dissipated face hung down in the frown that has been almost perpetual since his last facial paralysis, and as he tried to smile it was with a great upward heave that only managed to distort the festoons of flesh. He was dressed, as always, in white trousers and black coat, his one concession to the occasion being the ruby buttons. We had all hoped to see the fabulous emerald necklace, but it had not been his particular whim to wear it this year. The blue circles under his eyes were more apparent than usual, for the holiday season had been trying for the Jam Saheb, so that now, with his pink party hat on his head, he looked like some sad, performing Saint Bernard.

We knew what would happen. The Maharaja Jam Saheb would propose his regular toast to the British monarch; for Navanagar was a "state" and as in most of the others, the independence of India was just an ugly rumor there. There had been rumblings, that is true. Patel had made speeches and Nehru had spoken pointedly about "freedom for all Indians." Outside of the Palace there had been a few food riots and the life of the Navanagar Prime Minister had been threatened. But the Congress worker who had incited the people to this violence was safely behind bars as we sat down to our banquet. And the people of Navanagar were behind their mud walls as we raised our glasses of champagne for the toast.

3

"Ladies and gentlemen," intoned the Jam Saheb solemnly, "I give you the health of His Majesty, the King-Emperor." The seventy of us there cried loudly and obediently, "The health of His Majesty, the King-Emperor!"

It was appropriate. Though the India of today was free, it was an India of the past in which we were living. It was an India of the past and a feast of the past. It was fitting that it should end with a toast to the past.

On the fifteenth of August, I had stood on the maidan across from the secretariat in Bombay. I had watched, with the thousands of other spectators, the raising of the tricolored Indian flag. I had stood shoulder to shoulder with the sweepers and the coolies because I had not been able to get tickets for the ceremony, but I had one advantage—I could understand the speeches, for the majority were masterpieces of Oxford English. The crowds around me were restless and annoyed for it was their independence, but it was not their language. And I believe it was as early as that when I began to wonder just what this "Independence of India" would mean.

It had been a wonderful party at the Taj Hotel that night. We had drunk champagne on the fifteenth of August, too. We had talked glibly about the role of India in world affairs, and we had speculated on various government appointments. Masani would probably be the ambassador to America, and Madame Pandit would take over some department in Delhi. It was all arranged. We had thought of everything. India was free. It was all over, even the shouting.

There was one Indian industrialist who arrived quite drunk and began pouring his own whisky into our glasses of champagne, insisting that we drink it, "as a toast to India's triumph," though it tasted to most of us like too much of a good thing. The same gentleman later collapsed in an armchair and began declaiming between sobs upon the India of the Future. "Thish new nation," he cried passionately, "will

4

teach the whole world the values of Eastern spirituality!"
I myself drank enough so that the memory is confused.
When I think of it, the moralizing and the celebrating swim
together. Indeed, the whole week seems to blend in my mind
into a distorted pattern of rejoicing and revelry.

There were some Europeans who made dark predictions
and swore they would stay in their houses all week. They
were foolish. There has never been such joyous comradery
between Indians and Europeans as there was in Bombay.
One evening as I was trying to photograph a parade, shooting
blindly over the heads of the crowd before me, a dignified
old Parsi squatted down in the street and suggested that I
climb on his shoulders for a better view. I watched school-
boys, English and Indian together, singing patriotic songs
in both of their languages, and I shouted myself hoarse with
my Indian friends, crying, "Victory to India! Victory to
everybody!"

During the nights the streets were a blaze of decorations;
whole buildings were strung with thousands of lights. The
municipal streetcars had been converted into floats and even
some automobiles were painted green, white, and saffron.
There were teas at the clubs, parties at the consulates, ban-
quets at hotels, and speeches in the parks. It was like Christ-
mas and New Year's rolled into one.

And then it came time to take down the tree.

On the twentieth of August I opened my eyes to a gray
and dismal monsoon morning. The fortuitous break in the
rains had ended and sheets of water were beating against
my window. I opened my eyes, but I closed them again.
I had a headache, and there was a terrible taste in my mouth.
I rolled over on my pillow and went back to sleep, and I
expect there were many who did the same.

But we did not sleep long. By noon the radio was relaying
the terrible news from the Punjab. Matter-of-fact announcers
were telling us about mass murder in the same tones they
use for weather reports. We held our heads. It was the morn-

5

ing after. We had to pay for the fun we'd had. The champagne was gone. The hilarity was gone. And a lot of foggy optimism was gone.

For weeks the horrible news filtered down, though the government was busy censoring and denying. For weeks the leaders accused each other like mad children splashing in a pool of blood. The foreign press exploited the whole thing, but it did not exaggerate; there could be no exaggeration. Even a well-trained journalist can do little to improve on wholesale murder, rape, and mass torture.

It was a comfort to those of us who had argued for independence to say that the British were to blame for the whole thing. It was probably true that if there had been no partition there would not have been any Punjab massacres. But however satisfying it had been for us foreigners, this line of reasoning was not to the point, for it would not go far toward resurrecting the dead or even toward restoring peace in the North. Whatever the heritage from British rule, it was the heritage with which India had to face the future. Whether the British had or hadn't encouraged the trouble, the British were gone. It was up to India to stop it.

Mahatma Gandhi fasted to the death, but like any practical man he stopped before he died. Pandit Nehru, like Lincoln, paced the floors at night, bewildered and unsure of the men around him. Vallabhai Patel made speeches denouncing the massacres precisely as all of the other leaders had done, but there were some who felt that Patel's expressions of sympathy were like those of the cat that had swallowed the canary.

And then the influx of refugees began. On the platforms of Victoria Station in Bombay they slept for weeks till others drove them off. They cooked in the waiting rooms, slept on the floor, and climbed down between the tracks to defecate. Once-wealthy merchants sat mournfully on the tin trunks that contained whatever they had been able to salvage. Decent Hindu women tried to offer themselves on street corners, humiliated and unsure how they might best go about it. There were babies who had got separated from their parents, parents who had seen their children killed. There were Sikhs who had already begun to plan their revenge, sitting sullenly, sharpening and whetting their knives.

They brought cholera with them, and fleas and ticks. But worst of all were the stories they brought. Untouchables incapable of writing their names could tell stories that would put Edgar Allan Poe to shame. And they could prove them, too! They could show you the woman whose nose had been cut off for the jewel she wore in it. You could watch the boy whose tongue was cut out trying to make himself understood by the others. An American correspondent tells a story of having shared a train compartment with a Moslem from Delhi. During the night a Sikh had slashed his throat, while the American was spared because he agreed not to warn him. The women from some entire villages were stolen, the men of others were castrated rather than killed. The servant of a friend of mine returned to his master shouting, "I've proven I was brave! I've killed a whole family!"

And yet what is the use of recounting the stories, of dramatizing them out of their historical importance? What is the use of describing the barbarism and implying that it has never existed before? There are no new horrors. There are no new tragedies. There are only new generations and new discoveries, and if the tragedy of the Punjab was confined to these, we could commiserate the victims and accept the whole thing. But the tragedy of the Punjab goes deeper than that. It was more than the sum of immediate suffering. It was bloody and it was disgusting and it was horrible, but it was something infinitely worse. It was unnecessary.

It was unnecessary in the sense that it involved no genuine conflict of interests between the peoples involved. It was unnecessary in the sense that it did not even satisfy the traditional hatred of the Hindus and the Moslems. It was worse than unnecessary in that it betrayed both groups in the hands

7

of their degenerate traditional leadership and blinded them to the fact that their most dangerous enemies were the men who had planned and financed their "crusades."

I had watched the Hindu Mahasabha at work during those six months following the country's independence. I had seen the elaborate discipline it built up around the flimsy fear of "invasion from Islam." I had heard the slogans of the Rastraya Swayanseval Sangh and I had listened to the speeches of the belligerent nationalists and I had laughed at the ridiculous charges they made until it occurred to me that not even the speakers believed them. It was the case of Germany and the Jews all over again, of a racist means to an economic end, for if the Sudras and harijans could be directed against the Moslems, the Brahmins and the Vaisyas could retain their positions.

It was like a quiet alliance, an unspoken conspiracy among all the forces of reaction in India, among the feudal landlords, the predatory Brahmins, the major princes, and the petty chiefs. The communal issue was their common device, but the status quo was their common interest. There were no agreements, but no agreements were necessary when all recognized a common enemy in progress. It was peculiar at first to see ascetics and contractors, financiers and holy men banding together, and yet nothing could have been less peculiar underneath than such a natural combination based on privilege and power. Millionaires began talking, moist eyed, about "Asia's traditions," and damning "the materialism of the West" to their workers. Ayurvedic quacks began quoting the scriptures to prove that M.D.s should be driven from India. The British moved out. The old guard moved in, with Bhagavad-Gitas in their hands and contracts in their pockets, and though what they displayed was a doctrine of Hindu solidarity, the Sanskrit small print contracted for much more. It contracted for continuing obedience to the old order, continuing acquiescence in the traditional abuses. It contracted

8

for submission to caste and authority in exchange for a fakir's cow-dung blessing.

On the fifteenth of August, India had got her independence. I had heard the cheering and I had seen the flag raising. On the fifteenth of August the British had withdrawn, and at the time that had seemed very important in itself. But during the six months that followed, I had begun to realize that while the British had left, their empire had not. All the component parts of the reactionary old order were intact, in perfect working order. There were the contractors and businessmen who had been encouraged to expect an exorbitant profit on government business. There were the clerks and officials to whom graft and nepotism seemed the logical compensation for approximate loyalty. There was the whole synthetic middle class that had been bred in the corruptions of an imperial system, willing to support any special interest that would allow its habitual abuses and dishonesties.

It was so subtle that we didn't even notice it at first, for we were far too preoccupied by the more immediate tragedies. And anyway, it was nothing to incite the people to violence. It was nothing they could fight about, or shout in the streets. Indeed, it was less than nothing at all. It was an absence of something where something should have been. It was a strengthening of old fetters that should have been broken; it was a stable land-tax rate that should have declined. It was not a revolution or a counterrevolution. It was nothing violent, or sudden, or loud. It was as if Freedom, like an application for a driver's license, had got lost under a shuffle of official papers.

Flag raisings in Bombay and murders in Amritsar. Champagne in hotels and blood in the streets. Traditional values and the world's highest death rate. Spirituality, leprosy, solidarity, and caste. All these fragments had stuck in the back of my mind, the accumulation of six months' history. And now they all seemed to rise to the surface as the Jam Saheb proposed his poetical New Year's toast.

9

For it was more than a toast to a British monarch. It was more than the indulgence of a stubborn old man. It was a salute to the triumph of reaction in India. The tyrant is dead! Long live the tyrants!

[2]

IT WAS an intimate occasion. In previous years, the seventy of us who shared the Jam Saheb's bounty would have scarcely constituted the legal quorum, let alone the sum of a respectable party. For the Jam Saheb, like most of the other Indian rulers, has been bred to a tradition of habitual self-indulgence. His parties are generally ridiculous affairs with jewelry and sandlewood carvings as favors, beginning around ten and working their way gradually to a bilious climax sometime long after midnight. But when the Maharaja of Bikaner had sent his regrets and it was clear that this evening was ruined in advance, both the practicality and the sentiment in which the Jam Saheb abounds had suggested just this small consolation gathering. We had eaten in one of the smaller dining rooms and we had even been deprived of the gold table service. Now that the toasts were concluded we adjourned not to the ballroom, but to a smaller throne room to get better acquainted.

There was an interesting assortment of people present. In a sense it is misleading to talk of an "assortment" for the fact is, almost everyone fitted into one of several categories, each of which was immediately distinguishable from the rest. There were the international businessmen and the palace habitués, the itinerate peddlers and the sophisticated barflies. There was the man who was going to train the natives to make airplanes and there was I, who was to visit and then laugh at the Jam Saheb. Even the Indians in the gathering, and there were surprisingly few, did not seem to be free from this spirit of competition, for although they laughed and joked together and pretended amiability, each seemed to be trying to turn the jokes against the others. Then of course there were the regular palace hangers-on, the innumerable relatives and aides-de-camp, who smiled whenever the Jam Saheb looked at them and laughed whenever he turned his back. They had all of the characteristics of degenerate courtiers, the petty jealousies and the impotent philanderings; their most clear-cut purpose seemed the seduction of each other's daughters, and even about that they were slobberingly vague. All these aides-de-camp were dressed like the Jam Saheb, but next to him they looked like will-less little puppets, only the Jam Saheb himself having the form and carriage to endow the clothes with anything like dignity.

The British Navy was well represented. There was a contingent of officers from a nearby base, who were ideal guests, too busy with their drinking to be anything but approximately polite and satisfied. But not so the businessmen. They crowded around the Jam Saheb with blueprints and models and financial statements, for to them the evening was just one more opportunity to get the elusive official ear. The majority of these men were guests of the state, which is to say, they were kept in the palace, free; the Jam Saheb seemed to prefer having them around indefinitely to granting an audience and refusing their requests. Bicycles, helicopters, race horses, and lotteries were dragged in and thrown on the trash heap of the conversation. Navanagar grew affluent, or cultured, or powerful, at least twenty-five times in the course of each hour. The men grinned and elbowed each other away, flattered the Jam Saheb, or threw their wives at him till at last the poor fellow, with a gesture of desperation, waved them all aside and wiped his brow.

The dancing began. It was a command performance with the Jam Saheb arranging the couples to his taste. "Here you," he would cry, singling out some lone male, "I want you to dance with this lady over here." There was a method in these selections, for the Jam Saheb intentionally seemed to choose the most obvious and embarrassing mismatches, short men being coupled with Amazon women, rivals being paired with each other's wives. They circled the floor in pretended enjoyment, attempted and achieved with varying success while the Navanagar State Band tootled away at strange rhythms far better adapted to cobra charming than dancing.

But the most uncomfortable moment of the evening came later, when one of the Jam Saheb's brothers proposed a toast to the ruler. He was quite drunk and what began as an elaborate statement of gratitude turned more and more to resemble a catty satire. He first thanked the Jam Saheb for the night's entertainment and for his generosity in having us share it with him, but in the end he was talking about "that spirit of self-sacrifice which he displays in allowing us to breathe his air." The toast struck home, for before it was finished the Jam Saheb was standing, gone pale with anger, and during the last few sentences he began shouting across the room, "Sit down, you fool! That's enough! Shut up!"

But it was a relief. It was like rain on a foggy evening when it comes to dispell the dampness of the atmosphere and though the old palace guard pretended to be shocked, to me this seemed but a logical climax. For throughout the evening I had been constantly aware of an ingrown bitterness that pervaded the whole function, of a showing of teeth and flexing of claws beneath all the pretense of *savoir-faire*. Another American who was sitting nearby leaned over and expressed my feelings exactly. "Thank God!" he said, in a loud stage whisper, "that's the kind of fighting I'm used to!"

It was later in the evening. There were just a few of us left, so we were drawn up in a circle around our host, conversing, or more properly, preparing opportunities for his facile and invariably final pronouncements.

"I can't understand it," the Jam Saheb sighed, rocking disconsolately back and forth on his hams. "Your American journalists are so unfair! They never tell the truth about the Indian States."

"Well, I suppose . . ." I was about to apologize for the journalists, but my host interrupted me with another loud pout.

"They know nothing about the Indian mentality," he insisted. "Absolutely nothing. These journalists discover that the villagers are poor and, in their naïveté, they conclude that they must therefore be unhappy." Everyone tittered obediently at the naïveté of the journalists and waited upon the Jam Saheb as upon the Delphic Oracle. "Not at all!" he muttered, preoccupied with a cashew nut that was eluding his fingers in the bottom of a dish. He captured it finally and there was a general sigh. He said solemnly, "They forget we are a simple people!"

Now the Jam Saheb decided to expand this thesis; in preparation he stared myopically into space. "The Western mind cannot comprehend them, for they are like children, accustomed to their poverty and squalor.

"You see . . ." The Jam Saheb paused less for effect than to decide precisely what it was we should see. "You see, they live in the realm of the spirit, so they laugh at such things as physical discomfort. It is ridiculous to judge them by Western standards, for these standards simply do not apply to our people. Democracy? Security? They are fine words in Europe, but they are just not a part of the Asiatic mind. Do you know what would happen if I relinquished my throne? Why, the people would beg me to come back and rule them." Real tears were forming in the Jam Saheb's eyes. "They are my children," he breathed. "They love me very much."

He waved a deprecating hand around him, indicating the gaudy appointments of the room. "Do you know why I live as I do?" he asked. "It is because my people insist on such a display of luxury.

"For every anna that I spend on myself, I spend lakhs of

13

rupees on roads and schools. For every minute that is given to parties there are hours of work and planning in my office. Why, when I visit the villages, the people gather around me just to touch my feet and to receive my blessing. I belong to the people! I am a servant of servants! I am—" the tension was terrible—"I am their father," he bellowed.

At first I was inclined to laugh at his speech, to consider it just a political tour de force. But I realize now that rather than a display, it was the pathetic self-deception of a debauching old sentimentalist. I thought for a moment of the Jam Saheb's son, who would one day inherit his father's powers. It was easy to see how he would be bred to the job, conditioned to the smug and pious oppressions.

The mutterings were rising on all sides of the Jam Saheb where he sat humble and moist eyed in his moment of self-sacrifice.

"Why, of course!" I heard.

"A simple people."

"He is their father, it's true."

"What would they do without him?"

Childish? That was the word I had heard so often as the descriptive adjective for the Indian rajahs. And now I saw why. It was appropriate, for the Jam Saheb resembled nothing so much as a spoiled child. His every inanity was interpreted and restated till it assumed the proportions of a logical argument. His every blundering attempt at humor was repeated and accepted with encouraging laughter. When he was in a simple mood, stories were told of his simplicity. When he was in a regal mood, the courtiers would describe his jewels. When he was in a mood for bragging he had only to nod and his hired tennis star would praise his last game.

In Jamnagar it is considered the worst of poor taste to leave any group while the Jam Saheb is speaking. But by one o'clock I had decided that Jamnagar's idea of good taste and mine were different. I slipped away as quietly as I could, while the Jam Saheb was disposing of "the menace of Pakistan."

"War!" he was crying. "Immediate war! We have everything to gain and nothing to lose!"

[3]

I HAD been in Jamnagar for just about two weeks. I had seen all the things that the guidebooks recommended; the palaces and the museums and the public gardens, the picture galleries and the Jamnagar Club. I had even been conducted through the huge treasure vaults that are hidden beneath the principal palaces where, though I had been warned what to expect, I had stared open mouthed at the vast, endless jumbles of the exquisite and the atrocious. In Pratap Villas I was allowed to rummage through the extant remains of the Imperial Russian Silverplate, and in the rani's sitting room I was shown such masterpieces as Meissonier's "The Guide" and "The Fourth Murillo." There was much to see, both new and old, both breathtakingly beautiful and astonishingly ugly, and I had seen it all, in the cautious company of the ruler's various aides-de-camp.

It was inevitable that the Jam Saheb should eventually ask, "Well, what do you think of the state?" I had expected to make the conventional answer but when the moment came I felt suddenly stubborn.

"I don't know," I replied. The Jam Saheb looked at me with such a cold and uncomprehending expression that I hastened to explain, "I've been here two weeks, but until now I've seen nothing but the city itself."

The old ruler's face remained just what it was. He was silent but for the sound of his asthmatic breathing. I began to

15

suspect he would simply turn his back on me, a device to which he has frequent recourse, but instead he leaned forward with his palms on his thighs and asked dryly, "And what else is there?"

"That's just it," I replied. "I have no idea. But there must be more to the state than its capitol. I had hoped to get out into the countryside for a while, perhaps to visit a few of your villages."

The Jam Saheb relaxed. He understood now. I was asking for something and he was accustomed to that.

"Oh, the villages. . . ." he said vaguely. "Yes, I'll have it arranged. . . . A car . . . not much to see, of course."

It was just what I expected. A tour through the villages arranged along the lines of my tours through the museums; a comfortable three hours in an ancient Rolls-Royce, a few stops at hand-picked and atypical villages. Meston plows. Diesel tractors. Motor-driven pumps to irrigate the fields, and the necessary complement of happy peasants, dancing, laughing, and singing on request.

There was even one cultivator who had been taught to speak English so that he could extoll the virtues of Navanagar State. "The most modern and efficient equipment!" he would beam, or, "The progressive measures of Our Enlightened Ruler." He spoke his lines well. He made only one slip, and even that was a result of a commendable curiosity. "Sahib," he asked when I was about to leave, "what is the meaning of this—Our Enlightened Ruler?"

But it was a little too easy to blame the Jam Saheb; this occurred to me as we were driving back to the palace. It was just a bit too simple to generalize darkly on the significance of this unconvincing and slipshod fraud. The truth was, the Jam Saheb very likely knew less about these villages than I did, if that were possible, for I had been exposed to the pretense but once while he had been born and reared in the midst of it. I am convinced that he believed that his people loved him. "They live in the realm of the spirit" was not a lie but a story that had been told him from the earliest childhood and which he had never been given any reason to doubt.

But too many people had been told such stories. Every petty official of the Indian Union was one with the Jam Saheb in believing that he was chosen to "speak for the masses." While I had been in Bombay I had talked to one such, a member of the constituent assembly, who had assured me that the ballot was not necessary in India "because we already know what the people want."

No, the problem of the villages of Navanagar was not unique. It was the problem of the villages all over India, the problems of a leadership divorced from the people by the tremendous barriers of caste and class. In Kathiawar the name for these leaders was rajah. In the Union we called them Brahmins or banias, but the principle was the same. They had been bred to the belief that the good of their class was the good of India, that they are the natural leaders of the 80 per cent of the people who live in the six million villages.

I tried to think of one concrete advantage which the villagers of the Union enjoyed over these. I tried to think of one progressive measure in the light of which I would be justified in calling the Jam Saheb backward. There were none, of course—at least none of consequence. There were only the copious official tears of the leaders who, like Rothschild when confronted by a beggar cried, "Throw him out. He's breaking my heart!"

Six months had passed since Independence Day. The zemindars seemed as secure and powerful as ever in spite of the fact that their feudal land tenure was one of the primary arguments for Indian *swaraj*. Six months had passed. Men were still being jailed and held without trial for political offenses on the very statute which, when employed by the British, had been rightly characterized as intolerable and

17

oppressive. Six months. Newspapers were still being suspended for refusing to follow the Congress party line, while in the villages the police were still a source of terror to the common citizens of the Independent India.

Of course Congress had explanations for it all. But they were suspiciously like the explanations of the British, and even the leaders in Delhi could not help wincing when they insisted, "It takes years to accomplish these changes."

Of course it takes years if you table the Zemindari Act while you discuss the merits of national prohibition. Of course it takes years when the governments of the provinces devote their earliest revolutionary energy to the tasks of censoring kissing scenes in the theaters and outlawing the Western vice of mixed dancing. It takes forever if all things take precedence over the raising of the rural standard of living, if the national leaders go on moralistic witch hunts while a third of the population is on the verge of starvation.

And yet why should we call them leaders at all? There is no one who has less confidence in the people than they have, these khaddar-clad Congressmen who never seem to tire of blaming their ineptness on the Indian masses.

"The people resist all our innovations!"—a government engineer's refusal to build roads.

"They are superstitious about modern medicine!"—an apology to the world for an outbreak of cholera.

"Why, they would prefer to die in their homes!"—the reasoning behind the diminution of a hospital grant.

"They enjoy their poverty. They are hopelessly backward." —the slogans of the reconsidered revolutionaries.

No, the Jam Saheb was not alone in his generalizations. They had assumed the proportions of a political tradition. The Jam Saheb was not conspiring to keep me in ignorance. Like the others, he just didn't know the answers. What is the meaning of Our Enlightened Ruler? For that matter, what is the meaning of Independence? These questions were being asked all over the country, but nobody seemed to know the answers.

So what could you do but accept the generalizations, vague and prejudiced as you knew them to be? You could not start out in a bullock cart with the intention of interviewing India.

Could you?

Kathiawar

Kathiawar

[4]

ON THE seventeenth of January, about an hour after dawn, I stood on a hilltop two miles north of Wankaner. It was a cold, clear morning, yet already the sun had assumed its ominous orange-red color. In the east, where the dunes swept out toward the sunrise like an infinite succession of unpleasant mirages, there was just one spot of green in the whole sand waste. It was the village which we hoped to reach before nightfall.

I had arisen that morning by the earliest gray light that crept in through the small, barred windows of the dharmsala, not stopping to wash but putting on what few clothes I had bothered discarding before crawling into my bedroll. They were wet and uncomfortable, and in the flickering oil lamp I could see a few bugs crawling into the folds, but these I brushed away, then resigned myself philosophically to repeating the performance on each morning to come. There was no water to be had, nor light for that matter, so I had packed my comb and razor beforehand. I ran my fingers roughly through my hair, stroked my beard, and forgot them both.

When I went out on the veranda, the two coolies I had engaged were sleeping intertwined, like a pair of stray puppies. I called to them several times, but they only mumbled unintelligently and wound their arms the more tightly around each other. At last, after I had seized them both by the shoulders, they sat up and began blinking the sleep from their eyes, and after champing their jaws and scratching their heads, they rose and declared they were ready to start.

I myself shouldered one of the two large rucksacks into

23

which I had unreasonably crammed all of my equipment, leaving the coolies to divide the burden of the heaviest pack and of my light but cumbersome bedroll. On the night before I had carefully strapped each so that the weight could be suspended efficiently from the shoulders, but after an energetic debate over the merits of my method, each coolie alternately taking each side of the question, the two of them boosted the loads to their heads and, muttering inconsolably about the dangling straps, set off at their peculiar, loping trot. There was no one in sight at the time of our departure but the cook and the keeper of the dharmsala itself. They were standing at the gate as I expected they would be, faces tousled and tired but palms extended. "For luck!" I cried, throwing each of them a rupee. This roused them a little and they gave me their blessings. And it was that easy to pass from my accustomed world through a baked-mud gateway into India.

"It is there!" I sighted along the skinny brown arm that the oldest of the coolies was pointing toward the horizon. "Of course," he continued happily, "once we leave this hill, we will not be able to see it at all. There will be nothing to tell us which way to go, for all of the dunes are alike!" He stroked his throat. "One can die of thirst." Then he concluded spaciously, "But trust me, Sahib!"

Until now, it somehow never had occurred to me that there was any alternative but to trust my guide, but as I scanned the desolation all around our objective, I realized too suddenly how important he was.

"You are sure you can find it?" I tried to sound casual, but some of my anxiety apparently broke into my voice, for the old man drew himself up to his full height.

"Have confidence!" he commanded, striking his chest.

We started down the hill in single file, one coolie, then me, then a coolie at the rear, an order the old man had most carefully arranged though he had not bothered to tell us

24

why such precision was necessary. It was easy on the down-grade, but as we dropped into the valley, the sweat became cold and unhealthy on our bodies. However, by the time we were dry and adjusted to the shade, we had gained the next rise and were back in the sun. My pack dragged heavily at my shoulders after a while, the more so because of these changing temperatures, for I was unable to relax my muscles to the pull and they ached from fighting as well as bearing their burden. When the sun had risen to the proper inclination to strike the valleys as well as the dividing crests, in spite of the heat, the going became easier and we all broke into a constant, hard sweat. I had expected to stop somewhere out among the hills for the breakfast that I had decided to forego at the dharmsala, but when I halted, experimentally, the bearers disapproved. They wagged their heads and pointed to the sun. I supposed that they wanted to travel through the morning and camp during the hottest part of the day, and since I was not really hungry I consented in their plan and pushed on without so much as a rest.

It was probably an illusion, but it began to seem that the ground grew increasingly soft under foot. At each step my boots sank deeper in the sand, filling themselves with the coarse, dry stuff and dragging across it with such a considerable effort that it felt as if we must be walking through quicksand. My bearers had no trouble. Their broad, bare feet spread out on the surface rather than sinking in, but how they withstood its heat I shall never know, for when I stopped just to empty the sand from my boots their soles were so hot I could scarcely touch them.

We passed a number of dry stream beds, narrow little gulleys that wound through the sand where the monsoon torrents had cut down to bedrock. At this time of year they were dry, of course, bleached and white like old bones in the sun. As we crossed one I was suddenly struck by the clatter of my boots on the unaccustomed hard surface, and I realized all at once that since leaving the first hill we had none of us spoken except in whispers. There was something about the landscape itself that explained this. It was like a hostile force that stood at our elbows, like some personal enemy from whom secrets must be kept and whose attention must not be drawn more than necessary.

When I called to my guide it was like breaking a spell. He turned in alarm, then stopped and smiled. He dropped his burden and I unstrapped my pack and we squatted down on our heels to rest for a moment.

"How far do you suppose we've come?" I asked. He pretended to make the most precise calculations. But after scratching in the sand and counting on his fingers he looked at me blankly.

"Not so far," he replied.

"You think you can find it?" What had begun as a certainty seemed now to be less than an even chance, and though I was far too tired and uncomfortable to much care, I felt sure we were wandering in an eternity of sand.

He pretended to study his computations and figures again to verify our position before answering. "Oh, yes," he said, but it was with such a philosophic detachment that I was sure it was of no real importance to him. It was twelve o'clock. For the past half hour I had felt all too much the strength of the sun. I could no longer bear to look at the sand, so I had pulled my hat down over my eyes, managing to keep on the general course by an occasional quick glance at the heels of my guide. He had noticed this, so, after calculating the time, he suggested that we rest through the worst part of the day; and though we were sitting unshaded on the side of a hill, even this seemed better than the thought of moving on. I was so hot and tired that I could not think of eating, let alone of rummaging through my rucksacks for food, so I lay down in the sand and, in spite of the flies that buzzed in my ears and stuck to my lips, fell almost immediately into a stuporous sleep full of half-waking dreams and sweaty deliriums. When I woke hours later it was a hideous process, like

26

climbing through successive thick layers of consciousness; I had a headache and a taste of burned rubber in my mouth, and I was caked with a mixture of sweat and sand. But my guides were waiting and when I opened my eyes, they asked immediately whether I was ready to start. I was, but I could never shake off my torpor and as a consequence the rest of the afternoon was a blur.

By six o'clock it was apparent to all of us that we could not reach our destination before dark. Between us and the village which we could see from our hilltop lay another six miles of dunes and ravines, three hours of marching at our established rate, even without allowances for our diminishing energy. My bearers were willing to push on through the darkness, too willing in fact, since they were paid by the journey, but I decided that sleeping on the hilltop where we stood would be a simpler solution than stumbling through the sand, and would certainly be easier than finding a billet at an hour when most of the villagers would be sleeping.

I myself built a fire of the dry sage brush that I had noticed growing sparsely in some of the deeper valleys. For the past two hours, against the advice of my guides who insisted that we would reach the village at any moment, I had been collecting the stuff and dragging it behind me with one of the straps, which my pack could spare. My bearers felt guilty, and for the first twenty minutes they tried to pretend that the fire wasn't there. But at length, when the sun slipped down behind the horizon and a chilly wind sprang up in the east, they went foraging for a few propitiary sticks, then squatted beside me in undisguised comfort.

I opened a can of tomatoes, boiling a handful of rice in the juice. It was a tasty supper and though there was not much of it, it improved my disposition enormously. The bearers unrolled their dirty turbans and revealed undreamed-of stores of food. There was cold boiled rice packed into the folds, chilis and plantains in the vertical cones, even a few scraps of cheese to be licked from the cloth to which they adhered in sticky particles.

Then we talked for a while, my guide and I, about all the strange and unrelated things that come to men's minds at the ends of long days. About America, about India, about politics and religion, and as always on such occasions as this, about ourselves. We did not speak in sentences, as Europeans do, in a quick and logical give and take. We spoke like Asiatics, candidly and at length, signaling the end of our rambling orations by rising and poking in the coals of the fire. During the day Bapu had served me faithfully as a servant, obeying my orders without so much as a question. But now, gathered as we were around the traditional campfire, he assumed the prerogatives of the elder male and directed the conversation as it suited him.

"This America—" he said—"it is a very big city?"

"It is a country," I answered quietly. "Even bigger than India."

"And the people in America. They are all like you?"

"More or less," I answered vaguely.

Bapu tried for a moment to comprehend, but it was a strange and unlikely idea to him. He stared at the fire for perhaps five minutes.

"But if they are all like you, then who does the work?"

"We do it ourselves!" I said with a laugh.

"You build houses and carry packs?" He was suspicious.

"Of course," I answered. "There the sahibs do everything, but in America they are not called sahibs." Again the silence, this time so long that I opened my bedroll and crawled in to keep warm.

"No," Bapu sighed. "You do not understand me."

"Bapu," I concluded, "we do not understand each other."

[5]

IT TOOK us about two hours to reach Landra the next morning. Refreshed as we were by our good night's sleep and conditioned to the rigors of the previous day, the six miles that stretched between us and our objective seemed no more than a pleasant walk. But from the final hilltop in whose valley it lay, Landra itself was an unpleasant surprise, for it had far more the appearance of a ruin than a village, and I felt sure that it had been deserted for a great many years.

The village spread out in an incredible disorder from the mouth of the stone quarry directly beneath us, tapering off indefinitely into the crumbling old walls that lay scattered and buried in the sands beyond. There was none of the precise and obvious organization that the Central Indian villages achieve, however poor. Indeed, by their standards this was no village at all, lacking as it was in temple and tanks and even, for that matter, in discernible streets. It was a collection of huts in the middle of a desert, a gathering place of lonely animals, and in the sense that the village had once been rich, it was like some horrid cemetery of a dying race. From our point of vantage it was perfectly apparent that not a third of the houses were inhabited, or habitable, the majority of them marking in their stages of decay the grim succession of their owners' deaths. The whole scene was a litter of collapsing masonry, new houses half leaning on the walls of old. It was a maze of choked, directionless alleys, a vast, awful rubble more dead than alive.

We scrambled around to the end of the quarry and began making our way down the steep incline. As we approached, a cry went up from the village and the inhabitants began issuing like rats from a trash heap. Faces appeared beneath sagging lintels; children crawled up out of dark little holes.

Pye-dogs, annoyed at their own inattentiveness that had allowed us to approach so close unseen, squeezed up between cracks in the old foundations and vented their feelings of guilt upon us.

The villagers themselves were scarcely more friendly. They stared from a distance, seminaked and afraid, only the smallest children coming near out of curiosity, and then against the screaming admonitions of their mothers who sobbed in the doorways and wrung their hands. It was a deafening reception, for soon the men began adding their shouts to the already growing confusion, and it was but a fitting climax when a herd of buffaloes, frightened by the noise, came pounding down the street.

But the pandemonium died down at last. The sobbing mothers recaptured their children, the sagging bitches slunk back to their puppies, and the last of the buffaloes was brought in from the hillside where it had run in terror at our noisy approach. My bearers and I picked our way through the streets between piles of rubbish and the numerous dung heaps that lay scattered and decaying wherever the need of relief had come to a villager or his animals. As we walked, great swarms of flies arose, settling and sticking to our lips and our eyelids, hovering greedily around every small well of moisture, however we waved and scraped them away. The smells rose too, smells of spice and of urine, of garlic and curry powder and dysentery stools, all the assorted smells of the Indian village, all the smells of life, decay, and death.

It was a necessary corollary; the people of Landra were as sick and as degenerate as their surroundings, and as we passed, they limped and crawled about us in every form of pathological hideousness. There were wretched old men with twisted limbs that had been broken many years ago but had never been set, hobbling about on crutches that had been improvised from tree limbs quite as gnarled and stunted as the men themselves. There were blind children stumbling and shrieking in the rubble, running and clutching and

30

incessantly questioning, and there were hollow-eyed women with consumptive coughs and women with festering, encrusted sores. Even the fortunate majority were not really well; it was just that their diseases were less obvious and dramatic. There was scarcely a person who, if carefully examined, would not show some evidence of chronic dysentery, who would not possess some lesion or canker or the growing opacity of a cataract in his eyes.

I had been warned. In the terse, dry language of the textbooks I had read that "the people of the Kathiawar peninsula are among the most impoverished and backward in all of India, partly because of the poor quality of the land and partly as a result of their feudal economy." But my stomach still churned, for the textbooks had said nothing about the running sores and the piles of excrement. The charts had been accurate, even impressive in their way, but they had been nothing like the animal realities of Landra!

"This is the sweepers' quarter," Bapu explained.

We had deposited my gear at the home of one of his friends and had embarked on a casual tour of Landra. We were walking down an alley that, like all of the others, was wearily, monotonously dirty and disordered.

"The scavengers and untouchables live here," he continued. "You know what an untouchable is?" I nodded. "In most places, their quarter is far removed from the village, but here it is only separated by that wall."

Where Bapu pointed there was a mud-brick barrier topped with a screen of woven twigs. Like everything else it was in sad neglect so that, in addition to the openings which its builders had intended, it was melting and crumbling in many other places. Where it was broken and scattered, the village children were playing, good naturedly annoying the tired pye-dogs. Where it was whole, the wall was plastered with round cakes of cow dung, molded and drying in the sun.

"The scavengers collect the manure," Bapu explained.

31

"They sell it to the rest of the villagers for fuel. A few of them work in the quarry off and on, but generally the quarry is worked by caste Hindus."

We passed through one of the openings in the wall. "And this is where the Brahmins and banias live." It was like the sweepers' quarters in all the grosser respects, just perceptibly cleaner and better ordered. One or two of the houses were pretentious affairs with timbered roofs and separate kitchens, but the majority, both in plan and execution, were conventionally small and conventionally dirty.

"Can't the Brahmins and banias afford better houses?" I asked.

"Better houses?" Bapu did not know quite what I meant. He tugged at his crotch and thought before answering. "They are rich men. But better houses? I don't know. I don't know."

The last place we visited was the Landra quarry. It was a great open pit where men, women, and children scrambled dangerously over steep, protruding ledges or pried and loosened the large boulders with their fingers. At the bottom, looking up at uncomfortable intervals, sat the most elderly and indigent citizens of the village, breaking rocks into measureable piles of gravel with the chip-chip-chipping of their tiny, tired hammers. We watched for a while, then proceeded with our pointless touring through one village street after another, but I was so impressed with the totality of Landra that Bapu's careful refinements hardly registered at all.

"We stop here." My guide pointed hopefully at a tea stall, a little mud building not unlike the others, with a thin wisp of smoke curling up through the roof where providence, not design, had left a hole in the tiles. We stopped. After the old man's oration of the night before, touching as it had upon the duties of host and guest, I had no alternative but to acquiesce, since "an invitation is a matter of honor." When we entered, I was blinded by the vast clouds of smoke that poured out of the charcoal brazier near the door, but

Bapu only laughed, "You will get used to the smoke," and led me coughing to a bench in one corner.

When my eyes had stopped running and grown used to the atmosphere to the point where I could open them at irregular intervals, I saw that the tea stall was just a cavernous room with a few benches and a pile of straw at one end. There was a window, but the brazier on which the tea was boiled had been strategically located across the room from it so that it was a geometric necessity that the smoke either cross the whole space or sift as it could through the porous roof. By the brazier squatted an old, bewhiskered Hindu who was stirring the coals and adding new pieces. He would pick them one at a time from the box beside him, turn them over in his hands with the care of a jeweler and finally, in accordance with some whim or some secret standard, arrange them on the fire or discard them for others. But it was more than a ritual. It was an act of passion, for from time to time he would sway in a sort of ecstasy, inhaling the rising steam from the urns, then licking the distillation from his beard. In his own good time he poured out two cups of his dark brown brew and gave them to us. The spell was broken; it was a terrible decoction. I drank it, but only out of deference to my guide.

We talked again. This time I questioned Bapu, for I wanted to know all about Landra at once. Were the people happy? Had they always been poor? It was all as eager and foolish as that. Bapu tried to answer. "Well, you see . . ." he would say. But of course neither of us ever, in reality, did see. And it was only when I had abandoned my self-conscious attempts that I was able to learn anything that I wanted to know.

"Is this old man the owner of the stall?" I asked finally.

"Oh, no," Bapu answered. "He just makes the tea. The stall is owned by an old Jain bania, but he almost never comes here himself."

"Ah, the banias," I laughed. "It seems they own everything. Are they powerful here in Landra too, then?"

Bapu shrugged his shoulders. "They are powerful everywhere. They are merchants and moneylenders, but that is a means to all ends."

"A means to all ends? What do you mean?" I asked.

"Why . . ." Bapu seemed to feel that the phrase was self-explanatory. "They lend money to the rest of us and when we cannot pay them back, the banias seize our shops or our lands by default."

"Does this happen often?"

"Not any more," Bapu laughed. "But only because there is nothing left for them to seize. They already own everything worth having in Landra. There is no one now who does not owe them money."

"Ah, you must have borrowed very heavily!" I concluded.

"No," Bapu reflected, "the amounts were quite small. Still, when times are bad and you cannot pay them back, at 40-percent interest, little loans grow big."

I said that I had heard this story before.

"You will hear it wherever you go," Bapu agreed. "I don't know how it is in the rest of India, but as far east and west as my travels have taken me, I have yet to see a Kathiawar village that is not owned almost entirely by the moneylenders."

"Do you owe them money?" I asked.

"Some," Bapu admitted. "But my father and grandfather were more provident than most. They borrowed very little, and since I have added none to it, the income from my land almost pays the interest."

"Then you have some land! That is good," I observed.

"I have some land today," Bapu cautioned. "But I have two grown daughters who must be married shortly, so who can speak of tomorrow?"

"But it would be a shame to dispose of your land," I objected.

34

"Of course it would be a shame," Bapu agreed with a laugh. "But not nearly such a shame as if I failed to provide my daughters with dowries and jewels for their weddings!"

"But what will you do when you have lost your land, Bapu? How will you pay the banias then?"

"Oh," Bapu was not anxious to look into the future, "I suppose I will work in the quarry that the banias own."

"For nothing?"

"For the interest and a few handfuls of jowar."

"God!" I said. "That's the next thing to slavery!"

Bapu looked up with a melancholy smile. "If it is slavery, then everyone in Kathiawar is a slave," he said.

At this point a Rajput durbar came into the stall. He was a poor representative of the traditional village royalty, a tall thin man with sunken cheeks and the glaze of opium addiction in his eyes. When he entered, all the kolis and lower castes arose and touched their foreheads in a gesture of respect. The young durbar drew his short, soiled jacket around him and assumed too rigid a pose of dignity, for immediately after he lost his balance and, like an amateur Hamlet making his first-act exit, he lurched across the room and fell onto a bench where he lay with his eyes closed, breathing hard.

"Do they come here often?" I whispered to Bapu.

"He does," Bapu answered, staring into his tea cup. "He is so far gone with his opium and liquor that nobody has any respect for him anyway."

"A durbar!" I mused.

"He is the son of a durbar. But he is not like the durbars my father knew. They were Rajputs, warriors. They ruled the village. These!" he sneered. "These are tax collectors."

"But would you like the old durbars back?" I laughed.

Bapu's eyes grew wide at the very thought. "Oh yes!" he cried. "In the days of the old durbars, the village was beautiful and our houses were like forts! Why, those durbars didn't collect a rupee from each house. They collected ten at the beginning and perhaps came back for more. And no matter how much they wanted, you gave it, for they collected their taxes with knives in their belts!"

"And they spent all this on the village?" I suggested.

"Ho!" Bapu laughed. "They spent it on themselves. They had beautiful wives and fast Arab horses, and rings and jade brooches, and sandlewood carvings."

"But then why do you want them back?" I was puzzled. "If their sons take less money I should think you would be glad."

"Their sons!" Bapu spat. "Even the little they do take, they don't know how to spend. Look!" I looked across the room where the dissolute young durbar was trying to drink his cup of tea. His hands shook so that he spilled at least half of it through the hairs of his beard and down the front of his shirt. "These durbars are like children. They have to be cared for. It is a charity we give them when we pay our house tax. I would pay ten times as much to a real Rajput. But he—" Bapu laughed. "He would be my ruler!"

"Then you want a ruler?"

"Want . . . ?" Bapu was perplexed. "Sahib, every man must have his ruler. This!" He waved his hand in the direction of the doorway. "This is what happens to men without rulers."

"But is it impossible that the people should rebuild the village without the old sort of durbar?" I insisted.

Bapu was annoyed at my stupidity and he frowned in disgust. "Of course it is impossible. Who would make us?" he jeered.

It was growing late. Though I wanted to continue the conversation, I knew that I did not dare. There are certain logical places where a talk may stop; this was one, but there was no predicting when another might come. The younger of my bearers had been sent to arrange that I should travel with a caravan that was going east during the night, and though he had reported favorably, I was anxious to talk with the leader of the caravan myself before then.

"Well, Bapu," I said, "someday perhaps!" I stood and extended my hand. Bapu clasped it warmly, but he did not rise. "Someday, Sahib? Yes, anything someday."

[6]

IT WAS dark when we left Landra. The moon had just risen and was casting its shattered shadows through the streets when our procession of carts rumbled out of the village and onto the silvery carpet of sand. The village was quiet. There was nothing to hear but the regular creaking of our wooden axles and the occasional cry of a lonely jackal somewhere out in the hills to the west. It was growing colder. A wind had sprung up and was blowing directly into the face of our bullocks, but the drivers were wrapped warmly in their heavy, coarse blankets, and I was comfortable in the depths of my bedroll. I tried to sleep, and managed at intervals, but never for more than an hour at a time. Often when I woke we would be following our invisible track through a land that seemed to know no others, and often we would be passing in the shadow of a village as gaunt and as spectral as the one we had left. But always when I woke, the drivers were sleeping, gurgling softly to themselves in the folds of their blankets, with only the instinctive wisdom of their animals to keep us moving along the traditional course.

When morning came, it was with a startling suddenness; from an early gray twilight it was suddenly day. There was no real sunrise, just a burst of bright light you could almost have missed by turning your head. When I awoke, the bare dunes of the past two days were far behind on the darker horizon and we were rumbling along a well-marked road between fields of chili and tall stands of cane. There were tanks of water where the graceful coonch stood mirrored in the unbroken morning surfaces, and there were irrigation wheels that would dig deep down into them to fling water on the earth and rainbows in the air. The caravan seemed to come to life all at once, the drivers unwrapping from the folds of their blankets and twisting the tails of their slow-moving bullocks in their hurry to get to our breakfasting place. Even the bullocks seemed to sense an approaching rest, for they raised their great heads and bellowed to each other. "Hi yi!" called the drivers, and after a moment's interval, "Hi yi!" came back from the farmers in the fields.

Now the Moslems among us began their morning throat clearing, the ritual retching that is prescribed by their religion. So awful were their snortings and spittings and coughing that I almost joined in out of general nausea.

"How long does this go on?" I shouted to my driver.

"Till their stomachs are empty, I suppose!" he replied. Then, shaken by a particularly terrible bellow, he added, "Great Gods, there's a pious man!"

About five miles ahead we could see a river, like a silver thread in a dark brown tapestry where the morning wind blew its sleeping surface and the sun reflected in winking brilliance. Another half hour had brought us upon it, and we decided to rest on its bank through the day, so we drew up our carts into two parallel lines and unhitched and watered the tired bullocks.

There was a village nearby but few of us visited it. Instead we worked, tightening up the carts and scrubbing the dirty but unwilling animals till we looked less like a caravan than a circus parade. It was a regular routine for the next five days. We traveled at night and stopped through the day, sleeping round the clock in fitful shifts broken only by the few short intervals of work. At first I was treated with suspicion and deference, but the life was not such that this could last long, and when I insisted on helping with the daily jobs I was accepted almost completely into the carefree community.

A majority of the caravan drivers were Hindus, not a few

of them being durbars from the villages along the seacoast, descendants of the erstwhile Rajput rulers and inheritors from them of a tall slim physique that distinguished them at once from the kolis among us. They were casual traders, living mostly on their tax rights, the one rupee per house, which they collected from their villagers, but as a group they were remarkably friendly and democratic, quite unlike the typical durbar we had met in Landra.

Twice a year, I learned, they would caravan inland taking with them the season's supply of straw mats which the villagers had woven from the rushes that grow on the edge of the salt marshes along the coast. These they would sell at a profit to the traders and brokers who met them just beyond the customs barriers and, after buying the few things they considered necessities, they would spend what remained on the traditional debaucheries.

My driver was such a durbar. He was a handsome old man with a long white beard parted carefully in the center. If he was an opium addict, that was not apparent, for his eyes had a bright, transparent gaiety which belied even the age that his wrinkles attested. He was dressed all in white, in white trousers and a short jacket that was gathered in folds just under his arms, standing out around his chest like a ballerina's skirts so that it emphasized his height and the length of his arms. His turban was enormous—six yards, he told me. "Six yards of the finest Benares silk." He was proud of his turban and wore it cocked over one eye with the roguish vanity that all Rajputs affect.

It was from Lalji that I learned what became a rule of thumb, that it is never hard to make a villager talk; the difficulty, coming at the other extreme, is in inducing him to stop at a prosaic truth when he is capable of such interesting and infinite variations. It was not that Lalji was a liar by inclination; it was that for him conversation was a pastime rather than a discipline. It was that, his theory being that

39

men talk for pleasure rather than enlightenment, he could be counted upon to be pleasant but never reliable.

Once or twice during the week we traveled together I caught him in the most flagrant adaptations from the Mahabharata, turban askew and dagger drawn, enacting one of Raghu's struggles as his own. I didn't denounce these wilder fantasies for their very magnitude was proof against belief, but I was driven eventually to complain against the subtler vagaries, many of which I felt sure had taken me in.

"Lalji," I cautioned, "I am a stranger to your land, and you must therefore be particularly careful what you tell me. It is all very well for you to joke with your old friends, but you see, I do not know when you are joking and when you are serious."

"That is true!" he agreed. He saw my problem and promised that in the future he would be more careful. And he was as good as his word. On frequent occasions when he found himself being carried away by his eloquence he would stop abruptly in the middle of a gesture and say disgustedly, "Ah, it seems I am lying again."

But the rest of the drivers were equally candid and by the end of the first day of my traveling with their caravan they had managed to inform themselves, through the most casual discussions, who I was, what I earned, and whether my wife was frigid. For there seemed to be no subject which they did not consider to fall within the scope of even a passing discussion and though it was embarrassing at first, I soon learned to exploit them as mercilessly and as naïvely as they did me.

One night, for example, when we were gathered around our fire, I asked how many of the men took opium. Far from being annoyed at my curiosity, they were flattered that I should be interested in such an intimate detail. Of the durbars, who alone could really afford it, there were not five out of the twenty present who did not, while even among the kolis there were half a dozen or so who bragged that they had managed a mild addiction.

"Why do you take it?" I asked one of the older durbars who seemed to be suffering most obviously from the effects. All the others laughed and a few of them jeered, "Yes, Kanchan, tell us. Why do you take it?"

A slow smile spread over the old man's face and he began to fumble through the pockets of his jacket. "Here!" he said, producing a packet and handing it to me. "You take this in your tea and find out for yourself."

When the others had stopped laughing, I learned from Kanchan that the amount he had given me was just one day's supply. It consisted of a pair of amber droplets which, again he informed me, cost eight annas apiece. Even to my nonmathematical mind, this indicated that Kanchan's opium cost far more than his food, that indeed, the cost of his yearly supply would make a start toward reconstructing his entire village.

I was disgusted. I turned to a koli and asked him, "Why do you pay a house tax to these men?"

Now the durbars laughed more uproariously than ever, but the koli only replied disinterestedly, "It is a tradition."

"But it is also a tradition that men should have enough to eat, and it is a tradition that their rulers must see that they do. If these men do nothing but amuse themselves at your expense, then why should you continue to pay them a tax?"

There was still not a sign of resentment from the durbars, though they were following the conversation intently. They sat with their long legs drawn up in front of them, thin faces resting on their bony knuckles. The koli shifted uneasily on his hams, as if he were reluctant to answer at all. Finally he said, "It is a tradition. You see—" But he stopped in midgesture. "Oh, I cannot explain it."

I realized that I had exhausted this line of questions, so I asked, "Do you have a school in your village?"

He was relieved that I had turned to factual data. "No, we haven't," he said seriously. "We cannot afford one."

Now Kanchan, the old durbar to whom I had spoken

earlier, decided to re-enter the conversation. He edged closer to the fire and signaled for attention. "And why should we want a school?" he scoffed.

I proceeded cautiously. I knew that Kanchan would expect something very tangible for time invested. "If you had gone to school," I finally suggested, "you could earn far more money than these mats will ever bring!"

The appeal to Kanchan was undeniable. He pulled at his beard and reflected before answering. Then, with the crafty smile of a man skirting a trap, he objected, "Ah, but what good is it, if we cannot buy opium?"

But it was not only by indirection that I was to learn about the role of the durbars in the Kathiawar villages. Lalji, for one, when he was in a mood to do so, could make the most lucid and spirited pronouncements on the subject. Nor was he often reluctant; I might almost say that the degeneracy of his colleagues was a favorite subject, for Lalji was a durbar in the old sense of the term and he had nothing but disdain for those who were not. I knew better than to approach the topic directly, for Lalji innately distrusted questions, but this worked no hardship. There was plenty of time and I could afford to wait for Lalji's inspirations.

"This is a pleasant countryside, Lalji," I said one morning when we had just got under way.

He scanned the fields with a critical eye. "Things grow well here," he agreed. But he was not enthusiastic.

"Do you have such land near your village?" I asked.

"Oh no!" he replied. "It is dry around Salawa. There, even if we dig wells to irrigate our fields, we are so near to the sea that we get nothing but brine!"

"Then you must envy these people."

He shrugged his shoulders. "Envy? It was my fate to be born where I was. And besides," he added in a more practical vein, "I doubt that the people are much better off here!"

It was true. Though the fields were rich and ripe, fairly bursting with their harvest of cane and pulses, the villages were in the usual dramatic disrepair and the villagers were as poor and as sickly as ever.

"I think," Lalji continued, "that if you compared the two, you would find that my people are richer, if anything, in spite of the natural fertility of these lands and the great supply of fresh water that is here."

I was proud of myself. I felt sure that I had grasped one of the basic principles of the Kathiawar economy. "Then that is because there are no banias in Salawa." Lalji said nothing, but he turned and grinned in agreement.

"You see," he explained finally, "the real trouble with these villages is that there are far too many durbars about." He laughed. "They are more numerous than the pye-dogs in the streets!" Then growing reflective, he added, "And they are no more responsible."

"Technically, traditionally, the durbars are the village rulers. But how can a hundred men rule a village? Why, in Landra, almost every third man is a durbar. Think of it, Sahib! Every third man a ruler!" Lalji thought of it himself, and as he thought he laughed, leaning back against the mats, tears streaming down his face. I began to laugh too, but when I thought of Landra I decided that perhaps it was more tragic than funny.

"In Salawa, there are only four of us," Lalji explained, "and we have divided the duties of the village between us. We are well paid for our efforts," he admitted with a smile. Then growing serious he insisted, "But we give something in return."

"And you have managed to keep the banias out!" I said.

"It has been difficult," he sighed, "but we have managed. You see, these mats bring some money into the village and where there is money, it is hard for the banias to establish themselves. Oh, they have tried. I remember when they brought shops into the bazaar and tried to shame the people into borrowing for jewelry. 'Look here!' they would call when koli women went by. 'The women of Salawa are naked of jewels!' "

"And the people didn't succumb? I am surprised," I said.

"Oh, a few of them did at first," Lalji admitted. "But after one or two farmers had lost their lands and the people were angry with the banias anyway, we durbars rode around and collected the jewelry and gave it back to the banias, then chased them out of town."

"Ah, that's wonderful," I laughed. "It happens far too seldom. But knowing the banias, I am surprised that they left so easily."

Lalji laid his hand on the handle of his dagger. "Look at this, Sahib," he whispered. "You would argue with me? Eh?"

The days passed quickly. It had finally been decided that since the most desolate stretch of our journey was past, we could afford to reverse the order of our schedule, traveling by day and resting in camp. I had not been consulted but the arrangement suited me, since it meant that I would see the land as we crossed it, having the additional advantage that through the hot, dry days I could continue my conversations with Lalji and the others.

As we moved farther inland, the land grew richer, though there were still broad sand belts where nothing would grow. And, as Lalji predicted, regardless of fertility the people were as abysmally poor as in Landra. I was lulled by the pleasant company and the unpleasant terrain into following the caravan much farther than I should have and yet, even when I knew that I had delayed too long, it was hard for me to decide to strike out on my own.

Lalji tried to dissuade me from leaving the caravan. "Look, Sahib," he insisted, "you go with us to Viramgam. When we have sold these mats we will have plenty of money and in Viramgam there are pleasant ways of spending it."

"No, Lalji," I replied, "I must travel north, across the Rann of Kutch."

44

"Whisky?" Lalji suggested.

"North!" I repeated.

"A woman, perhaps."

"The Rann of Kutch," I laughed.

Lalji had never asked me where I was bound, but I imagine that he assumed I was fleeing from the police, for while he never said anything that suggested as much, his respect for my own silence on the subject was incredible. But he was curious now.

"You go north?" he asked. "Across the Rann of Kutch? That is very strange. I cannot imagine why a sahib should travel across the Rann of Kutch."

"Perhaps I just want to see it," I parried. The word that stood out for Lalji was "perhaps."

"I asked no questions," he answered simply. "I assume that the sahib has reasons of his own."

I did have reasons of my own, of course, and the most suspect reasons in the world to Lalji. Far better, I thought, to be a murderer and a comrade than a curious foreigner prying into Lalji's life. I decided that Lalji's friendship was an indication that if I wanted to continue as successfully as I had begun I had only to leave my presence unexplained and encourage the assumption that I was vaguely disreputable.

"But one thing," Lalji said without turning around. "Tell me one thing, Sahib. You are not with the government?"

"I am not with the government, Lalji," I said, "but tell me, why do you ask?"

"Sometimes," Lalji said, "the government sends spies to check the tax valuation in the villages. And if the Rajah discovers that the villagers have money, then he knows that he can raise the taxes the next year."

"No, I am not with the government, Lalji," I repeated, making the words as suggestive as possible.

Lalji turned around and placed one hand on my shoulder and we laughed together like the conspirators we were.

45

I left the caravan at a village called Vasuri, about two miles west of the town of Wadhwan. Though it really would have been simpler for me to continue into Wadhwan, Lalji's sense of drama would not permit it. Now that my virtuous dishonor had ceased to be a conjecture, and had assumed the status of a tacit understanding, he was full of such dark warnings as "It would not be safe," and "Wadhwan is the capital; there are police in Wadhwan." I tried at first to ride down these objections, but when I sensed that I was shaking Lalji's faith, I desisted and, with appropriate backward glances, sought to restore his notion of my desperate character.

We parted with a handshake, a gesture which I taught Lalji but which he took to his Rajput heart with fervor. To him it was the same sort of mystical performance as swearing in blood is to the Western mind.

"Lalji," I said, "you are a good durbar and a good friend. Kathiawar and India need more men like you!"

"Sahib," he said (and they were his last words to me), "if you were not so short you could pass for a Rajput!"

[7]

HALVAD is just another Kathiawar village. It is neither larger nor smaller than the vast majority. It is neither richer nor poorer, cleaner nor dirtier than the dozens of others I passed through going north. There was no good reason for me to stay in Halvad; it was simply that I was too tired to continue on foot. But since I arrived at the peak of the midwinter harvest, that was precisely my choice, to walk or to wait.

From a distance, Halvad blends almost perfectly with the landscape as nearly all of the Kathiawar villages do. So gently does it rise from the country around it, so completely is it built from the native materials, so casual is its plan and care-

46

less its construction, it could easily pass for some natural formation. Yet in Halvad the effect is not entirely unpleasant for there is an austerity in this very dilapidation, as if it were less the result of simple neglect than of an urge to preserve its antiquities intact. In every direction from the village, the fields spread out in a circle of decreasing greenness, since, drawing their life from the tank of the temple, they flourish in ratio to their proximity to the gods. The effect that this produces is striking; it is as if all life took refuge from the sun and the desert there, as if the grass and the trees and the buffaloes and the men flourished together only by right of Vishnu's blessing.

When you enter the village there are the usual disillusionments, the rubbish and the feces and the garbage underfoot. There are the smells and the flies and the dirt and diseases in ugly contrast to the traditional beauties that command the scene from a distance. As you walk through the streets, the pye-dogs crawl past you, muzzles low to the ground and hind quarters dragging, a moment later to resume their fighting over garbage or to make frantic love, to the delight of the children. And the streets are as disordered as dirty. They reach out into circular alleys and crazy cul-de-sacs, winding and twisting their nightmare courses with the violent inanity of a chronic drunk. The main street in Halvad runs north and south, but beyond that no generalizations can be made, for Halvad is like some madman's jigsaw puzzle, hammered together in pathetic and impossible ways.

On the outskirts of the village a few houses have been built in recent years from woven reeds but as you proceed toward the temple you will discover that the majority are built of dried mud, occasionally plastered with cow dung. Overlooking the bazaar there is one two-storied place that, in some more prosperous period, was built partly with lumber. But, since this is left over from an earlier period and has been repaired but infrequently and in the successive prevailing modes, it seems to combine all the disadvantages of each style so that at the present it stands unowned and unoccupied.

The bazaar itself is a shabby affair, unlike anything that the word suggests in the West, being a collection of low huts built of corrugated iron sheets whose removal from the railroad would not stand close scrutiny. The majority of the shops there are owned by the banias who sit cross-legged inside of them like great Buddhas in their shrines with expressions of profound and passionate displeasure—in ludicrous contrast to the gaudiness of their wares. Still, in the bazaar you can buy all manner of useful things, keys without locks and locks without keys, bits of colored glass with magical powers, and such mundane commodities as grain and pulses. As always, in the bazaar there is a village tea stall, a combination of restaurant, open forum, and pawn shop, and finally, in the middle of the square, stands the pavilion where the durbar holds corrupt and dreamy court.

In Kathiawar, in Halvad, there is an omnipresence of all ages and nowhere is this so clearly expressed as in the architecture. From the ruined cornices of the Rajput fortresses, from the crumbling arched gateways of the Mogul period, from the ancient Jain temple that stands near the tank, the shadows of the past are cast upon the present. Even the shrines give evidence of the same degeneracy. In the oldest the gods are strong, lovely figures, but gradually as they proceed from one age to the next they sicken of neglect like lonely old men, till in the newest renderings they are blobs of mud devoid of all strength and imagination.

In the Brahmin quarter there are some interesting old relics that literally have been built into the modern houses, carved beams and adzed lintels from the earlier periods supporting the ugly mud walls of the present. It is a tragic thing to see stern old relics come down so far in the scale of architecture, but it is strangely appropriate in another sense, this graphic decline of an ancient culture.

There is no such thing as a history of Halvad. At any rate,

48

there is no clear, organized statement of the origins and subsequent fortunes of the village to be got from the Brahmins who are responsible for such things. They are interesting old men and they can talk for hours in a fabulous mixture of fact and mythology, but when they have concluded their tales you are always aware that they have told you nothing that was not contradicted. There are legends that Halvad was established by Lord Krishna, who at one time made his home in nearby Dwarka. There is a story that it was founded by an envoy of Chandra Gupta when Kathiawar was a part of his far-reaching empire. There is even one Brahmin who habitually insists that the village did not have a beginning at all, and who discourses at length on the subjectivity of time to prove that Halvad could always have existed. I gave up after a while, for it became apparent that my quest for an objective recounting was unreasonable.

"But which story is true?" I would ask the Brahmins.

"Why, all of them are true!" they would invariably reply.

It was not important. In so far as Halvad was like most of the other old Kathiawar villages, its history was the history of the area generally, and it was not hard to construct a plausible account. Unfortunately, it was not a story of progress. It was rather a story of continual retrogression, of the depletion of the land, of a shifting of population, and of the consequent decline in the standard of living.

It is quite conceivable that Halvad existed as long ago as 200 B.C. If it did, it was a part of the highly organized and widely established Mauryan empire. It was certainly much richer than it is at present, as almost the whole of the peninsula was at that time, partly because its population was small but even more as the result of an efficient government. During the reign of Chandra Gupta particularly, Kathiawar was a well-administered province, its governor being appointed and sent by the emperor and charged not alone with the collection of taxes but with their wise and economic expenditure. Under the Mauryan kings there were operative bu-

49

reaus of mine, animal husbandry, trade, and irrigation, and one of the most notable achievements of the latter was the huge artificial lake at Girnar in Kathiawar.

To judge from the oldest inscriptions in the temple, Halvad, in the earliest phases of its history, had a more diverse agricultural and industrial life than its present inhabitants would dare to imagine. Mat weaving was a highly developed skill. Cotton was manufactured and dyed for export, and it is even quite probable that the abandoned stone quarries furnished blocks for paving Mauryan roads. For roads there were, not the narrow ruts that in this age are the only means of transportation, but well-planned highways connecting the ports of the western coast with the Indian interior.

Most simply considered, the Mauryan kingdom was classically feudal in its organization. The institutions of Halvad, in 300 B.C., must have been much like those of Europe during the twelfth century. Under the Mauryan kings the cultivator was expected to pay a sixth of his crop to the government in taxes, in return for which he received numerous benefits of both a military and a civil nature. The Mauryan state was a police state; according to Arthasastra there were five kinds of political spies, idlers, astrologers, ascetics, and prostitutes being frequently hired to supplement the regulars. The caste system had already been highly developed, but it was probably not the abusive thing that it now is, being primarily a system of professions and guilds that, though religiously sanctioned, were economic in function.

But it was in the fifteenth century that the political institutions of Halvad must have assumed their present form, for it was then that the Mewari Rajput empire defeated the Gurjura and annexed its territory. Under Lakha Singh the Kathiawar rajahs were confirmed to rule the local peoples, and it was these rajahs in their turn who established the present durbar system in the scattered villages. It is likely that in Halvad in the fifteenth century there was just a single powerful tribal chief, the present system of family rule being a later ruinous corruption of the idea. The duties of this durbar were widely varied. He was a tax collector, but that was not all, for he was held strictly to account, by the rajah and his officers, for the welfare and prosperity of the people of his village.

There was never a collapse of the durbar system. There was simply a diminution of the vitality at the center of the state, the Mewari empire being weakened by the Moguls to the point where its peripheral jurisdictions relaxed. The rajahs persisted, but it began to occur to them that the profits of the taxation of the states were all theirs and that they need no longer worry about affairs of finance beyond the needs of their privy purses. Thus the men who were once energetic tyrants, ambitious for their states and ambitious for themselves, began to assume the characteristics of the modern rajahs to the inevitable detriment of the states and their people. As the rajahs relaxed, the durbars relaxed. The corruption spread from top to bottom till, like the jackal who will feed from his own wounded body, the state settled down to devouring itself.

So the appearance of Halvad is no deception. In the crumbling houses and the decaying temples the history of the village can be accurately read, the history of decadence and disintegration. The shrines are appropriate. The temples are appropriate. Most of all, the gods themselves are appropriate, for in their successive stages of retrogression they symbolize the declining fortunes of the village. When I first saw Halvad by moonlight there seemed only one phrase in literature to describe what I felt. Eliot's line could well have been written there—"This broken jaw of our lost kingdoms."

[8]

MY ARRIVAL in Halvad was an event of some importance. From the beginning it was a subject of suspicion and curiosity, for at the least I brought news from the outside world and provided a new subject of gossip in the market. And at the most? Opinion was about evenly divided whether I was a government spy or a fleeing criminal. Quite unwittingly I solved this problem almost immediately by refusing the hospitality of the police patel; he was an unpleasant old man and my reasons for snubbing him were based chiefly on this simple and personal consideration. But, fortunately for me, he resented my impertinence and warned the people to have nothing to do with me. It was all that was needed. The villagers were my friends and as friends they agreed to lodge and keep me.

For the first few weeks I had a house to myself. It was an unwholesome place with neither chimney nor windows, but with a disconcerting number of perverse little cracks that, while they would not permit the egress of smoke, seemed to invite and admit every chilly draft. Its overall measurements could not have been more than a scant fifteen by twenty feet, notwithstanding the fact that through most of the year it was the habitation of a joint family of some fourteen souls. It was constructed of dried mud like most of the others, and like them it was in a perpetual state of rebuilding, a crack plastered here and a chink stopped there till the walls had the appearance of a bad patchwork quilt. The floor was mud too, but it had been surfaced with cow dung that was worked to an almost cementlike finish, being shiny and hard, and though inclined to chip off, considerably cleaner than the flaking walls. Since there were no closets or shelves, the belongings of the owners were strewn about with the most willful abandon, saris and cooking pots, jewelry and dried peas scattered all over the floor in an unsorted litter. My unwitting host was a koli farmer who had gone east with his family to visit one of the temples, but when his neighbors offered me his hospitality in absentia, I accepted it immediately and without compunction.

Still I was a long time in establishing rapport with the villagers, for however well we might be disposed toward each other there was the considerable barrier of language between us, which no amount of good will could dissolve. There were some men, to be sure, who spoke Hindustani, but almost without exception they were men with whom I could not deal. There was the police patel who had already been eliminated, and there were a few banias who had traveled in the north. But in the koli community where there was an abundance of sympathy, alas, there was an equal lack of learning, so that for the first few days I was able to communicate nothing more abstract than my physical needs.

Then Baghwan appeared. At first sight, he looked little like the valuable ally that he eventually proved. His hair was full of lice, his clothes were filthy, and his incessant scratching had caused large, open sores which it was his particular pleasure to divest of their scabs with an intensity of interest that was frightful to behold. He was a village orphan, one of a number of children whose families had been vaguely dispersed around them, some to the burning ghats, others to the cities, a few following will-o'-the-wisp rumors of employment. Baghwan's father was living but was off soldiering somewhere; it was while following his camps that the boy had learned Hindustani. Only recently, having tired of the youngster's presence, he had returned him to Halvad and to the charity of the villagers, which consisted in less than occasional scraps of food and more than occasional beatings for thievery. Baghwan was nine years old, but it was a long nine years, for he was more sophisticated than the majority of adults of Halvad. He was not suspicious of strangers as they were, and since there was no one who cared to restrict his movements he was willing to move into my hut bag and baggage, which is to say with his dhoti and one small brass pot.

It all began as a commercial arrangement; Baghwan was to act as my servant-cum-interpreter, his duties including everything from scouring out pans to interrogating the priests on subjects of metaphysics. He did both of these ably and with considerable enthusiasm, but it was inevitable that our relationship should become increasingly personal, for as Baghwan himself was wont to point out, "We are men of experience. We understand each other."

Of a morning, it was the custom of we "men of experience" to set out on a quest for food and gossip, a combination less arbitrary than it sounds in Halvad where these two form the staples of life. Our shopping itself was a leisurely business and we would often spend hours in one or another of the stalls, arguing good naturedly with the owner and his friends and consuming his margin of profit as we did so. In personal relations even the shopkeepers were generous, though it was their professional inclination to be otherwise, and it was not uncommon for them to send out for tea while we were arguing over prices worth a fraction of its cost!

The durbars were good for gossip too. When we left the shops we would frequently repair to the broad pavilion in the middle of the square to pay our respects to them. Often we were denied this. They would all be sleeping or at least lying back in a stuporous condition, dirty and disheveled and breathing hard like a pack of hounds at the end of a hunt. On these occasions Baghwan would explain to me that they had just drawn their biweekly allotment of opium. They did not trust themselves; they paid in advance and were given the stuff in a regular ration. Still, when the durbars were able, they were wonderfully garrulous and, though they never talked about anything of consequence, they could talk about nothing with such a subtle wit that it was always interesting to visit them. They were like the ruined temples, these durbars of Halvad, disjointed remnants of a former glory that, while largely merged with the degenerate present, would occasionally blaze up in its previous brilliance. No peasant humor was theirs, no raucous, backslapping laughter like the koli laborer's, but a delicately subtle and decadent wit, sighed with a languishing gesture or smile.

But it is the evenings that I remember with the greatest fondness. Then Baghwan and I would brew coffee at home and he would tell me stories about the people whom we had met, advising me when to believe them and when to be skeptical. He was a good advisor. His lies were transparent enough not to mislead me seriously, or for long, and his truths were based, in spite of his youth, on an experience that was exceptionally broad and humane.

Occasionally some of our neighbors would stop in to talk. They had learned that there was always good coffee to be had, and I was more than willing to share it with them in exchange for their welcome company. The kolis of Halvad were quiet and unimaginative, so much so that I had rather disliked them at first. But during our evening gatherings I began to understand them and to value all the more the few words that they spoke.

Only the banias I found impossible to like. There was about them a brusque, unfriendly quality that I could not understand in the light of the ready good will I had found in other quarters. I was particularly annoyed to discover, eventually, almost all of the banias spoke fluent Hindustani and that it was simply an expression of their natural perversity that they had pretended they could not understand me when I first had arrived.

The banias were innately suspicious. Nor was their curiosity the naïve, innocent curiosity which I had come to understand; it was a sort of belligerent assumption that they were entitled to an explanation of anything that did not make immediate sense to them. They avoided me in the streets, but came often to my house to stare sullenly and unashamedly through the door, relaying to each other an account of my movements and particularly, of any new peculiarity which they could discover.

The thing that annoyed me most about the banias was the delight that they took in watching me shave. A safety razor was a novelty to them so my use of one amounted to a moral wrong. As soon as I began to lather my face, one or two would come in and stand at my elbow, mimicking my actions and peering over my shoulder with expressions of the most clear and undisguised disgust. When I was finished, they would examine my brush and razor, holding them up and laughing inordinately together, and it was only when they were sure that the performance was over that they would leave, muttering, "Conceited fool!" or "Cocky foreigner!"

There was nothing I could do. Baghwan warned me what to expect and suggested that I simply ignore the insults. If I did not, he assured me, the banias would see to it that I was driven from the village immediately. To have their contempt was one thing, he reminded me, but to have earned their genuine dislike quite another, for if they decided that I was distinctly *personna non grata*, there would be no one in Halvad who could stand against them.

I learned that the majority of the banias were Jains; that is, members of a small but exotic sect that has gained some attention in the West because of its strange preoccupation with the protection of all forms of animal life. I thought Baghwan was joking when he told me that many of them hired coolies to sweep the insects out of their paths through the streets, but I discovered that it was true, so anxious were the Jains that they should not take the life of a single small being. I questioned one once with regard to this practice, suggesting that some insects would be killed in the sweeping.

"That is true," he admitted. Then after reflecting for a moment he added, "But that is all right. The sweepers are Hindus!"

Of a morning it is the custom of the traditionary Jain to

scatter sugar on the ground in front of his house to feed the procession of roaches and ants who regularly congregate there. He will be dressed in white, for the Jains have discovered that some dies are manufactured from animal matter and, in the case of a most highly religious type, he will wear gauze over his nose so that he may not inhale germs.

And yet, if there is one thing that distinguishes the Halvad Jain bania even more clearly than his kindness to the lower-life forms, it is his casual and yet almost unbelievable cruelty toward the less fortunate of his fellow human beings. Starvation is not uncommon in Halvad. There are probably more than twenty-five deaths each year resulting from the immediate failure of a crop or from the compounded effects of malnutrition. The children of Halvad have the spindly legs and the swollen bellies of the underfed and in the evening they can often be seen picking through the garbage, vying with the pye-dogs for the edible morsels. Hunger is all about. There are unfortunate women who have borne as many as a dozen children and who have not one of them left to fill the old cradles or to inherit the cast-off clothing of their fathers. And yet on feast days, the Jain banias can often be seen sowing bajri and jowar grains broadcast in the streets. And woe unto the hungry child of Halvad who robs the insects while the bania is watching!

Nor is the cruelty of the bania just a negative thing. Many villagers would insist that he is the author of their poverty, that it is his habitual usury that is most clearly the cause of the disruption of the traditional village economy. It may well be true. At any rate, it was the bania who encouraged the people to cultivate tastes beyond their means, lending them money with the misleading assurance that they never need bother to pay back the principal. It was the bania who subsidized the dope addiction of the durbars so that they would relinquish even their small pretense at government, and it is the banias who are most anxious that the villagers

57

should continue their senseless competition over marriage expenses.

"But what about the Brahmins?" I asked Baghwan one evening. "Aren't the Brahmins charged with protecting the people?" The Brahmins, Baghwan explained, have followed in the faltering footsteps of the rajahs and the durbars. In the years gone by they were a power among their people, and by and large they had used this power for good, but in the general breakdown of the past few centuries, they have been glad to salvage just a few of their old privileges. A small sphere of exploitation still remains to them; they collect their fees on funerals and weddings or, if they are not attached to the temple proper, they might own a small field which the kolis work. But in general the Brahmins are not a force to be reckoned with. They are just a handful of weak and ineffectual old men who are permitted to exist because the banias have decided that it would be cheaper to buy than to defeat them.

The effect on the religion itself is striking. The Hinduism of Halvad is a degenerate thing, the real content having been long since replaced by a mystical mumbo jumbo that is convenient to the ignorant priesthood. Ayurvedic medicine is unknown in Halvad. The old Hindu law has been virtually forgotten while the study of Sanskrit has come to the point where most of the temple Brahmins only pretend to speak it. One result is that the people have by-passed the temple, building shrines in their homes and ignoring the priests, though the priests are aware of the dangers in this practice and have managed to keep it within narrow limits. Whenever a plague breaks out in Halvad, they insist that it is a punishment which they have called down, and though I suspect that the people only half believe it, still they do not care to argue about cholera or typhoid.

During my last days in Halvad I was invited by the Brahmins to witness a demonstration of their powers. Though it was not yet apparent, they explained that a disease was about to break out among the villagers' cattle. There was just one way to avert it, as they had warned the herdsmen. They, the Brahmins, could outwit the spirits of the sickness and, though it was an arduous undertaking, they were sorry for the herdsmen and would perform the service for only one hundred rupees.

On the night of the exorcism they erected two poles from which a rope was stretched taut across the main street of the village. Then they anointed the backs of the cattle with todi, a powerful drink of fermented palm sap. On their command, the cattle were driven between the poles and under the rope in a virtual stampede and, when this had been done, the Brahmins officially pronounced that the spirits of the disease were dead.

"But what is the significance of the rope?" I wondered.

One of the Brahmins undertook to explain it to me. "When the cattle run under the rope, the spirits who are riding on their backs are knocked off and trampled."

I tried to show the proper respect but I was still curious. "And what about the todi?" I asked.

"Oh, the todi," explained the priest, "is to drug the spirits. If they were sober they might duck beneath the rope!"

I was not the only unbeliever in the crowd. All the herdsmen themselves laughed loudly at the explanation.

"But you paid a hundred rupees!" I reminded them.

"With these Brahmins you never can be sure!" they answered.

[9]

OF ALL the people who visited Baghwan and me, the one that I liked most was a farmer named Dharamdas. He was a large-boned young koli who came often in the evening to sit and listen to other men talk. Dharamdas had little to say himself, but it was not because he lacked the imagination for he would sit quietly intent through the other men's arguments, clasping and unclasping his large, bony hands. Occasionally he would decide that he wanted to speak. His eyes would light up and his lips would part. But they would usually close without uttering a sound, for the conversation would have passed him by. One night our eyes met just after this happened. "You had something to say, Dharamdas," I whispered. He knotted his hands and looked down at the ground.

"I have much to say. *But the words!*" he groaned.

I remember one night in particular, however, when the majority of the kolis had already gone home, and Dharamdas and two or three others were waiting while I brewed one final pot of coffee. It seems almost like a dream, I was so tired myself. I don't even recall what I said to Dharamdas. But all at once we were sitting together in the courtyard and he was telling me, ecstatically, about the village where he was born.

"All green!" he was saying. "You cannot imagine it! Green. Not for a mile or two, but forever." He stretched out one thick and calloused hand as if trying to touch the elusive vision.

A flicker of doubt passed across his face and he stared thoughtfully down at the sand for a moment. "Of course, we remember things better than they are. You believe there is a land such as that which I describe?"

"I am sure of it," I said with the air of a conspirator. "I have seen such lands myself, Dharamdas. There are places where a man can ride for days without coming to the end of the cultivated fields."

"Yes," Dharamdas hissed, managing to keep his voice low in spite of the rising emotion behind it. "I have described it to them, but they do not believe me. You and I, Sahib!" He laughed. "We know of these things."

"To the East," I continued, caught up in the romance, "there are lands where the water runs over the ground, where there is so much water that all a farmer need do is dig channels from the stream, to bring it across his fields."

Dharamdas' eyes were closed but he was smiling broadly, the firelight reflecting on his moist, open lips. "Yes, yes!" he was chanting. "It is just like that. It is just like that in the village where I was born."

"Kuwad," he said fondly. "That was the name of the village. Kuwad." He handled the word carefully, like a talisman, turning it over and over in his mind and on his tongue for the joy of feeling its familiar surfaces.

"Kuwad is on the coast, a long way from here. A hundred, two hundred, perhaps three hundred miles." He pointed his finger out into the darkness and said positively, "Right over there!

"But it is such a rich land, Sahib!" His enthusiasm was rekindled. "It is so rich that the date palms grow wild in the fields." He picked up a handful of sand and looked at it. "Black! . . . the soil in Kuwad," he muttered.

"When I was young, my father was a wealthy man—oh, perhaps not wealthy as the sahibs use the word. But our house was well built and we had plenty to eat; to have plenty to eat is to be wealthy in the villages! My father owned fields, large fields for a koli; ten or twelve acres, perhaps even more, and the land was so black that things grew by themselves. We were very happy in Kuwad."

"But then why did you leave?" I wondered.

"Well, my family inherited this land," he replied. "And since our fields in Kuwad were to be divided among four of us, I agreed to come and settle in Halvad.

"In Kuwad," he continued, "we worked ten hours a day, weeding and plowing and harvesting mostly. Here I spend ten hours in irrigating alone from these ridiculous little bucket wells. And the salt! A well will be fine one year, yet the next it will be so brackish that you cannot even use it.

61

Or the brine will rise in the middle of a field and ruin a whole year's work.

"All year long we must irrigate. Even fallow fields must have water poured over them as if they were seeded. If you stop for a month the salt will rise and it will be years before you can plant again."

"But it is not just the soil that causes this, surely." I waved my hand to indicate the village. "There is more to the poverty of Halvad and Kathiawar than just the fact that the land is poor."

Dharamdas did not answer, but he picked up another handful of sand and, holding it high above his head, he let it run out, the crystals flickering in the firelight as it fell.

"There are the banias," I said. The sand kept falling. Dharamdas seemed to feel that it answered my objection.

"And the Brahmins," I added. Still the sand sifted down. Dharamdas did not feel it was necessary to speak.

I knew what he meant. The land was poor and to the farmer this was a good explanation of all ills. The Brahmins? The banias? You could withstand almost anything if you could only count on the sky and the earth.

When Dharamdas left, I noticed that he still had a handful of sand which he was examining intently. A week later he had sold his land to the banias and returned to Kuwad to farm with his brothers.

North Gujarat

North Gujarat

[10]

THE Rann of Kutch is a geographer's nightmare. No two maps seem to agree on even its general description. In the publications most common in the West, it is colored and labeled as an inland sea; in at least one that I know of it appears as a desert while, for the conciliatory purposes of the Survey of India, it is permitted the noncommittal designation of a swamp.

The truth is, the Rann is all of these and more, depending on the season when the map maker happens to see it; it is an enormous flat plain from which the ocean is receding in an absent-minded and hesitant way and over which the elements are in a constant dispute whether it shall be a dry salt flat or a shallow lake. During the monsoons the Rann is entirely impassible. Even during January it is a dangerous journey, for there are numberless bogs that, though crusted on the surface, are deep enough and soft enough to swallow a camel. Worst of all, there are no charts of the Rann. There cannot be any since it shifts from week to week. All sensible people are content to avoid it; it is only the occasional curious foreigner or the highly experienced and professional smuggler who, for their respective reasons of whim and profit, are willing to attempt its treacherous crossing.

Still, on the edge of the Rann there are a few scattered villages which, lacking all visible means of support, are commonly if not officially supposed to live on the profits of a "Trans-Rann" smuggling. It has never been proved that the Kathiawar rajahs themselves participate in this ill-concealed trade, but it is a matter of record that they have never done anything to help the central government destroy it. Indeed, when I arrived in one of these villages, a large shipment of candy was being prepared for export, very carefully concealed in large burlap bags which were ostensibly full of camel fodder. Two state cars were parked on the outskirts of the village and the men who were directing the whole operation were dressed in the white trousers and black coats which I had come to consider the uniform of the rajahs' courts. But since I was contraband myself, or traveling as such, my presence in K—— was not resented. Though my greatest delinquency was a habitual failure to register my change of address with the police, I hugged even this minor crime to my breast till I felt very much a part of the illegal scene.

On the morning following my arrival at K—— I embarked on my trip across the Rann by camel. It had been easy to arrange and the principle was simple: cash on the barrel head and no questions asked. My driver was a small Punjabi Moslem and his camel one of the hard-riding Sindhi varieties that are particularly distinguished by their stamina on the trail and by their ability to traverse long distances between water. I was not used to a camel. Though I flattered myself that I was a reasonably good rider where horses were concerned, I very soon discovered that even a tall Irish hunter presents none of the problems of these thirty-hand desert ships. It was impossible to rise in the stirrups; the principle seemed one of complete relaxation to the gait. But my riding was apparently too unsteady for the camel, for by the end of the first day his hind legs were lame.

"But the worst is yet to come!" warned the driver. "Tomorrow and the next day will be the hardest of all for so far we have been skirting the edge of the Rann, but at dawn we must finally strike out across it."

He was right. By noon of the second day I was almost swooning with heat and fatigue. We allowed ourselves a pint of water per day, but I found that I was losing that much

66

each hour. My face was burned from the reflected glare and my hands were blistered where they clung to the saddle, and now a hot, dry wind blowing from nowhere to nowhere drove rough salt crystals into my flesh till it sprung drops of blood. My driver spoke once. I tried to answer, but I discovered that my lips were hard and scabrous, burned into their grimace of fatigue and despair like some molded and lacquered tragic mask. I bathed them with urine when we halted for the night since my driver assured me it would take out the sting. It was nauseous but effective; after several applications the pain subsided and I was able to go to sleep.

But our crossing was uncomfortable in another sense, too; there was something other-worldly and unreal about the Rann. Being alone is one thing amidst foliage and vegetation. It is another when there is nothing but earth and sky. During the day the horizon was no more than an abstraction, a dancing, fluid, changing thing deceptively broken by lakelike mirages and by even more confusing miragelike lakes. It was like wandering around in a hall of mirrors a hundred miles long and a hundred miles wide. It was like standing on an island in the middle of the sky with light washing the ground from beneath our feet.

As the sun went down, every tiny mound, imperceptible through the day, cast its small, dark shadow so that when you looked to the west it was as if darkness were bubbling from the very ground in tiny springs. The fringe of the sky was hysterically colorful, but it was awful rather than beautiful to behold, the bleak, curved horizon arching up into the aurora like the desolate edge of some forgotten world. And the Rann was quiet. Though the wind blew constantly it was like a ghost wind that passed without making a sound, with neither trees nor bushes nor blades of grass to arrest or apprehend or signal its passage. The camel's soft feet made no sound as we went and neither the driver nor I were in a mood for talking. We were too burned and tired and uncomfortable from our riding, too withdrawn from the sickening immensities around us.

Even our camel was suffering. There were frequent dried ponds where the hardened salt crystals were like glass beneath his feet, cutting into the soft pads till he bellowed with pain and left tracks of blood across the even, white surface. In the end it was necessary for us to skirt these deposits as an alternative to breaking the animal completely. This was not easy to do when we were already having trouble picking our way between lakes and mirages.

I began to be worried. I knew that we were depending on striking an oasis on the evening of the third day, which would be a difficult feat, considering these detours and the informal nature of our celestial navigation. The driver asserted that the wind held steady and that with this as a crossbearing we could not go wrong, but since his words seemed to me more confident than his manner, I was worried about our limited quantity of water. And my fears were justified. On the evening of the third day we still had not sighted the oasis as we had expected. We could always have borne east to save our lives, but this would have meant risking capture by the border police. Leaving me in camp that evening, my driver rode out to scan the horizon for some glimpse of greenery, but when he returned he announced that he had sighted nothing but some stakes which might or might not indicate a trail. In the morning we decided to follow the stakes, hoping they would be the marks of some recent caravan, but around noon we were confounded again when we discovered that a bog had formed across our path. We detoured once more, our camel bellowing suspiciously as the ground continued to crack beneath his weight, sending crazy fissures snaking out on all sides with a succession of rumbling and crackling sounds. On two occasions, we broke completely through. On both we had to unload the camel, then, much against his will, roll him over several times till he was back on firm ground where he could stand again safely.

But it was the camel in the end who found the oasis. Around noon of the fourth day he began veering to the wind-ward and in spite of any amount of coaxing and beating, he set out on a northerly course of his own. We finally gave him his head, having no convictions of our own as strong as his, and in an hour we had reached the oasis where, as we sus-pected, a herd of females were already stopping.

The oasis itself was a disappointment. To me the word had always suggested a grand and almost magical verdure rising suddenly and unexplainably from the middle of a desert. Alas, in this case the oasis was no more than a single scraggly scrub acacia tree and a shallow well whose water was so brackish that neither Raza nor I could keep it down.

But there was a keeper of the well. He was a garrulous old Moslem who had lived at the oasis for more than two years, trading whatever services he could provide for the scraps of food passing caravans would give him. He was so starved for company that when he saw us coming he ran out in the sand to meet us, beginning a steady stream of conversation while we were still a good two miles away. Sounds carry on the Rann, but not that well. By the time we were actually close enough to hear him he had disposed of the formalities of introduction and had begun a statement of his philosophy of life.

Still, he proved valuable to us in the end. He kept a herd of female camels for the milk they gave and though he pro-tested that there was only enough for himself he agreed to share it when we threatened to move on. As a consequence we were able to lay over a few days. Our camel badly needed the rest, and as for myself, I was only too glad of the chance to shelter my blistered skin from the sun.

[11]

DURING the first four days of our trip across the Rann, not a hundred words could have passed between me and my driver. I was far too impressed by the dangers of our undertaking, too conscious of the spirit of illegal conspiracy to risk all of the usual eager questions that had become almost habitual by now. For my driver's part, he was a tight-lipped, forboding man whose whole manner and bearing suggested secrecy. He went about with his eyes on the ground and his head tucked down between his shoulders, darting suspicious glances back and forth around him with all the quiet, expectant malice of a foraging timber wolf. It was rare that I had occasion to speak to him; when I did it always seemed to take him by surprise, for he would look up at me quickly, but he would never reply before working his lips in a sort of silent rehearsal, and even after that, he would mumble his words so that I could scarcely understand him. While we were traveling, I had been only too pleased by this reticence for I had formed an almost immediate and unreasonable dislike of the man, but at the oasis, after a bath and a few hours' rest, I began to regard him with a more active curiosity.

Raza was incredibly dirty. This was certainly the first thing that would have struck anyone who looked at him. It was not just the innocent dirt of childhood, a dab on the arm and a streak on the face; rather, it was that ingenious, almost sensual dirtiness that only the most practiced and sophisticated adult can achieve. His hair was matted into long, greasy plaits that surely had never known a comb or a brush, yet it was his particular vanity to douse it liberally, night and morning, with a mixture of rancid coconut oil and cheap perfume. This was to assure the vitality of the scalp, Raza would explain, and that it did this one would surely have had to grant him, for to judge by its abounding insect life, a more vital scalp would be hard to imagine. Yet in all ways the effect was far from lovely; invariably Raza used more oil than was needed so that, from long exposure, his shirts were stained with it, and during the day little streams would run down over his face. Moreover, since the oil had a jasmine scent, it attracted great swarms of steam flies and gnats with the result that from a distance he always had the appearance of a particularly disreputable but haloed saint. Raza and his camel were inseparable companions. At night he would lie down by the very side of the beast and, pressing himself close against its sweaty, odorous fur, sleep as calmly and as happily as in the arms of a beloved. Indeed, as some men come to look like their wives, Raza had grown to resemble his camel; his movements had the same, strange awkward efficiency, his skin was infected with the same diseases, and his teeth, for some reason neither discoverable nor imaginable, always seemed to be stained the same ruminant green.

And yet dramatic as Raza's dirtiness was, it was not this that I remember most clearly about him; it was something less tangible, less easily explained. It was an aura of intense sadness that hung about him, a belligerent and malevolent melancholia that issued from his body in the same unmistakable manner as did the hosts of body and camel odors. It was like a disease, this sadness, like some subtle plague that had spread its infection in the heart of the man and that had written its record, as diseases will, in the sunken cheeks and the ravaged body. It was not that Raza frowned or scowled disproportionately; far from it, if anything he smiled too much. But it was a vacant smile that was the refinement of unhappiness, a smile that had no connection with feeling, the smile of a man who remembered an expression but had forgotten the occasions on which it was appropriate. His eyes must have had something to do with this impression; they were a weak gray-blue, entirely out of keeping with the rest of his dark and strongly marked features. When you looked into these eyes, you felt no comfort at all, no sense of communion with another human mind. In an abstract way, I was often tempted to probe into the mind that must lay behind them, but when it came to doing so the prospect always terrified me, precisely as would the prospect of embracing a leper!

It was late in the evening of our third day at the oasis when the old keeper of the oasis had talked himself out. He was chattering away of one thing and another while Raza and I tried our best to ignore him when suddenly, with no warning, he hesitated, groped for a word, and unable to find it lay back and went to sleep. Raza and I were as tired from listening to the old fellow as he must have been from talking, but we decided to stay up just to enjoy the silence that was now unbroken but for the occasional word that our host would still mutter to himself in his sleep. We sat down by the well and filled up our pipes with the one package of moldy tobacco we had between us. It was dry and tasteless and had never been much good, even on the day that I bought it from the farmer, but we puffed away with an ascetical determination just to be doing something that would keep us awake.

After a few minutes, Raza came scuttling over, crab fashion, along the ground. He was in one of those rare moods when he wanted to talk, but since he had nothing to say he only looked at me wistfully, as if begging to be diverted from his own introspections. There was nothing about him which invited my sympathy. I never felt genuine sympathy for Raza, but after he had been pleading with me silently for perhaps ten minutes, I felt that I must break the silence somehow. I said the first thing that came into my head, asking how long he had been crossing the Rann.

His face twitched and he stammered, "All of my life, Sahib," in a tone so gentle that it seemed to implore me to ask more questions that could be answered as simply.

I tried. "Then you were born near here?" It occurred to me too late that I had phrased my question carelessly.

Raza saw what he considered was a chance to please me. "Oh, yes!" he replied. "At this very oasis."

The fact, of course, was not that he had been born here; perhaps he had been born some thousands of miles distant, but he was playing the part of a faithful friend and servant, laying this verbal offering at my feet. I decided that I must change the subject, for I knew that once begun this chain could not be broken, that if I began to suggest more reasonable alternatives, Raza would enthusiastically agree to each of them in turn.

"What did your father do?"

Raza waited a moment, hoping that I might suggest some occupation, but I was wiser now, so after a pause he replied, "When he lost his farm he came here to pan salt."

"And your family came with him?"

"My mother did," he answered. "My brothers and I were born in these parts." He smiled. "You know, till I was nine years old, I thought the whole world was just like the Rann."

"But you must have lived near the edge," I reflected. "Otherwise you would not have had drinking water."

"We were about twenty miles from the nearest village," Raza agreed, "but all the water was brought in by my older brothers."

"And you never went with them till you were nine years old?"

Raza corrected me. "At nine I ran away by myself. There was a caravan passing within a few miles of our place and I joined it. Since then I have been traveling back and forth." It was said so simply that the significance almost escaped me. I said "Oh," and was about to change the subject to politics, religion, or the business of smuggling. And then suddenly I felt the full impact of the words.

"You have spent all of your life on the Rann, then?" I asked, trying hard to conceal the horror that I felt.

73

"Well, most of it," Raza agreed. "I have a wife in a village, but I almost never stop long enough to stay with her there."

"Good God! What a depressing life!" I blurted.

"Depressing?" Raza murmured. He was not offended.

"Well, look!" I said, waving my hand toward the horizon. "Not a tree or a blade of grass in sight."

Raza looked up. He wore a defensive expression, as if he were being asked to criticize a friend. "One gets used to it," he shrugged, but he continued to stare as if he were trying to see what one would have to get used to.

I decided to press him as far as I could. "What is the farthest you have been from the Rann?" I asked.

"Perhaps a hundred miles," he replied. "I once took a train to the town called Viramgam."

"And what did you do in Viramgam?" I queried.

"Oh, I got off the train and came back," he explained. "But I could see the whole place from the station platform. It is a wonderful town, this Viramgam, Sahib."

Now it was Raza's turn to question me. His own curiosity had apparently been aroused, for after regarding me intently for several moments he said suddenly, "And you. You come from near here?"

I laughed. "No, I come from America," I said. But the name apparently meant nothing to Raza.

"America?" he said.

"America is a country many thousands of miles from here," I explained.

Raza repeated after me, "Many thousands of miles . . ." His brow was furrowed in concentration. All at once he seemed to comprehend. "Ah, it is even farther than Viramgam," he said.

[12]

IT WAS several days after this that we left the Rann behind us. True to the perversity which I had begun to expect of it, it came to no definite, decisive end, but merged gradually with the country that lay to the east, tree by tree and house by house, reaching its greedy sand fingers into the bordering farmlands. One of the first signs of life that we encountered in our course was a herd of wild asses, foolish little beasts that inhabit this fringe and that, in keeping with the whole impossible character of the place, having thrown off their role as beasts of burden to style themselves beasts of prey instead, foraging in the villages and tilled farmlands by night, by day taking refuge on these broad salt spaces against the occasional hunter or angry farmer. As we passed them, they stood together in a band, six or seven of them in the shade of a coconut palm, blinking at us and switching their tails in a sort of lazy, somnolent greeting.

We came next upon a deserted village lying spoiled and broken beneath an advancing sand spit, only the tops of its houses and a few crenelated old walls standing erect like small forts that had fallen to a siege. In a sense they were just that, the enemy in this instance having been the malevolent phalanx of advancing sand; one could imagine the villagers fighting against it, clearing their fields for a few futile years before surrendering and going to the cities to beg. And there was one village, too, only nearly deserted, still inhabited by its last two men when we passed through. They were father and son; during the day the boy spent his time panning salt from the underlying brine while the old man, who was blind, went crying through the streets, his white, blank eyes staring wide at nothing as he ran curious fingers over the old façades and muttered incredulously when a familiar one had changed or crumbled. So cruel was fate, he was mad as well as blind, and he would sit for hours in the dust-choked streets, his gray head drooping and his knuckles pressed into his eye sockets, crying loudly to himself in the hot, awful darkness.

But there were so many like him. Since the Rann is a public domain, on its borders dwell all manner of pathetic creatures, men who have fled from the unfriendly towns and cities to these neither friendly nor unfriendly immensities. There are cripples, widows, farmers dispossessed elsewhere who drift hopelessly about from one place to the other, advising each other but never quite believing, "They say that to the north . . ." or "I have a cousin who tells me . . ." Behind them in the sand they leave their pathetic wreckages strewn about to mark their unhappy trails, broken pots and torn clothing, castoff toys, even crumpled boxes that must once have been the cradles of children now hobbling about somewhere in pitiless old age. In the abandoned fields, old plows jut up, plows long since conquered by their patient furrows, and in the deserted villages there are the jagged remains of shops and houses in silent rows, through whose windows only the vacant sky is now framed like a gallery of surrealistic paintings.

But this too, in its turn, we left behind us. For perhaps four hours we sighted along this fringe, picking one ruin after the other from the horizon, then riding it down till we caught sight of the next. At last Raza decided we might chance swinging eastward; he reasoned that we were far enough north of the police lines so that any stray officer we chanced to encounter would be free to accept a bribe for passing us. But fortunately not even a bribe was necessary. We crossed the barrier by the much simpler expedient of slipping in behind the mirage at high noon and proceeding invisible between two distant outposts. And after this, the villages began abruptly—the live villages this time, loud, hot, and foul smelling; yet far from being repelled by their squalor as I had been once, I was only too glad for their noisy humanity, for the loud laughter of the women, and for their bright-colored saris, for the hosts of smells that assailed our nostrils, even for the bravado barking of the pye-dogs, at whom I happily threw stones from the safe height of our camel.

Racially, the people to the east of the Rann were not very much different from the Kathiawaris. Strictly speaking, they were not a race at all, but an imperfect mixture of a great many races. Among the kolis and untouchables, those men I met working as sweepers in the villages or as cultivators there, was—as I had noticed to be the case in Kathiawar—a distinct preponderance of broad-faced Gujrati. From the zemindars and durbars, the landowning groups, they differed racially as well as economically and socially, these latter being the descendants of the various invasions which had swept through this countryside in historical turns. Like Kathiawar, the region was something of a polyglot, bearing the separate and distinct marks of all these invasions, and yet here, though the physical conditions were the same, the results were surprisingly different. While in Kathiawar there seemed to be a vast accumulation from all of the periods of conquest and merger, along the borders of the Sind there was precisely the opposite—a skeptical rejection of all of the forms that, one after the other, had been brought and forced on them. Where Kathiawar had accepted and digested each invasion, this area had suffered them and yielded only externally. Where Kathiawar was suspicious and medieval, jealous of all of the old traditions that had lodged there, these people had only been made frank and skeptical by the same host of contradictory notions and systems. It was an interesting and puzzling thing that in similar areas, the same histories should have such divergent results; the one explanation that occurred to me most readily rose out of their differing geographical situations. Peninsula that it was, Kathiawar was perhaps a more natural repository than the mainland would have been for

77

all the myths, superstitions, religions, and authorities that had been brought to each section in historical sequence. Where the Merwara and Gujarat and Rajput civilizations had merely washed over this land that bordered the Sind, in Kathiawar they had found themselves contained as in a cul-de-sac so that even today they had not been dissipated. At any rate, whether for this reason or another, I soon discovered that those qualities of the Kathiawar durbars, which I had liked, here were to be met with not only among the Rajputs but through every level of the population. There was the same irreligion, so refreshing a thing in a country as ridden with religions as India, and there was the same sense of humor at once worldly and simple, which reduced every pretense to the most human terms. There was the innate kindness that was well concealed beneath a studied pretense at unconcern, and there was the wonderful, irrepressible Rajput vitality that flashed up from the patterns of decadence and disintegration.

While Raza and I were traveling near the Rann, both he and I were well received in spite of the fact that he was a Moslem and I a foreigner. For these border villages—transient as was their nature, and accustomed to a world somewhat wider than their horizon—were almost totally lacking in that self-satisfied provincialism in which the communal spirit characteristically flourishes. Near the edge of the Rann, our coming to a man's house was a cause for celebration, Hindu and Moslem alike, and even in those houses where there was nothing with which to celebrate, we were quartered, fed frugally, and sent on our way with a blessing. It was only as we began to work farther inland where the community was a more or less settled thing that the people grew conscious of the distinction between Hindu and Moslem and began to regard Raza with hostility or suspicion. At last, however, noticing his beard and the unmistakable Semitic cast of his features, they began meeting us in the doorways before we could dismount and explaining that while they themselves had no objections, there were some fanatics in the neighborhood who would render it unsafe for us to stop and unsafe for them to have us.

I had expected to leave Raza at the first opportunity. I was still anxious to do so, but I reconsidered now. Partly, I feared to leave him alone to work his way home through a hostile country when the carryover value of a white face was so great, even now that there was no government to back up its authority. Even more, I had begun to form a strange attachment to him, smells and lice and all, so that the prospect of resuming my lonesome journey did not particularly appeal to me as once it had.

It was at this point that we began having trouble with the camel. It was nothing that Raza had not expected, for since we had begun our Rann crossing he had been warning me that the season was approaching when "his heart will be full of passion." This passion, when it came, took the sudden and perverse form of a vicious bolt while I was riding alone, during the course of which he managed to unseat me, biting my arm in the process. I was not hurt badly, but I was frightened, for it is a belief of the Gujrati that the bite of a camel is poisonous, and though in the abstract I could see this as a baseless superstition, as one man against the many I could hardly remain calm. This decided my course. I was slung on our camel, my balance being affected by the temperature that I was running, and at Raza's insistence, I agreed to continue the remaining fifty miles to the village where he lived.

[13]

O F M Y first week in Bursad, I remember nothing distinctly but the uncomfortable charpoy bed on which I lay and the flimsy vermin-ridden roof above it. My arm had swollen to an enormous size, probably less as a result of the bite of our camel than as a consequence of the ministrations of a local midwife, and for about six days I lay in that not unpleasant daze which a persistent high fever is apt to induce. Once my temperature fell to normal, however, and I was able to look after my wound by myself, it was only another week before the swelling had gone down and the pus was entirely drained. It was some time before I could use the arm; for a while I could not even lift its own weight. But, after the dire predictions of Raza and the others, I was more than satisfied with the progress it made.

The house where I was quartered was unusually large. It had an unusually large population to match, there being three full families of husbands and wives, plus a regular contingent of widows and orphans whose relationships to each other were so complex that not even they could keep them straight. I was separated, after a fashion, from the family by a blanket hung down from one of the overhead beams, but it was a rather more touching than effective effort since it did nothing to discourage the chickens and turkeys that came in to roost on my bedrails at sunset, or the children who appeared as regularly each morning to stand staring at me solemnly when I was scheduled to awaken.

The family that kept me were Rajput Kshatriyas, members of the warrior caste. This was fortunate for me since, as in most Kshatriya households, one of the staples of diet in this one was meat. There were few enough Jains in Bursad so that they had not interfered with this custom as they had to the south, and I am sure that one reason for my steady recovery was the daily mutton stew I was given.

As always, I was at first regarded as a curiosity. I set out to make friends with the youngest children, for I had learned much earlier that it was through their good will that I could find the most ready acceptance from the adults. In Bursad I had an easier time than usual, probably as a result of my indisposition, for I am certain that I could not have looked especially dangerous when I was as frightened and unhappy and disheveled as I was then.

Only at one time did I knowingly jeopardize this good will. I insisted that a Western-trained doctor be called. There was one nearby and though I was warned against him by the host of self-appointed midwives and Ayurvedas, their objections I set down to simple superstition and insisted that they tell him there was someone who needed him. But he never came. He opined within hearing of my messengers that a sahib was a dangerous patient and that if anything happened to me while I was under his care, it might be that he would be held responsible. It was just as well, for my reaction was enough to reinstate me in the esteem of my friends in Bursad; never again did I joke about their local quacks, having seen Western medicine as it appeared to the villager.

During my illness, one of the cardinal social rules of the region was broken; I was attended by women, a thing unheard of, even in a Hindu household, in this district so strongly under Mogul influence. That I did not stay with Raza was only the result of his own wife's understandably greater reticence on this score, purdah to a Moslem being a matter of decency while to a Rajput it is no more than a half-hearted convention. Even so, it was surprising that once I had recovered completely I was not moved to some more conventional bachelor's quarters. Presumably I worked my way up from semiconsciousness so slowly that my presence never became an issue.

The woman who was in the most constant attendance upon me was a classic hag that one would expect to meet only in the pages of some nineteenth-century fairy tale, a pathetic old creature all bent and gnarled, used to the full extent of her eighty years. She was deaf and almost toothless, a single canine protruding obliquely from between her lips and another black stump where she could suck it incessantly and, according to its reactions, predict the weather. She wore a

81

scrap of an old sari that only partially covered the desiccated legs on which she hobbled about and, since she was incredibly stooped, her breasts hung down like withered remnants of leather. She was ignored by everyone except at those times when she would go into a sort of neurotic tantrum, moaning and beating her frail little body and protesting her uselessness to God and to man. Then the younger women would gather about her and snicker to themselves as she raged on happily, blaming the perversity of Vishnu which, she asserted, was the only thing that kept her alive. She was interesting, but a little bit wearing after a time since the two ranges of her voice were a whisper and a scream; she would sit for hours by the side of my bed, mumbling so quietly that I could not hear a word, then shouting loudly when in self-defense I would close my eyes and try to sleep.

Still, if Bhanu had been consulted, I am sure that I would never have been considered well enough to leave my bed, for after a week of attending me she had so warmed to her job that it was apparent that it satisfied every desire of her old heart. In the first place, it gave her something to do beside going to the market place and arguing with the banias, but even more, it provided a listener who was bound to one place and could not escape from her tongue.

There was another girl too, niece I think, though Hindustani is impossible for expressing these relationships, a fearful, secretive, yet pretty little thing perhaps somewhere between the ages of ten and twenty. I sensed immediately that she was a little weak-minded and more than a little bit oversexed, for she had that intense and nervous awareness of her own body which less excitable women find it easy to mask. When she entered my part of the room she would always slide furtively about from wall to wall as if fearing that once she approached too close to a man she could not be responsible for her impulses. I spoke to her seldom since she knew no Hindustani, but when I would speak at all she would stop, electrified, and stand looking at me with her mouth half open, rubbing the palms of her hands caressingly on her thighs.

It would irritate Bhanu, the old hag, if I noticed, for she had assumed a sort of proprietary air, and as often as not she would make some remark such as, "You are far too sick yet to think of these things!"

On these occasions I would put my arm about her, drawing her struggling and protesting to the bed beside me. "Now Bhanu!" I would say, "it is you that I love."

Then we would laugh together.

And then she would cry a little.

[14]

WHEN I was once again well enough to get about the village, I found that there was much to be seen in Bursad. It was a completely unconventional place, about half its inhabitants making their living by smuggling while the other half were equally divided between panning salt and distilling liquor. As practiced of course, each of these pursuits was illegal since revenue laws restricted them both, but though the Bursadians must certainly have been aware of this, it seemed to sit lightly indeed on their consciences. If anything, the village was more carefree and jovial than any I had seen before, its people being characterized by a Bohemian gaiety unthinkable to their settled and ascetic neighbors. They slept by day and lived by night, roaming freely and indiscriminately through each other's houses, lying down wherever fatigue overcame them, and eating from the pot that appealed to them at the moment. Even the police in Bursad, and there were always a great number, came only to collect bribes and to enjoy themselves, drinking and carousing in the illegal todi stalls and cautiously ignoring each other in the streets. This gave the place an air of intrigue, as if it existed from day to day on contracts and bribes, and one always had the feeling that if some contract fell through, the whole village could be vacated at an hour's notice.

And yet in spite of all this I had noticed a strange thing. There was a conspicuous lack of real wealth in Bursad; it was as if all of the money that came into the village were daily dumped down one of the abandoned wells. The streets were the usual twisted alleys with dirty, open drains—where they were drained at all—and the houses were, if anything, in even worse repair than the hovels of the farmers with whom I had stayed earlier, all fissured and cracked and seamed by the rains till they could scarcely support their inadequate roofs. There were some signs of self-indulgence, it is true, like Raza's habit of using perfumed hair oil. A few of the women had acquired gold front teeth and some of the men wore gaudy silver earrings. Still, beneath these strange and erratic displays, there was nowhere a decent standard of living.

When I asked Raza about this, he laughed at my assumption that smuggling must be a highly lucrative business. "It would be," he granted, "if the profits were ours, but unfortunately the shopkeepers and banias take most of them."

"And just how do the shopkeepers and banias come into this?" I asked.

"Oh, it is through them that we must buy and sell," he explained. "You see, there is no one else in the village with sufficient funds to finance our purchases."

"But just the same," I objected, "it would seem to me that you could almost set your prices. After all, if the shopkeepers had to buy through legal channels they would pay all that you pay plus a considerable duty."

Raza laughed at my ignorance. "In any case," he assured me, "they would not have to buy through legal channels. They would hire someone else to do the smuggling for them and then we would not get anything at all. Besides, when we buy our goods in Kathiawar, we have to pay a premium our-

selves. Oh, we don't have to, of course. But we have discovered that if we refuse to allow the seller his margin of
graft, the police are informed that the sale took place and we
are caught before we can get out of the Rann."

He continued. "And at this end, our price is set too. Only
the banias and merchants can dispose of our goods. There
are many of us and few of them, so we are not in a position
to argue."

"Then why do you stop here in Bursad at all?" I asked.
"You could take your goods farther inland yourselves and by
selling them there on the open market, eliminate these deal-
ings with the banias entirely."

Raza smiled. "Yes, and some have tried that too, but unfortunately it is not as easy as it seems. The police are, of
course, in the pay of the banias, so if they discover that some
of us are by-passing them, why they order our arrest and
charge us with smuggling, and then we are brought back and
are flogged or imprisoned."

"But I should think the banias would be afraid of that," I
insisted. "After all, there is much that you could tell about
them. How could they dare have you brought to court on
a charge in which they are involved themselves?"

Raza shrugged. "Oh, the banias have nothing to worry
about. They are safe whatever we villagers might say. You
certainly don't think that a local magistrate would ever
accuse a bania, do you?"

I cast about for some new objection. I did not want to
admit that it was as hopeless as this, yet the more I searched
the more apparent it became that there was certainly no
simple solution. It was easy to question each fact, of course,
the corruption of the police or the power of the banias;
on the surface each one of them seemed highly improbable,
yet in the totality their relationship was all too apparent.
Here in Bursad, as in all of the other villages, the established
powers were standing together, each protecting the others'
flanks, together presenting an unassailable front. There was

85

no loyalty between them, but there needed to be none when by dim and vicious instincts each sensed that fate and history had bound it to the others, that it would exist as long as they existed. Even the briberies were not to the point. The smugglers paid bribes, but received only nominal favors. No, the basis of the relationship was social more than economic. The motives were not gain, but self-preservation.

And yet, if it had been only Raza who told me these things, I would have found it easy enough to discount them, for even assuming his honesty, a questionable assumption, he would certainly be far from an unbiased observer. More difficult to discount were the schemes and the agreements, the constant and shameless exchanges of money. And finally there were the men of the village like Sharma, who were far more sophisticated and honest than Raza.

Sharma was one of a number of political refugees who had come to Bursad years ago. His crimes were vague ones and he would never discuss them except in a light and joking way, yet it was easy to imagine why the British had feared him when you felt the intensity in his cracked, squeaking voice. He was an old man. Long since he had left the life of an agitator, which had won him the disfavor of the raj, yet it was apparent that though he lived a peaceful enough life, he did not feel it safe to go far from Bursad. There were rumors about Sharma. Some said that he had come to Bursad from the United Provinces originally, where he had plotted the murder of a government officer. The rumors did not say whether the plot had succeeded.

Yet this much was true. Just after independence he had gone north, hoping for a welcome and a pardon, only to discover that he was as unwelcome as ever and in just as serious danger. Not officially, of course, but casually it had been suggested that he might best go back to wherever he had been hiding since, though the charges of the British would not be pressed, it would be an easy enough matter to find some new ones. And so he had returned more bitter than ever to the exile that he had known for so many years, seeming a little bit sad that the hated authorities had not valued him highly enough even to kill him while they could.

At times he seemed senile. At any rate he seldom spoke in calm or rationally connected sentences. Rather he would ramble on, interjection upon interjection, in a rhapsodic condemnation of all parties and programs. Yet I sensed that for all of this detachment, this almost hysterical and demented manner of his, that there was something of the old revolutionary left, that there was a clarity in Sharma's very confusion.

"You think it is just Bursad that is like this?" he would ask me. "It is India you are seeing, not just Bursad, my friend. You are an intelligent young man, so listen to me. I like you. I will tell you what is wrong with this country.

"For a long time we believed we were fighting against the British. Do you think that we *were* fighting against the British? Well, you are wrong. We were fighting against the banias and against bania rule, and the first step was the elimination of the raj. But we have only taken the first step, as you see. It is the corrupt officials that must be defeated next. And do you think that nonviolence will work against them?" He would smile. "Unfortunately, it will be necessary to kill them.

"You are an intelligent young man. I can see that you believe me. Of course! I know the villages through and through. I am not one of your philanthropic congressmen, understand. I am a farmer with the interests of the farmer at heart."

But he was best on definitions. "A congressman," he would say, "you know what a congressman is? He is a man with a great deal of money and very little sympathy, who distributes the sympathy and keeps the money!"

Or, "Gandhi. He is not so difficult to understand. He is really a very consistent character. Just remember that he is the most loving, the most religious, the most honest—in a word, the most reactionary figure in India.

"So you want to know something about the police," he once offered. "Well, my friend, you do well to come to me. I have spent years in their company. Delhi, Ahmadabad. There is scarcely a jail that I have never seen. I can speak from an extensive criminal background, for I have been convicted on every charge from swindling to rape. Ah no! There is one charge which was never brought against me, the one of which I am guilty, conspiracy against the government.

"And yet in a sense it has all been so unnecessary. If it were not for a mistake I would be as placid as anyone, for I am not by disposition a revolutionary, as you can see. The truth is, I was forced into it against my will. When I was a boy, perhaps twelve or thirteen years old, I was accused of a crime which I did not commit. Of course everyone knew that I was perfectly innocent, but that obviously had little bearing on the case." He smiled. "You know how it is. The police do not like to have unsolved crimes on their books, so it fell to my lot to go to prison. Oh, but I am not complaining. The books must be balanced."

He was increasingly earnest. "Well, you see," he explained, "it was in prison that my eyes were first really opened. I met all kinds of men there. Thieves, dacoits, even some enemies of our enlightened village governments." By this time I was interested, but I did wrong to show it, for I knew that Sharma would not be taken seriously. It was as if, in penance for his ineffectuality, he was forcing himself to play the fool. When he saw me frowning he broke into a smile. "Oh no," he said mockingly. "Why so earnest, my young friend?

"Oh no. Do not take me seriously for a moment. I just thought that an old man's lies might amuse you."

Still, it is another conversation with Sharma that I remember best, a conversation that we had on the first day we met. It is embarrassing for me even to think about it now, so completely unprepared did I prove myself to be for the subtlety of his mind and the malice of his wit. Somehow or other we had begun talking about the smuggling trade and I assumed from his words that Sharma was involved in it, and with all the zeal of the misguided psychologist, I was trying to find out whether he was conscious of any guilt.

"I should think—" I said at one unfortunate moment, unaware that I was baiting a trap for myself—"I should think that a man with your imagination could find some profession more honorable than this."

"Honorable?" A twinkle showed in Sharma's eye. It should have been my warning, but I missed it entirely. "There is something dishonorable about smuggling then? After all, we cheat no one but the government, you must grant!"

I laughed. "And the government doesn't count?" I said.

"Well, after all, who is the government?" Sharma queried. "It is not you nor me nor any man. Even the police and the magistrate are satisfied with our arrangement."

"Oh, of course they're satisfied," I granted. "It is the police and the officials who gain most by the smuggling in the end. But it is the people who suffer. In their taxes they must pay the profit you make by evading the customs."

Sharma pretended to weigh the merits of my argument. He hummed and slowly nodded his head. Actually he was probably just taking this opportunity to plan further his strategy.

"Well, look at it this way," I suggested. "In an independent country, the government and the people are one. If you cheat the customs, now that India is free, that is the same as cheating the other villagers."

Sharma smiled at my naïveté. "We don't see it that way," he said. "The government and the people are always opposed. Why, the very definition of government, my friend! A government is the men who have the power!"

"But look," I insisted, "can't you imagine a country where the government is run for the good of the majority?"

"For the good of the banias and Brahmins!" Sharma said. "Or for the good of the tax collectors and officials."

"No," I objected. "That's not what I mean. I'm talking about a government that is run for the best interests of everyone, a government that neither fears nor exploits the ryot, a government that is the ryot!"

Sharma offered, "I can imagine what it would be like to be a rajah, if that is what you mean."

"I'm afraid not," I said. "That would make no difference. One rajah is in the end as bad as another. I'll try again. In my country, for example, we have a rajah whom the people can throw out of office. If we don't like the way he is running the country, after four years we simply tell him to get out."

"And does he do it?"

"Of course he does it!" I replied. "It is an old institution in America, the election."

Sharma shrugged. "Well, then, there you have the difference. In India there is no such institution!"

This suggested a new point. "That's true," I granted. "But remember, your country has just got her freedom. A lot of things are bound to change quickly now that India is an independent country."

Sharma feigned confusion. "They say this," he said. "But I do not know just what this independence means."

I was not sure that I knew either, so I stalled, "Well, it's a difficult idea to explain. Suppose I say this. It means that the destiny of India is no longer to be controlled by foreigners. It means that your own people, your Nehrus and Gandhis, will make the decisions concerning your future." Sharma was still dissatisfied, and so was I, so I tried to make the idea still clearer. "It means," I floundered, "that from this time forward, the government will be working for the people of Bursad!"

Sharma pressed me. "Does it mean that there will be new district officers, new police inspectors and tax collectors?"

I began to feel uncomfortable. "Well, perhaps not at once," I temporized. "These things take time."

"Does it mean that the village will have its taxes lowered? Will the government build roads or schools?" Sharma asked.

"I can't say," I insisted. "I am talking in the abstract, but I am sure that these problems will be of interest to the government."

"In Bursad—" Sharma began, but I interrupted him.

"In Delhi things have begun to change already. All the government offices are staffed by Indians, by men who have served in the congress ranks."

"Well, here—" Sharma offered, but I cut him off again.

"But it goes even further than that," I enthused. "In Delhi there is a body called the Constituent Assembly that is revising the whole form of government in India!"

Sharma blinked. "And this is our independence?" I was glad of the chance to compromise, so I agreed.

"Well, it is a very fine thing for Delhi," he wailed, "but I thought that Bursad was to be independent too!"

[15]

STILL, there were a few encouraging signs in Bursad. Not the least of them was the gampanchayat court, a village council where disputes between low-caste villagers could be mediated. It was extralegal, and illegal in this case, but in practice it exercised a broad jurisdiction, for experience had taught the villagers that obedience to its injunctions was the only alternative to appearances before the local magistrate, which would usually result in losses to everyone and justice for no one. By and large it dealt with minor disputes, infractions of grazing rights and such, but there were occasions too when large judgments were handed down and, by the sheer power of public opinion, enforced.

Officially, it was the policy of the government to encourage these courts. In theory there were even provisions for their growth to the point where they were allowed a legal jurisdiction over many of the internal affairs of the village. But like so many policies enunciated in Delhi, this one was not much more than the expression of a wish. At the village level the panchayats were suppressed by very reason of their governmental sanction, which made them far more dangerous than otherwise to the local magistrates and police officials. For example, in Bursad the people had once tried to establish the panchayat legally. They had gone to the collector and filled out the forms and retained the services of an expensive lawyer; then, in their excess of enthusiasm they had even proceeded to build a hall where it might regularly meet. But the life of the legal panchayat was short. It was inevitable that the banias should recognize it as a threat, and it was just as inevitable that having recognized it as a threat, they should find some means of crippling or destroying it. In this case it was easy. After a decision that was particularly unfavorable to their interests, they challenged the judges and, purporting to have evidence of bribery and conspiracy, they brought them before the magistrate's court. Of course in the end the charges were dismissed, but by that time the judges had been held for so long that their fields had ripened and gone to seed and their families had contracted enormous debts. They were released, acquitted, but the banias had won, for after that no one would serve on the panchayat except the banias themselves, who proceeded to pack its membership with those representative of them. And of course the court had collapsed soon after that, for it was as corrupt as the regular magistrate's court. This was the beginning and the end of Bursad's experiment in working within the framework of the law.

But the panchayat was reconstituted. It went underground, meeting each week in a different place, taking no notes and keeping no records, but handing down decisions by word of mouth. In spite of these handicaps it was remarkably effective within the limit of its operations, for the members of the panchayat were all venerated old heads and when they passed judgment on a man it was like the judgment of God. It was impossible, of course, for the panchayat now to render and enforce a judgment against the banias. But then, it had been proven that this was impossible in any case, so that the people of Bursad were glad to settle for a council that offered mediation and solution of the problems that arose just among themselves. I say that the panchayat was an encouraging sign. In a sense it was discouraging, for it served to prove the unbridgeable gulf that lay between the institutions of the government and the needs of the people. Yet, it was encouraging in the sense that it proved that the villagers were still capable of working out their own solutions when, as in the majority of cases, the government had proved that it was not genuinely interested in their welfare as an end.

I remember the first panchayat meeting that I attended. Like all of them, it was characterized by a sort of protective informality. There was no set of judges. There was just a group of aged and respected lower-caste leaders who seemed, by the merest chance, to be present. They wandered in at casual intervals and, for a long time, they discussed all sorts of unrelated things such as the weather or their families. Only gradually did they broach the actual case before them. In this instance, a young koli had been brought before the court on a charge of beating his pregnant wife. Normally, of course, wife beating is not a crime, but a recreation in which every normal man indulges, yet it was the judgment of the court that when a farmer takes to throwing a woman eight months gone with child around a room, it was something in which the community might just conceivably have a right to take a stand.

At first the offender had refused to appear. One would suspect that under the circumstances it would have ended at that, yet it was a proof of the force of public opinion that he was here, whatever abstract logic might suggest. I asked Sharma how this had been accomplished. He shrugged, "Oh, it is a simple enough matter when we make up our minds. For example, he is unable to buy in the bazaar. His cattle are stampeded on the common grazing land. Worst of all, there is no one who will talk to him. Some object, but as you see, they appear in the end."

When the room was full, one of the old men beckoned for silence, then turned to the accused and said casually, "Arandas, it has been said that you are beating your wife. She is eight months pregnant, I believe?" Arandas nodded and the old man put his finger tips carefully together, blowing across the top. He shook his head and said, "This seems a shameful thing to me!"

Now, Arandas was a koli. He resorted to the koli habit of replying to an argument with humor. He made a few sallies about man's prerogatives, but he did not seem to feel that these sallies were funny and, to judge from the expressions, the rest of us agreed with him. At last he stopped smiling and hung his head and his jokes dribbled out in halting phrases. He knew that the sense of the meeting was against him and he began to grope for a more serious excuse.

"I was drunk," he explained, with his eyes on the ground and his fingers twisting self-consciously in his dhoti. "I was drunk, you see. . . . I appeal to you my friends, is there any harm in taking too much todi?"

There was a murmuring in the circle that sat immediately around him, then a friend offered a desperate but ineffective defense. "He was drunk!" he cried with a stupid enthusiasm as if to suggest to the others that this made a great difference. But apparently it didn't. There were some sympathetic murmurs, but they came only from the drinking companions of the accused. "Oh, he was drunk!" they muttered, but it was obviously more a demonstration of loyalty than an argument.

I noticed the circle of women at this point. They were

standing, of course, at the back of the hall, raising their veils at nervous intervals and resisting the temptation to whisper to each other. It was their presence, I sensed, that kept the meeting serious and discouraged the men from siding with the accused, for though they said nothing, they were proving their interest in this case and that had individual implications for every husband.

At last one of the five old men cleared his throat. All the independent arguments were immediately stilled and all eyes were turned on the judges.

"It seems," one of them said, "that there is no excuse for the behavior of Arandas in beating his wife." He paused dramatically. Arandas opened his mouth to object, then waved his hand despairingly.

"It seems—" the judge spoke slowly and carefully—"that it would be best if he sent his wife away. Arrangements will be made for her to be transported to her mother till after her child is born."

Now Arandas objected. "But Bapu!" he cried. "Where shall I get the money for this, can you tell me that? I am a poor man, as you know. I have scarcely enough to feed and clothe us here in Bursad!"

The judge smiled and cocked his head to one side. "And yet you apparently have money for todi," he mused. At this the whole assembly laughed loudly and Arandas seemed momentarily deflated.

"Ah, but no more!" he said. "My money is gone. And even if I had it I would not buy todi. Bapu, believe me; there will be no more drinking. Will you not take my word and leave it at that?"

The judge said sadly, "If this were the first time, we would be content to warn you, Arandas. But you have repeatedly promised your neighbors to stop drinking and yet you drink as much as ever."

"But this time—" Arandas began.

The old man interrupted. "This time is like all of the

others, we know." Then he added softly, "Go home Arandas. Tell your wife to prepare to leave in the morning."

Now Arandas suddenly leaped to his feet. This was the ultimate test of the court's authority. He opened his mouth, but no words came; his fists clenched and unclenched spasmodically at his sides. For a moment I thought he would seize the old judge, for he was so angry that his body was trembling all over. But as suddenly as he had tensed, he relaxed. He shrugged his shoulders.

"As you say," he sighed.

Of course, it was not always so simple as this. As often as not a case would drag out, involving so many witnesses that just the hearing of evidence in itself would take months. One of the greatest procedural weaknesses of the panchayat was that any villager who wished could speak, and there were always a few oldsters who, having no connection with the case, nevertheless would monopolize whole days with their prattling. Indeed, it was seldom that a man was acquitted; either he would be convicted summarily or the case would simply languish, with the result that it was only the most patently guilty who were sure of receiving their just deserts. But there were other peculiarities of the panchayat, too. To one acquainted with Western justice it seemed to proceed on personal grounds almost to the total exclusion of what we would call evidence. For example, an eye witness to a crime could be neutralized by a single character witness for the accused. In disputes over property, some intangible thing called "reputation" could outweigh the very village records. I often argued with Sharma about the validity of these principles, not because I was confident of my opinions but simply because I was curious. But I was never able to get a better clarification than, "It is the way we have always done these things."

And yet for all of their faults, the panchayats served their purpose. They were at least an improvement over the alternative of anarchy. Unfortunately there was no such alternative in the case of intervillage disputes. In the case of boundary controversies and the like, it would usually be fairly easy to arrive at some settlement, for the respective panchayats would meet and negotiate, or a council of elders would be chosen. The real problem rose in those cases when one of the villages simply refused to arbitrate, for in those cases it would be necessary for the other village to arrange for its own retribution or have none.

And yet in even these cases there was an accepted pattern. The offended village would send some of its men to steal into the other after dark and bring back as many cattle as they could find as hostages. In this area, cattle were rarely stolen for profit; they were too easy to identify and too hard to dispose of. But they were frequently stolen just to force the arbitration of some insult or injury that a village had suffered. Unfortunately, the abductors never seemed satisfied to steal just enough cows to achieve their primary end. Once embarked on one of these schemes of retribution, they seemed to go wild with the spirit of the thing, and they would frequently take sixty or seventy animals, denuding the enemy village completely. The ransom of the herds varied, but in a majority of cases it did not even compensate the abductors for their trouble. Quite often no more than an apology was demanded, but the villagers took their honor quite seriously.

In one instance, for example, the people of Versova had been speaking disrespectfully of the people of Bursad and somehow it reached the ears of my hosts, who proceeded to make the most dramatic nonsense of it. I was inclined to laugh it off, for the insults were quite logical imputations on the honesty of Bursadians, but even Sharma—to my surprise—played the part of the village nationalist, waxing eloquent about the stain on the good name of Bursad.

Accordingly, one night after nerving themselves for the deed by two hours of heavy drinking in the todi stall, all

97

Bursad's manhood marched out toward Versova to avenge themselves in the accepted manner. It seemed impossible to me that they should succeed. Many of them were too drunk even to stay on their horses; there was much boasting and singing of warrior songs, much throwing of bottles and arguing along the way. But as we neared Versova a change came over them. They divided themselves into groups of three and, working their way close behind the cover of a dune, they quietly entered the streets of the village. They relied on stealth. I had expected that they would simply stampede the cattle. Not so. They combed the yards and enclosures one at a time, working carefully lest someone should spread the alarm. Of course the pye-dogs barked desultorily, but then they are always barking so no one pays much attention to them, and after an hour or so my friends were able to return with a total of some forty or fifty cattle.

By this time they saw the humor of the undertaking. Todi and revenge having tempered their anger, they proceeded homeward, the loud bawling of the cattle being more than drowned out by the cries of their herders. I must confess that I laughed as much as anyone. I could not understand a word that was said, but I could not help wondering how the Versovans would take it when they got up and discovered that their cattle were gone.

But the fact is, I did not have to wonder very long. A few hours after dawn I could see for myself, for the whole population of Versova, it seemed, had mounted and tracked their herds to Bursad. They rode into the village looking more embarrassed than angry, as well they might, having proved such sound sleepers, and it seemed that their major concern was not the return of their cattle but rather the assurance of the Bursadians that the story of their ignominy would not be spread throughout the other neighboring villages. They were all too ready to apologize to Bursad and to admit the untruth of their previous assertions. Anything, so long as Kurla and Varavoli and Gunawa were kept ignorant of their shame. *Noblesse oblige!* The people of Bursad were so pleased with the penitent attitude that they adopted, that they not only agreed to keep the secret but even neglected to press for the formal apology that was to have been the terms of their settlement. Instead, both groups, the Bursadians and the Versovans, adjourned to the todi stall to drink together and by noon they were so drunk that even between them they could barely get the cattle back to Versova.

[16]

IT MUST have happened during my fourth week in Bursad. All I remember is that it was one of those cold, clear nights. I had gone to bed early and I must have been sleeping for three or four hours to have been so stubbornly tired. Slowly, very slowly, with an animal reluctance, I shook myself awake and looked around. For some time I could not think where I was, for I had expected a window on my right and it was on my left. Everything seemed strange and out of place; then, gradually, my mind began to focus. Whether it was a hand on my shoulder or just a whisper I can't remember, but all at once, I was aware that there was someone near my bed.

"Sharma—" I whispered, for I could tell that it was he silhouetted in the light that came streaming through the window.

"Yes, but quietly!" he cautioned, laying his finger against his lips. "There is no time to lose. You must get up and dress."

"At this time of night? You're crazy!" I objected, but he seemed not even to hear my protest.

"Bring all of your things. It will be necessary for you to leave Bursad tonight—immediately," he said.

"Sharma!" I demanded, but he did not wait for an answer.

99

So, with the natural haste of one wakened unexplainably, I got up and pulled on my trousers and shirt, then buttoned my jacket with shaking fingers.

I went out into the street, dragging my packs behind me, trying to rub the sleep from my eyes.

"Sharma!" But he was far down the street already so I followed after him as fast as I could.

The streets were deserted but for the occasional pye-dog that went snuffing along with his head to the ground. Once a rat scurried past me, lean and angular, accompanied by an even more angular shadow. Sharma was standing in the porch of the old council hall, talking to the driver of a waiting bullock cart who looked as sleepy and surprised as I did. His animals were still steaming in the cold night air.

"Look, Sharma—" I said.

"Yes, hurry!" he cried. "Put your things in the back and climb up at once. There is no time to lose. I cannot explain, but you must trust me. It is for your own good that I am doing this."

"I believe you," I said. "But it's all so mysterious. I don't see why I must leave tonight. Why, I haven't even had a chance to say thanks and good-by to my host. Wouldn't tomorrow morning do just as well?"

"Tomorrow would be hours too late," Sharma insisted. "You would thank me for this if you knew why I was sending you off."

"Then you won't even tell me what this is all about?" I asked.

"I can tell you nothing." He spoke harshly now.

I stood looking at him for a moment, wondering if this were a trick. Then I threw my packs in the cart and climbed after them and at Sharma's command, the driver joined me and twisted the bullocks' tails.

Sharma walked alongside when the cart rumbled off. At the edge of the village he said good-by. "I have a friend named Sadokhar in the village where you will be taken. Stay with him for a while. And good luck!" he said.

"Just once more," I insisted. "You can tell me nothing?" Sharma shook his head gravely from side to side.

"All right," I agreed, "we'll leave it at that."

"You would thank me . . ." he repeated, waving his hand.

South Gujarat

South Gujarat

[17]

THE road from Suigam to Abu is like a river. It draws its substance from a thousand small tributaries, from wandering trails and meandering pathways that reach up into the rocks of the Aravalli range and beyond to the dry wastes of Rajputana. Officially, it begins at the town of Suigam. Actually it begins everywhere and nowhere; in front of small huts in the mountain regions, in overgrown paths through North Gujarat woodlands, everywhere where there is a rivulet of travel or commerce that eventually joins its flow to the east.

Like a river, it gathers momentum as it goes. Near Tharad it is no more than a hesitant little pathway, wandering its weak-willed and equivocating course over the uneven ground on the edge of the Rann. It is narrow and dusty, like all of the trails that cross and recross this desolate region, and certainly there is nothing here to suggest that its destiny is in any way different from the others. And yet in fact it is different. As you follow the road, more and more of the byways join forces with you, and after a while the trail grows wide and deeply rutted and you begin to suspect it is taking you somewhere.

At one place the plains run into a forest, a Lilliputian forest full of stunted trees that have been spaced by the exigencies of moisture and nourishment in even lines some ten feet apart. The Abu road plunges through the thicket. All the others reconsider and skirt its edge so that for about fifty miles—a good two days traveling—you are completely alone and on your own resources. In this thicket you must stay very close to the road, for the brake is infested with ferocious wild pigs. There is no grass at all, scarcely any soil but for the spits that sweep out to the lee of large rocks, yet the tuskers somehow manage a precarious existence, living on heaven alone knows what.

After this, the road plods doggedly along through a barren, rocky waste not unlike the Rann except for the fact that it undulates in gentle hills and bears occasional cacti. This whole region is dry and drifted with alkali. There is no water to be found except at the few settlements, and even there, while the water is not precisely poisonous, it is so salty that it has a woefully purgative effect. But this land in its turn you leave behind. The gentle undulations swell gradually into hills that force the road to a line of least resistance, crawling and winding along between them. Here an occasional rockslide may have blocked its course. Like some rudimentary animal form with a life of its own, the road has simply developed new appendages as soon as the old ones were amputated.

And so you come at last to the plains. Gradually, then suddenly they are unfolded to view. At one place you climb steadily for perhaps two thousand feet, plodding your way up a steep hog-back ridge, and then all at once, when you are not even expecting it to come, when your eyes are still narrowed against the glare of the sun, a cool breeze sweeps over the crest of the ridge and you realize that you have reached the top. You look out and the whole of India is at your feet, with her thousands of villages and her millions of people. The land itself is a pattern of colors, greens and browns and every shade between. To the north, an enormous thunderhead may be forming with the sun slanting through it in oblique, fanning rays, while to the south, the land may be parched and cracked into hexagonal blocks by a terrible dry heat. It is frightening in a way. For a moment you are God with a thundercloud at your elbow and a rainbow at your feet, and before you are spread all the conditions of the earth from ripe fertility to actual famine.

You stand there gaping at the difference between the monotony behind and the beauty ahead. And you realize what is peculiar about the Abu Road. It seems to have led you from death to life.

Once I left Bursad behind, I decided that I must alter radically my established habits of traveling. It had become apparent that if I were to get to South India before the monsoons began in June, I must not only keep to a more rigorous schedule, but I must actually make up the month that was lagging behind my itinerary already. It was not an easy decision to make, but I decided I must abandon my pose as a fugitive. It had served its purpose in allowing me to establish rapport under circumstances where it would otherwise have been difficult, but now that I was anxious to expedite my movement, it was beginning to prove more of a hindrance than a help. For the next few weeks, I concentrated simply on putting as many miles and villages as possible behind me, and it was a refreshing experience to hire guides and bullock carts without all of the old cloak-and-dagger pretenses.

Of course my new plan had its disadvantages too. Chiefly, it limited me to the most cursory observations. Yet, as I learned in time, there was some merit even in this as a complement to my earlier and more intensive investigations, designed as they had been to provide me with a deep rather than a broad understanding of the village areas. I discovered, for example, that when I was traveling more rapidly, certain patterns began to take shape before me, that now instead of a series of intense, detached pictures, I was getting a sort of panorama of the region. After the lazy and casual habits I had formed, this village-hopping was something of a nervous strain, but it is perhaps the best comment that when I could relax again I was glad that I had been forced into such an ambitious few weeks.

To be perfectly honest, there was one thing in particular that made it easy for me to cover the North Gujarat so quickly; that was the nature of the people who dwelt there. They were not unfriendly; that would be an oversimplification. Better say that they were friendly, but only at a distance, for it is a fact that they were always ready to provide me with a bed and some means of transportation when I was among them. It was just that beyond this they were entirely unapproachable, that their hospitality seemed institutional rather than personal. Like the iceberg that is eight-ninths submerged beneath the water, the Gujrati seemed eight-ninths submerged in their environment.

In the first place, they were a highly conventional people. There was nothing in their environment to make them otherwise, for they lived in that unrebellious, unimaginative middle stratum that lies between the economic extremes. On the one hand they were rich enough not to have the psychology that almost any change would be a change for the better; unlike poorer farmers, they had fields and a few cattle to give them some stake in the status quo. Yet on the other hand, they were not rich enough to have known real freedom from the force of the banias and from the power of tradition, and so, freedom being an acquired taste, they didn't give any evidence that they yearned for it. Indeed, they were annoyingly sure of themselves and of the ideas that had prevailed among them for generations. This struck me immediately, for they were the first group I had encountered that was not even curious about my peculiar appearance. In Kathiawar and elsewhere I was a subject of wonder because of the whiteness of my skin and the strangeness of my clothes. But the Gujrati didn't wonder. They knew. Since their skins were black, a white skin was simply unnatural. Since they ate jowar and died of diseases they contracted from contaminated water, tomatoes and onions were obviously inedible, and boiling one's drinking water a sheer affectation.

It follows that for the central government, these people had nothing but the most profound distrust. "Those men in Delhi" were non-Gujrati at least; whether they were Englishmen or Punjabis seemed to them unimportant. There was Patel of course. Him they trusted, reactionary and opposed to their interests however he might be. Patel was at least a Gujrati, so though he might be selfish and cunning, he would at least be sane. And there was Gandhi, too. They trusted him; not because he had won independence for India, of course. They were not even sure that they wanted this independence. No, the significant thing about Gandhi was his blood line.

"But is there nothing that you want from the government?" I used to ask, before I learned that the reply would always be the same.

"We want nothing from the government," I would be told categorically. "All we ask of the government is to be left alone!"

"Then you do not want roads and schools? You do not want the government to send doctors to cure sickness and deliver your children?"

And the answer would come. "We want neither roads nor schools. All we want is that the government keep out of our affairs."

Nor were they content just to talk. I remember passing through one village where the government had built an enormous dam across a torrential river that in previous years had inundated all the fields, then passed on leaving them dry. It could be a godsend to the farmers. In the first place, they could safely plant before the monsoons began, and in addition to that, they would be assured of enough water to permit them to sow a second crop.

But the farmers would have none of it. Before the monsoons began they had torn up the dam and used it for firewood. "We must thank the government for that!" they would sneer. "But who ever heard of stopping a river?"

Religiously, the people of this section were far stricter Hindus than any I had seen until now. In both cause and effect, their Hinduism was far less degenerate than it is over the rest of India. The Brahmins of the Gujarat, for example, retain most of the characteristics of the classic Hindu Brahmins, having not only rights and privileges, but definite duties which accrue to them because of their rank.

The relation of the Gujrati to his religion is a human one. It has not degenerated into a formal thing as it has in Kathiawar where, for all the mock piety, there is a deep hatred of the established religious powers. There is a genuine respect for the Brahmin in the Gujrati and, in general, he is more or less worthy of this respect, being a learned man who takes his religion far more seriously than he takes his economic condition.

Even the gods themselves are close to the people. Almost every Gujrati home has its little shrine, before which bananas and incense are placed to invoke the good will of the gods on the inhabitants. The favorite god is Ganesh, and this too is significant of the simplicity and humanity of the religion, Ganesh being a lovable and foolish little fellow with an elephant's face and the spirit of a child. He is nothing like the awesome and fearful gods that are worshipped at a distance in the South Indian temples. He is so tolerant and friendly that when a guest is late in arriving at a Gujarat home for supper, the host will think nothing of immersing him in water till he uses his influence to bring the guest quickly.

And yet there is another side to the story. Though the Hinduism of the Gujrati has managed to avoid the new evils that have crept into the more degenerate forms, it retains many evils which these forms have lost. In South India alone have I seen more dramatic examples of untouchability than in the Gujrati. In the very schools where the Brahmins teach, the Harijan children are refused admittance, those of particular ambition being left to look in through the windows and absorb what they can. In particularly liberal villages, the Brahmins sometimes will correct the examples of these veranda-scholars, but always it is without touching their slates. They are laid on the ground and perused at a distance by the teacher. But for that matter, all education in this area is a farce, for almost no one takes his schooling seriously. As one laborer put it, "If you are from the lower castes, no amount of education will help you, and if you are from the upper castes you will automatically inherit your father's business and position anyway." This is true in substance, and as a natural result, it is the rare child who bothers with books and sums. The Sudras are too busy in their fathers' fields and the banias are simply too busy.

Still, it would not be correct to say that relations between the castes are particularly bad in the Gujrati, for though the formal discriminations are almost without parallel, they do not seem to engender any very deep hatreds. Persecutions there are. Large landlords there are. The banias, like the poor, are always with us. The difference seems to be that here there is a margin, arising from the fertility of the land itself, which permits the banias and Brahmins to live well at less cost to the villager than in poorer sections.

Indeed, the relations of the cultivator and the landholder in this area sometimes verge on real cordiality, both groups being far less touchy about the other, less anxious to maintain dignity and pride respectively. In one village that I visited, I was surprised to see a cultivator making public sport of the banias. He was imitating an old Jain with an ant in his beard, and yet, even the banias themselves were laughing. Though the actor was clean shaven, his demonstration was convincing. First he lay on the ground and tried to coax the mythical ant from the mythical beard with the offer of a mythical lump of sugar. When this failed, he screwed up his mouth to blow downward, spreading his dhoti to break the insect's fall. And finally, having achieved no success by these methods and being maddened by the incessant tickling of his chin, he began beating his face in a most irreligious anger, gesturing and declaiming his outraged dignity.

It was an interesting performance. What was most interesting about it was the fact that the mimic would have dared such a thing. In Kathiawar, for example, he would probably have been rewarded for his talents by being driven out of the village. Was it that the banias of the Gujrati were more broad-minded? I hoped at first that this might be the case, but on the contrary, I suspect that they were really so powerful they knew they could afford such petty abuses.

It is not the weak man, but the strong man who does not fear to laugh at himself. And it is not the weak but the confident regime that knows it can tolerate such mild heresies.

From Suigam to Abu. From Abu to Mehsana. From Mehsana down the edge of the Aravalli Hills, across the tracts of scrub forest and desert that slope gradually down to the plains of the Gujarat. From the desolate gray of the Rajputana border, through the mottled brown-green of the watershed itself, to the variegated richness of the lowland cotton belt. This was the course that I had followed since leaving Bursad.

It was perhaps only natural in the light of this sequence that I was tremendously impressed by the Gujarat landscape. After all, I had come from the poorest part of India to what is generally considered the richest and most lovely. And yet I am sure that my reaction was not entirely subjective. There is an undeniable *fin-de-siècle* beauty to the Gujarat. Once you have adjusted to the perversity of the people who inhabit it you cannot help being enchanted by this incredible landscape, filled with the best of the Rajput ruins, where peacocks roost on lovely old pillars and spread their tails like graceful fans to shade the carved faces of posturing goddesses. As for the villages themselves, even the newest of them are generally built on old Rajput or Mogul sites, so that however squalid their houses may be, there will be a sprinkling of inherited grandeur about them. Indeed, these ruins are not ruins at all, so sound is their construction and so perfect their condition; they are ruins only in the sense that they are part of a culture that has fallen into a spiritual and artistic decline.

Nor is the countryside between the villages less lovely. It is abounding in animal life, almost every form of which is sacred to the Hindu and is consequently incredibly, idyllically tame. If you are mounted, you can ride within a few hundred feet of the enormous nilgai, literally blue cow, an animal the size of the North American bison but with a coat the color and texture of blue suede. Then there is the sambar deer, with his corkscrew horns and his peculiar plaintive bark. Him you would encounter on the very roadway itself or taking his ease of a morning beneath a peepul tree. It is the best country imaginable for traveling. The ground is soft and spongy underfoot, and though it is a bit uneven for a camel or a bullock, it is quick, easygoing on a country-bred mare. There is ample fresh water and wild grass about so that you can by-pass the villages entirely if you like, grazing and watering your mount by the roadside and simply appropriating your own food from the fields as you pass.

I was particularly lucky. I managed to buy a Kathiawar pony for some seventy rupees, a canny little mare who seemed to know every hole and gulley in the country by heart. She had amazing endurance. Day after day I could push her as far as fifty miles, so it no wonder the stretch from Abu to Mehsana was the easiest that I had traversed to date.

[18]

IT WAS in Varavoli, as I recall, that I first met Khan. He was making one of his two monthly tours of the district, so when I arrived in the village and requested the dharmsala I was told that the deputy superintendent of police was living in it. I had just come down from a place called Bhili-Ghunga, covering some fifteen-odd miles between noon and six o'clock, and since my feet were blistered and my shoulders sunburned, I was in no mood to accept such a final pronouncement. I must confess that I approached Khan with a chip on my shoulder, for I really did not want to share his accommodations, but I had decided that just as a matter of principle, I would assert myself against this village bureaucrat. So I went over to the dharmsala, not knowing what to expect, but knowing precisely what my reaction would be, all my accumulated wrath against the baboo official concentrated on this one man whom I had yet to meet.

Khan indeed looked official. I had expected far less, even from a deputy superintendent of police. He wore brown shorts and a topee and a Sam Browne belt with a bandoleer of bullets slung across his chest, crossing his body from upper right to lower left and terminating in a distinctly lethal-looking pistol. He was incredibly fat, and these leather accoutrements did nothing to diminish the size of his waistline; rather they made him look like a dray horse in harness, some great Belgian stallion trapped out for the fair.

Yet I took an instinctive liking to Khan. There was about him an air of tremendous vitality, and as he walked out on the porch to greet me that first day, his short arms beat the air in his very enthusiasm. The thing that amazed me most, though, was his voice. It was the deepest and most resonant that I ever have heard, and as he laughed and called out his

welcome from the veranda, it was like something from the
score of a Wagnerian opera.

"Come in!" he commanded. He could do nothing but
command, endowed by nature with a voice box like his.
"Come in! What on earth are you doing in this place? You
must stay with me here! Come in! Come in!"

I must confess that I stood for a moment and stared, so
different was this man from the one I had pictured.

"Well, don't stand there!" he roared to a servant. "Get his
luggage!"

And it was thus that I first was introduced to Khan.

For two days Khan and I laid over in Varavoli, he because
of business and I just from choice. He had offered to let me
accompany him in his touring; no, the fact is he had pressed
me, he was so anxious for company. At first I was reluctant
to agree. I felt that I had wasted too much time already on
such detours, and even more I was still unconvinced that
there was really much to be seen from the official's point of
vantage. During the time that we spent in Varavoli, however,
I had ample time to watch Khan at work. He was conducting
routine interviews, or so I thought at the time, and yet his
approach to the villagers even then was unique. There was,
about Khan, none of that brusque and officious quality I had
noticed in so many of the petty bureaucrats, particularly in
Kathiawar and in Bursad. He was kindly and sympathetic
in his talks with the cultivators; it seemed that he spent half
his time in trying to allay the fears and quiet the suspicions
which they all had formed of the government generally. Even
in the face of the most obvious and stubborn resistance to his
simplest questions he maintained his calm. It was interesting
to watch the reaction of the villagers. They seemed as surprised by all this as I was myself.

Khan's job at the moment was an interesting one. He was
trying to pick up the trail of a killer who had been operating
for years in this district, then taking refuge in Baroda when

the police came after him. He was a clever sort. He never committed an offense within the boundaries of the state itself, for he realized that as long as he gave them no trouble the Baroda police would give him none in turn, particularly since it was known that among his victims were a round half-dozen unwary officers who had tracked him too far into his native environment. His name was Zonia, and he was something of a dandy. He maintained a string of pure-bred horses, which he stabled in various villages so that he would always be sure of having a fresh mount when he wanted one. He dressed in bright colors and in Rajput fashions, claiming to be a Rajput himself, and he was never to be seen without a pair of silver-handled pistols, which he would tuck in his cummerbund at a rakish angle.

Still this cockiness, Khan assured me, would eventually be his downfall. Khan already had seen him twice when he had decided to present himself and play hide and seek rather than flee undetected, which he could have done. He was incredibly vain and it is very likely that these performances were to satisfy that vanity as well as to demonstrate to the villagers that he was far stronger than the police and that they had therefore better side with him against them. On one occasion Zonia had even tried to slip into a dharmsala where Khan was sleeping, but in this he went too far, for Khan was no fool and certainly would never have slept without a guard. The guard had discharged a shotgun at Zonia, but since there was no cry, he assumed that he had missed his mark. It was only in the morning that by the pool of blood they could reconstruct the night's events; Zonia had been hit, but had staggered to the veranda and lay there through most of the night, bleeding profusely. Then in the morning, when he recovered consciousness, he had apparently managed to drag himself off.

After that, the issue had become personal on both sides. For his part, Khan felt humiliated by the near miss, and to make up for it he was devoting almost the whole of his time and energy to tracking down the outlaw. As for Zonia, his arm was so badly shattered by the shotgun blast that it was now quite useless, and it was Khan's thesis that a mono-maniacal thirst for revenge would lead him soon to some fatal indiscretion. I must confess that this last caught me rather off balance; the idea of a hardened and experienced killer braving gunfire to get at my traveling companion was one which I would require some time to get used to. But Khan himself took it quite in stride. "If he finds me," he would shrug, "why it saves me the trouble!" Then he would spread his palms comfortably across his enormous belly, cry, "Khan will protect you!" and laugh his great laugh.

Yet, for all of his exhibitionism, Khan was a shrewd man. His very genius perhaps lay in his harmless appearance, for he resembled nothing so much as the stereotype village police officer, lazy, corrupt, anxious only for order, and that on whatever terms it could be had. He now seemed to be pro-ceeding on a routine tour of inspection. His interviews were desultory and his manner was casual; such an appearance of indolence and disinterest did he give that the people he talked to were invariably overconfident. But he was like a sleeping watchdog. Just one stray word, just a sentence out of place would jar him awake. He would swing his feet down off of the table, shift his enormous bulk in his chair, point a finger and ask a question, and a whole week's work would have been thus accomplished. He was not nearly so much a detective as a psychiatrist, but then his job was to pick the brains of the villagers, to extract just a tenth of the inval-uable information that to them was simple common knowl-edge. I noticed that he never asked a direct question. He seemed to sense that there was enough animosity so that to identify the very information he wanted would be the surest way of closing it to discussion. Rather he would talk around the question in his mind, probing and prodding, testing for reactions, piecing together every raise of an eyebrow, every halt or stammer or hesitation in speech.

"And you really learn something from this?" I asked incredulously on the evening of our second day in Varavoli. In answer, Khan took out a map of the district with a course plotted across it in red ink.

"What's this?" I asked.

"Zonia's movements," he replied. "You see, he crossed over from Baroda up here. Since then he has been continuing west and slightly south. By now I should judge he is somewhere near here."

"Well, then what are we doing in Varavoli?" I asked. "If you know where he is, why don't we go after him?"

"I don't know where he is," Khan corrected me. "I know where he has been, and there's a considerable difference."

"But you say that he is somewhere near here—"

Khan sighed. "Somewhere near here is a general term. One does not hunt snakes by reaching in dark corners. No, I must know the very bed on which he is lying."

I groaned. "And where will you ever learn that?"

Khan pulled thoughtfully at his lip for a moment. Then as if the idea had just occurred to him, he said brightly, "Why of course! Someone will tell me!"

[19]

FROM Varavoli, as soon as Khan's work was completed, we set out for a village called Bhal-Gundawa, roughly seventy miles to the west, perhaps halfway between Varavoli and the sea. Khan did not tell me why we were going to Bhal-Gundawa, but I suspected; I remembered that on the night before, he said we would probably find Zonia in that direction. At breakfast Khan seemed particularly cheerful, and I decided that the portent for the day must be good. An hour later we had loaded our gear into the jeep and had got under way.

The trip itself was something of an experience. Khan did not believe in traveling light and his jeep was crammed with odd personal effects till there was scarcely room for himself inside with them. It was not that he actually lived well in the villages; he seemed to carry most of this truck out of habit. There was a crate of army rifles, for example, the mechanisms of which no one present understood, and there was a collapsible bathtub whose canvas had rotted till it was hanging in strips from the rusted frame. Still it was impossible to convince Khan to part with anything and as a result, it was the fate of his deputies and me to ride on the hood and the fenders, dearly clutching whatever gave some illusion of security.

Worst of all were our frequent stops in the villages to ask directions or to issue orders. Then Khan would no sooner dispatch his men when he would grow impatient with them and begin blowing his horn. They would come tumbling from the buildings that served as jails, their sheafs of papers still clutched in their hands, but Khan would drive off, and they would be expected to board the passing vehicle while in furious motion. In most cases Khan would not even look around, but would shout "Roll call of deputies. Sharma! Bhavana," and then, when they both called a breathless "Here," he would slap his leg and laugh, "They never miss!"

Still it was the country itself that I found most interesting. It was apparently a patchwork of tiny states which, though they exercised no judicial or legislative powers, had been allowed a token existence by the government. They were like pieces of an uncompleted jigsaw puzzle, an odd island here and a splinter there; there were even some states that were landlocked by others, and some that were shattered into several small fragments.

Out of curiosity we visited one state. Unfortunately we were unable to meet its chief; the servants apologized and said he was ill, but Khan had told me he was a chronic drunkard. The palace itself was unutterably filthy. The

119

rooms had not been swept in years, and through cracks and holes in the foundations, stout creepers were growing up over the long-closed doors. The whole palace had apparently been abandoned to the servants, at least all but the room where its master lay, for the sweepers were squatting insolently in the corners, picking their noses and contemplating the wreckage about them.

We visited a number of talukdars too, the government's grass roots administrative officials. As a matter of fact, we visited them all, since any we missed would have brooded and felt ill used. At each taluk headquarters we were offered repeated cups of sticky, sweet tea. And though Khan's capacity seemed virtually unlimited, I took to pouring mine out surreptitiously.

Then there was the village where we stayed the first night out. There even Khan would not eat or drink, for the whole place was infected with "Guinea-worm germ," an intestinal parasite that breeds in bad water. The villagers themselves were rotting away with it; their bodies were covered with ugly white scabs that would erupt periodically into maggoty pustules, which as often as not would be washed in the well. Still the patel was offended that we refused his hospitality and he went out of his way to let us know. "You call yourselves educated men," he sneered, "and yet you are superstitious about foods." We left the village as soon as we could, rising long before dawn and making our excuses, though actually we had only a few miles to go and were entering Bhal-Gundawa long before noon.

Bhal-Gundawa itself was more a town than a village. Its population was upwards of two thousand families, and what was more important, it was a taluk headquarters and the seat of a government co-operative bank which, though defunct, was the pride of all surrounding regions for the height of its façade and the size of its deficit. It was a town in the old and traditional sense, and since it was entirely submerged in the Gujarat landscape, it owed none of its size and importance to the influences of the West that had shaped the larger cities. For example, in Bhal-Gundawa there was no railroad, nor even a road connecting it with the outside world. But then, for that matter, to the villages in its orbit, Bhal-Gundawa itself was the outside world.

Accordingly, our accommodations there were good. There was a local dharmsala, but we did not stay there. Rather we were installed in a pretentious town hall, a huge two-story building in the bazaar. I was amazed as its dimensions, but Khan explained that it was a holdover from the time when Bhal-Gundawa was simply part of one of the petty neighboring states. In those days it had served as a durbar hall.

Inside it was even more surprising, I discovered, for the old ruler of the state had been fond of chandeliers and he had indulged that taste to the utmost on these ceilings, notwithstanding the total lack of electricity. There were large chandeliers and small chandeliers, square and round and oblong chandeliers. There were cupids and cherubims and uncoiling pythons, all holding unfunctional light bulbs in their mouths. Still the place had at least one redeeming feature. There were no beds here. Though they seldom used them, the villagers would all too often turn out some old durbars and bring in their bug-ridden charpoys to us. In this case, though the patel suggested something like this, we were able to convince him to leave us as we were, so that we were able to lie down on the hard, clean floor and sleep intermittently till the busy next morning.

[20]

K H A N ' S one official act in Bhal-Gundawa was to attend a meeting of the magistrate's court which, to our misfortune, just happened to be meeting in the village on the morning following our arrival. Once again, he explained that it was a matter of form. If he failed to attend while it was known he was here, the magistrate would consider it a personal affront and feel impelled to send gifts to win back his lost favor. It was all very complicated, Khan assured me, and apparently it was all very distasteful as well, for it took me a full twenty minutes of argument to convince him that I should be allowed to attend.

The court was held in the local police station, a mud-brick building in a nearby compound that was guarded by a pair of unhappy naiks who had apparently been sewn into uniforms for the occasion and still felt foolish and ill at ease in them. When we entered, they came to a ragged attention and one even managed an abortive salute, but the other was too busy with the crotch of his trousers and could only smile weakly by way of apology.

The room in which the trials were to be held, I noted, was about the size of the average dwelling. And it was just as dark, the one window being located up under the eaves where it would admit no light. Though I went in with Khan, it was several moments later before I discovered we were not alone. When my eyes got used to the darkness I could make out a half dozen or so villagers sitting near me.

The magistrate himself was just about what I expected. Before Khan he was deferential to an embarrassing degree, while to his subordinates he seemed intentionally rude and thoughtless, inconveniencing them repeatedly as a matter of principle. He was dressed in that peculiar mixture of East and West which so many village bureaucrats affect. Above the waist he might well have been a justice straight out of His Majesty's court in London. He wore a broad gray cravat, a starched white shirt, an oxford gray coat and vest. But below the waist he had conceded to the climate. He wore a dhoti cloth and a pair of soft sandals. His manner also was a peculiar blend, for he alternated between shooting his cuffs like an Englishman and comfortably cupping his genitals in his hand as is the traditional habit of the Indian villager.

"The court will come to order!" he declared in English. This was apparently meant as a favor to me, for he looked over in Khan's and my direction to make sure that neither of us would miss the gesture. There was a scraping of feet in the rear of the room; as always, the villagers were uneasy when English was spoken. But the judge immediately repeated himself in Gujarati and the gallery settled into silence again.

The first case of the morning involved two villagers, a Kurmi and a Rajput who had been drunk and disorderly. This was a serious charge, for in the villages nothing less than an attempted murder is a "disorder." To judge from the testimony that Khan translated, the two had attacked the owner of the todi stall when, on the reasonable grounds that they were already too drunk, he had refused to sell them any more liquor. That they had indeed been drunk there could be no question; the episode had transpired on the day before, but both of the defendants were still so tipsy they could scarcely support each other in the dock. After a display of scars on the part of the stallkeeper, they were sentenced to two months in jail apiece, a lenient disposition according to Khan and, according to the complainant, a sheer injustice.

The second case involved a cattle theft. It was precisely the kind of case to show the complete ineptitude of the Western forms to cope with the problems of the people of the countryside. The whole village, it seemed, wanted to testify in the case, and in the end it turned into the most ludicrous carnival, with witnesses bawling at each other across the room and the partisans setting up rump courts of their own. At last it became so bad that the magistrate simply recessed and slipped out unnoticed by the mobs. But it was apparently just as well for after another half hour, they too recessed with a solution of their own!

I was disgusted by the performance. The whole thing seemed to follow the pattern I had seen so often before, and I could not help telling Khan, at lunch, how silly and fantastic it had appeared to me. I told of the corruptions I previously had witnessed, and none of them seemed to come as a surprise to him. Rather, he smiled with a bored and preoccupied air as if it were all too obvious to discuss. He was silent while I talked, so I had rather concluded that this signaled his general agreement at least, but when I finished he launched into a peroration of his own which, though it did not really oppose me, quite by-passed my argument.

"You know," he remarked, "it is not really fair to say that these magistrates' courts serve no purpose. They do. After lunch the court will reconvene and give official sanction to what has transpired this morning."

I laughed. "Well, it seems to me," I said, "that after lunch the court's sanction will be a little superfluous. After all, the issue has already been decided. Whatever the court does is quite beside the point."

Khan blinked. "Not at all. To begin with, if it were not for the magistrate, there would be no record of the decision." I tried to interrupt, but Khan held up his hand. "And there is something more than that!" he said. "Do you suppose that without the threat of a court hearing, the two parties to this dispute ever would have been reconciled?" He laughed. "It is precisely because they are distrusted that these courts are able to serve their purpose. They clean these things up. They prod the villagers into formulating some standards of justice of their own and applying them, whatever they are, rather than allowing disputes to simply languish unsettled for years."

I could not decide whether Khan was serious. "Then this is the purpose of the courts?" I asked skeptically.

Khan frowned and passed his hand over his lips. "I don't know about purposes. I am telling you what they do."

He grew more explicit. "Take this case as an example. You know when this cattle theft took place? I've been hearing about it since I came here two years ago, and it probably happened some time before that. Oh," he nodded, "I have threatened to bring it to trial, but they know I am soft so they have put me off with promises that everything would be settled any day. Well it has been, but not till the magistrate was brought in."

I laughed uneasily. "Khan," I said, "I think you're simply trying to justify your job."

He took it more seriously than I had hoped that he would, for he snapped, "I justified the job before I took it!"

But he quickly relaxed. "Oh, I know what you mean. You'd like to see a more regular pattern. You'd like a rigid code of justice rather than this hit-or-miss system that prevails. Well, I'd like it too. It would make my job easier, for then everything would be written down in a book. If a man stole a cow or committed murder there would be a convenient statute telling me what to do."

He came over and waved his finger in my face. "But tell me, where are we to get these statutes? Are we to borrow them from the West as the British suggested? Or perhaps we can pick them out of the air."

"Oh, of course not," I objected. "But the villagers themselves—"

Khan interrupted me before I could continue.

"Ah, the villagers themselves! Exactly!" he cried. "And it is they who decided in the courtroom this morning."

I was angry now. "Then you think that justifies all the corruptions and abuses that we must expect from these magistrates, the whole districts where the banias make the laws and judge offenders, the police who are willing to arrest anyone for a price?" I was sorry I had said it, but Khan was not angry. Rather, an enormous grin had spread over his face.

"You are a very observant young man!" he chuckled, clapping me on the knee and sitting down before me. "No," he said. "I do not suggest that the small value of the courts justifies their corruption. But think! Who is responsible for the courts, the government that appoints them, or the villagers who tolerate them?"

125

I wanted to answer, but Khan continued. "It is the villagers themselves who are chiefly responsible. The government is a myth! Delhi is a myth! The faults of the country begin here, in the villages. Ah! When I was young I thought as you do, that there were evil men somewhere who were responsible for this, but the truth is our sufferings and injustices are like maggots, generated directly out of our own decay!

"When the villagers really want justice," he declaimed, "more than they want their old traditions, then, and only then, will they get it.

"When the villagers really want wealth rather than a convenient excuse for being poor, they will get wealth too.

"When the people of the Indian countryside are willing to sacrifice the security which the caste system gives them, to assume the burden which democracy imposes, only then can they expect the privileges of democracy.

"You laugh at the court. You are angry with the magistrate because the one is ineffectual and the other corrupt. And yet, I'll wager you feel nothing but pity for the ryot which, in the end, is responsible for both. Well, save your pity. What you saw today was the sins of the village being visited on the village, the narrowness and the refusal of the villagers to face the issues turned back upon them through this foolish magistrate.

"Injustice? Good! It may serve to shock the villagers out of their habitual apathy. Corruption? Thank God! It will suggest to the people that they have got to insist on something better. They live like animals? Of course they do, for their motives and desires are like those of animals; enough to eat today and tomorrow and a place to sleep tonight.

"Listen here. The villagers do not want honesty. They are afraid of honesty. It is the one thing they distrust. It is the result of this revolting religion of theirs that teaches them that they all are miserable and insignificant, that they can hope for nothing if it is left to merit, that they must steal their happiness if they are to have any at all.

"But the trouble with you, the trouble with so many is that you see it as a conflict between the people and the authorities. It is not that at all. The government is what they make it. The struggle is between the good and the bad in the villages. I know what you think. The villagers are all innocent; they have been abused and corrupted by outside forces. But in this country there are no outside forces; the virtues and vices are to be found right here. The trouble is, you want to keep things just as they are, only changing the government, but it is impossible, for the villages are so corrupt themselves that they would contaminate a government of gods, I can tell you."

Now Khan paused and wiped his forehead with his sleeve. He grinned at me as if in apology. Then he began in a quieter tone as if his enormous energy were dwindling at last. "I am an honest policeman. That's rare, you know? I am honest chiefly because I'm a Moslem among Hindus. I take no credit, for I'm considered an outsider and I just haven't had the opportunities. But do you think that my honesty is something in my favor? Far from it; it's the chief thing they hold against me, not so much because my superiors are embarrassed as because the villagers themselves can't get used to the idea. In most districts, a villager has only to stay on the right side of the system to get along. If a dispute over cattle or boundaries arises, it is decided by his caste or his position in the community. And the tragedy is this; they prefer it this way. While the Vaisya will complain about the domination of the Brahmins, he will be the first to protest if his own caste is not given a privileged position over the Sudras and harijans. What can the government do? It must gear in with the system, rotten as it is, or impose one of its own. I have chosen the latter, but sometimes I think it was a more selfish choice than the former would have been."

He sighed and sat down on his cot again. "No, I am not

defending the 'old order' as you would call it. I am simply asking in all humility what new order we will be able to substitute for it.

"You know," he said with a quizzical expression and an unmistakable note of challenge in his voice, "it takes a wise man to sympathize with the villages. But it takes an even wiser one to be critical of them too!"

Until now I had been wondering whether Khan's point of view might not be a simple rationalization of the bureaucracy. Certainly I had been tempted to call it that, for it would fit in much the better with the theories that I had. And yet, now I felt sure that there was something more to it. I felt sure that he was speaking with perfect candor. That he indeed was that rarity, an honest policeman, I knew, and that being the case there was no need of self-defense. One question remained. Khan might have been speaking as a Moslem, out of unreasoned disdain for the Hindu. It was possible that a certain communal bias had crept into this eloquent plea of his. But when I had thought more about it, I discarded this too, in the light of the inferences I could draw from his behavior. And in the end I decided that my reluctance to believe him might indeed be a rationalization of my own.

Whether he was right or not, Khan had taught me one thing—the danger of generalizing too quickly and with insufficient knowledge, the danger of accepting the word of one class and of judging everything else in terms of it. Khan himself would have been the first to object if I had tried to apply too quickly the standards which he had given me, for however disdainful this one speech had been, he himself felt an enormous sympathy for the villagers. And yet, he was right in insisting that it was impossible to learn some one great lesson to the exclusion of all others. He had reminded me that the issue was as complex as it seems, that no passion was an adequate substitute for knowledge.

[21]

JUST one thing remained to be done in Bhal-Gundawa. On the morning following our trip to court, Khan announced that his interviews had been a total failure and that he must plan a general meeting of the villagers. After breakfast he sent one of his deputies for the police patel, who appeared summarily leading his idiot son whom, he had advised us, he was grooming to inherit his job. Khan instructed him to see to the details of the meeting.

These mass meetings, it appeared, were important to Khan's method. Quite frequently, when he had been able to learn nothing from individuals, in a group he was able to play faction against faction, clique against clique, with much better results. I had seen him do this once or twice in Varavoli and again in the smaller villages we had touched, but he promised me that these had been nothing at all compared to what he would attempt tonight. He had chosen to hold the meeting in the dharmsala notwithstanding the fact that the town hall was bigger—chiefly, I suspect, because the villagers seldom went to the dharmsala and were, in consequence, a little in awe of it. He himself was a little like a prima donna. He checked all the details of the meeting several times and, though he pretended to rest for a while in the afternoon, it was obvious that he was suffering from a severe case of nerves.

Around half past seven the villagers began arriving, still grimy from the fields, and tired from their day's work. There was a certain unmistakable tension in the way they would hesitate at the doorway, glancing around them. They would come into the room and stand for a moment trying to accustom their eyes to the bright oil lamps, then they would slide quietly along the walls and squat down, muttering a few phrases and lapsing into silence. Khan himself was obviously contributing to their discomfort, for he sat tense and unsmiling behind a large table, staring off into one of the dark upper corners, tapping one finger rhythmically on the wood.

When the room was quite full, he relaxed a little. He rose and took off his Sam Browne belt, laying it on the table and rolling up his sleeves. And yet even in these actions he seemed playing a part. All eyes were upon him following each move, but like an actor, he seemed entirely oblivious. It was only through a rather exaggerated grace that he suggested he was not as calm as he would appear. Apparently he was producing the desired effect, for the villagers began twisting and whispering uneasily. At last he leaned forward, both hands on the table.

"You have been hiding an outlaw in this village," he said quietly.

It was like a hand grenade. The meeting exploded into a dozen simultaneous arguments and protests, men suddenly standing and shouting at others who were as suddenly defensive and withdrawn. It was interesting that even without knowing the language I could sense what had happened before it was translated; the meeting had been riven to the core on the issue of the defense or the prosecution of Zonia. The quiet men were those who had chosen to offer the outlaw a refuge in the village, fearing his wrath more than the wrath of the police and betting that Khan would never find out. The others, the laborers who were shouting abuse at them, chords straining in their necks and arms extended—these were as obviously the ones who feared Khan and had vainly protested the harboring of Zonia.

Khan himself was silent. He did not have to speak for gradually the energy of the partisans diminished till, after perhaps five minutes, the attention of the villagers was again on him, only now submissive. He wasted no time in questions or argument. He explained what each villager would be required to do. He would come up to the table and write down the direction in which Zonia had gone, beside his name. Of course there was an immediate protest, everyone insisting that he knew nothing about the route Zonia had taken, but Kahn thumped on the table for order and said acidly, "Then you will guess," and the line was formed.

I was at first confused as to the merits of this method till the police patel explained it to me. The fear of Zonia being as great as it was, no villager would be willing to give the right direction, even though they knew that by their refusal to do so they would tell Khan the truth in a negative way. It was logical enough, for the villagers were not really interested in protecting Zonia so much as avoiding any sign that they were siding with the law and thereby risking the outlaw's enmity. Of course there were a few, more sophisticated than the rest, who tried to offset the majority by choosing right. But when the predictions had been made and results were calculated there was, as always, one direction that was significantly low.

Still Kahn was not satisfied. "And now—" he announced— "the village to the south where Zonia has gone." Again the protests. Again the recording. And again the one village from which everyone shied.

For the first time Khan's face showed some semblance of feeling. He looked over toward me and smiled broadly. And thus the meeting was closed, the villagers sent home, with Khan and I returning to our billet.

"But I should think," I said to Khan that night, "that after a while the villagers would see through your stunt."

Khan laughed. "They see through it already," he said, "but there are few who are willing to risk the right answer. You see, these lists are posted in the village and the patel sees to it that they stay up for a month, so the villagers are deadly afraid that if they tell the truth they will get the name of an informer. How on earth can Zonia blame them this way? Each man can prove that he personally is innocent, and if I am able to learn something from checking the totals, well, whom can he hold to account for that?

"Of course," he admitted with a self-satisfied smile, "on occasion Zonia himself has tried to mislead me, like the time when he explained my system to the villagers and suggested that some of them tell the truth." Khan laughed. "But these villagers are a simple people. Since all of them want to earn Zonia's favor, when he does that almost every last one tells the truth and I am able to learn as much as ever."

He leaned back in his chair, very pleased with himself, smiling and obviously inviting my applause. Nor could I disappoint him. "It's amazing," I agreed. He threw back his head and shook the room with his laughter.

[22]

THERE is a road leading directly south from Bhal-Gundawa, running toward Bhug, where Zonia had fled. It is an exceptionally fine highway, one of the few that have been maintained since the eleventh century when so many were built. It by-passes most of the smaller settlements on the way, or more accurately, these settlements have been set back from it by order. Since Bhug is only about fifty miles from Bhal-Gundawa, it should not be more than a two-hour drive.

Khan and company, however, did not take this road. By now I had learned to expect such a thing, for whenever a course seemed overwhelmingly obvious, Khan seemed to shy away from it as a matter of principle. In this case, perhaps, it was just as well, for this road offered a good many opportunities for ambush- in one place, for example, where it passed an old fort, running a good half mile beneath its crumbling old walls, and again where it wound its way up a dry stream bed, both banks of which were incredibly steep.

At the time I was disappointed since the dangers of the journey seemed a little too dramatic to be very real, but I said nothing, for of course I was well aware that Khan knew this business far better than I did.

We broke camp one morning around four o'clock. It was a surprise move, for Khan had not even warned me, so cautious was he being to veil our departure lest the news of it get to Bhug ahead of us. When I awoke most of the preparations already had been made, for Khan was anxious that I should get as much sleep as possible, and I was still a bit drowsy when our horses were brought around and I was given a hand up by one of the deputies.

The plan, Khan explained when we had got under way, was to swing south and east in a circle around Bhug, approaching the village from behind, and perhaps camping where we might be able to arrange an ambush of our own. There was a plain, Khan said, to the south of Bhug, across which Zonia would have to travel, assuming he did not get word of our presence and backtrack again through Bhal-Gundawa. It seemed like a good plan, for the plain, when we reached it, surrounded the village on all but one side and from our point of vantage we were able to command the escape on all but the highway to the north.

Still, it was a trying piece of strategy. For nearly a week we laid over at a deserted, ramshackle well house, posting a watch on the roof by day, and by night sending the deputies out on patrols. Worst of all, there was only local food available, which in this case turned out more meager than usual; I had adjusted without complaining to regular village fare, but all we had here was flour and garlic stems. Khan armed me with a rifle, an enormous old Mannlicher of a caliber that is usually reserved for tigers, less, I suspect, because he expected me to need it than as a gesture designed to relieve the monotony. Yet even with this diversion I grew nervous after a while, and at one point I even contemplated leaving.

That I did not was only the result of my reluctance to offend Khan, who had been so kind to me till now.

At last Khan decided that something had gone wrong. We had kept our position for six full days, yet we had not only failed to catch a glimpse of Zonia; we had not even sighted a single villager. This meant something to Khan. Ordinarily, he argued, at least a hundred horsemen would have passed our way. That they had not could only be explained by the villagers' knowledge that we were stationed out here and their consequent fear that if they rode across the plain they might accidentally be shot for Zonia. It would be necessary, he sighed, for us to return to Bhal-Gundawa and pick up the trail once again where we had lost it. By now it should be safe to travel on the highway so it would only be a matter of a day's delay.

"But why not go straight into Bhug?" I asked. Khan laughed, for Bhug was "enemy territory." In Bhal-Gundawa he himself held the balance of power, but here the outlaw could muster the most help. Once again I realized how foreign I was. To me the idea seemed wholly impossible, two villages within a radius of fifty miles divided over support of the law or of a bandit! Nevertheless I agreed to continue with Khan, to Bhal-Gundawa and, as it happened, as far back as Varavoli. It seemed that Zonia, rather than making a stand, had decided to race for the Baroda border.

For some days now, I had sensed that the time was approaching when it would be necessary for Khan and me to part company. From my own point of view, the time had passed quickly—too quickly in the light of my ambitious schedule—for it was clear that if I were to get beyond the first leg of my touring I must avoid prolonging these tempting digressions. And for that matter, there was more than my own reluctance. Khan himself was growing increasingly uneasy about my presence, which was perhaps only natural in view of the fact that I was a foreigner for whom, practically, he had become responsible. I had assured him, of course, that he needn't take any special cautions on my account, but the assurance was unrealistic in the extreme when it did nothing to change the nature of his obligation. The facts were clear. We were closing on Zonia and each step that we took was more dangerous than the last. When he already had to worry about ambush and strategy, it was senseless for Khan to have to worry about me.

Suddenly the hostility of the countryside was brought home to me. Until now I had easily discounted these dangers, schooled as I was in the expectation that a criminal should be fleeing rather than fighting with the law. I was reminded that here this was not the case, that in the villages there was really neither hunter nor hunted, but a wilderness of people with no distinct loyalties among whom Khan and Zonia were groping for each other. It was an uncomfortable thought that the outlaw might recently have been sitting where we sat, seeing just what we saw, perhaps even talking with the same villagers and, awful thought, getting as much information from them. But it was true. And likewise it was true that we were not simply trailing Zonia as I had preferred to think. We were rather just trying to make contact with an enemy. The issue was undecided and the odds all too even.

"So you see," Khan explained, "though I enjoy your company it would not do for me to let you continue any farther. For myself I am paid for taking these chances, but you— It is really too much of a risk."

"Do you think you will get Zonia this time?" I asked.

He replied, "Ah, don't make me say—it is dangerous. If I ever get anxious to the point of predicting, it is Khan who will die instead of the outlaw. He is a clever one. He knows how maddening it gets, month after month following at a distance. And [he was serious] the man has a sixth sense that seems to tell him the very moment when his pursuer is apt to get cocky. I have been chasing Zonia for more than two years. Would you believe it, the pressure sometimes gets so great that I drop the chase when I am almost upon him because I realize that I am on the verge of something foolish, perhaps fatal?"

"My predecessor," he explained, "was a cautious man, but Zonia killed him just north of here. A woman came to him, far gone with child, Zonia's child according to her story. The outlaw had sired it and then deserted her and she would be willing to lead the police to his hideout. It was a plausible story. I would believe it myself. But the result?" He drew figures in the dust as he spoke. "The deputy superintendent and four of his men killed or wounded as they entered the house."

He sighed and mopped his face with his handkerchief. "And you ask me whether I will get Zonia this time. Frankly, I don't know if I'll ever get Zonia. It's a job just seeing he doesn't get me."

I decided to risk seeming foolish again. "Khan," I said, "is there really no alternative to all this? I can't believe that the villagers wouldn't help you if they knew you were only interested in their welfare."

"Well, I can understand that," Khan agreed. "Ten years ago I couldn't believe it myself. But the truth, and it's a hard truth to face I grant, is that I am not 'only interested in the villagers' welfare.'" I objected. "Don't be sentimental," Khan warned. "I'm here to enforce specific laws. Whether they are right or wrong is not my affair. They are given to me and I must follow them to the letter."

"But doesn't this work for the welfare of the villagers?" I asked.

"The villagers don't seem to think so," Khan replied. "You constantly make the same mistake. You believe that our troubles result from a misunderstanding."

"And don't they?" I asked.

"Of course not," Khan said "The villagers and I understand each other perfectly. They want to avoid paying their taxes to the government and I make them pay. That's the source of the trouble."

"Well, I'm afraid I can sympathize with the villagers," I insisted. "After all, they get nothing from the government in turn."

"Well, sympathize to your heart's content," Khan laughed. "But you see, our sympathy is not to the point."

"The police are not a revolutionary army, dedicated to abstract justice," he continued. "They are men who work within the framework of a system, and if the system is rotten, well, so are the police. Do you think we like taking orders from the banias? It's not just a matter of bribes and the like. The whole essence of our profession is that we do as we're told, and if it is the banias who have the power, then they do the telling. Damn it, the whole thing fits together. I grant, the individual villager is not to blame. But the system is, and if the villagers are its victims, then so are the police in equal degree. When the people of Varavoli and Bhug decide they've had enough of Brahmin and bania rule, perhaps they'll insist on a government of their own, and the police will really be 'working for their welfare'."

"And till then?" I asked.

"Till then," Khan replied, "we'll serve whoever makes the laws. And—" he added rather wearily—"I'll continue to hunt Zonia and have a running battle with the villagers while I do it."

[23]

OUR last day together was something of an occasion. Khan decided that he could afford a few hours' delay to take me to Zainabad, a small Moslem state whose borders were not very far from Bhal-Gundawa. He assured me that there we would be feasted royally, literally royally, by the chief of Zainabad himself, and he hinted that if we somehow could get rid of his deputies who, being Hindus, would probably object to the idea, we might even manage to bag a peacock en route or, as he euphemistically called it, "a Kathiawar turkey." It was a day well spent, not only because of the excellent meal that was provided indeed, but also because of the chance to see Zainabad. It was easily worth a day's time in itself.

The state, I learned, was one of those anomalies, a dominion of Hindus ruled over by a Moslem, the sort of creation which could only exist by virtue of a tradition far stronger than will. Many years ago it was part of the Mogul empire, in the tenth or eleventh century to be exact, and its continued existence could only be explained by the incredible fact that its Hindu inhabitants apparently never reflected, in those intervening centuries, that there was no longer an empire to support their ruler.

At night it was always easy to find Zainabad, for from the top of the palace a great beacon had been erected in the utterly forlorn and pathetic pretense that it would be needed to guide visitors across the surrounding plains. It was one of those vanities so common in these states that are dictated by the fact of their very uselessness, like the elaborate but unfunctional chandeliers at Bhal-Gundawa, or the unpiped toilets in the guesthouse at Baroda. Unfortunately, since we arrived in the early morning, we derived no benefit from this beacon; the fact is we had to be content with far less—a mosaic inscription on the front of the palace itself that was a monument to the good will and illiteracy of Zainabad, proclaiming in four-foot letters, "Well-Come!"

And indeed we were welcome. At the borders of the state we were met by the dewan, the chief administrator, who drove us to the palace in the official state car, a rather ancient Packard with a broken spring. Except for its emblem the palace was really an impressive reconstruction of an old Mogul ruin and in the sitting room, where we were officially received by the Chief, there was a most remarkable collection of Persian hangings. The dewan was careful we should notice it all; he was almost beside himself with excitement for, as he kept assuring us, it was a great many years since they had had any "distinguished visitors from abroad." The last, I gathered, was the local British resident who had paid the state a semiyearly call. At any rate the halls were covered with pictures preserving his discomfort and boredom for posterity.

But it was the Chief himself (and he was called just that) who was the most fabulous thing about the state of Zainabad. I had tried to picture him in the most unlikely manner, but my most vivid imaginings were far short of the truth. When he arrived, he came in a pony cart, for the Chief of Zainabad was just six years old, and in spite of the fact that everyone seemed to pick on him, he was really quite a prepossessing child. When he entered the room we all had to stand, but that was apparently the extent of his royal prerogatives, for in the same breath with which the dewan introduced him he also bade him stop picking his nose. He retired to a corner following the introductions where an Anglo-Indian governess sat over him scowling, nor was he heard from again till a few minutes before lunch when he asked the dewan if he might go to the bathroom.

At lunch, the dewan and I sat adjacent, the Chief having been sent upstairs to his room. It was a little bit trying for, though I tried to make conversation, the dewan and I were a natural mismatch. In an effort to be polite I asked what crops the villagers of Zainabad chiefly grew, but it turned out badly for he groped about till it was perfectly clear he had no idea; then he managed to turn the question to generalities and affirm that, "Agriculture is our primary industry."

I tried again. Had this been a good year? Were the villagers' yields what they should have been?

The villagers' yields were always what they should be. "The sun, you know . . . and they dig little wells. . . ."

Just to save the dewan from further embarrassment I asked him to tell me about the problems of his job. As I expected, this served to revive his self-confidence and incidentally gave me a chance to finish my meal.

"You have no idea," he happily lamented, "how hard it is to do anything for these villagers. A hopeless people! Completely hopeless." Parenthetically he added, "They are Hindus, you know." He had picked up a number of English mannerisms and his conversation was bristling with them. "The sanitary conditions are shocking in the villages. Absolutely shocking."

He breathed a sad, long-suffering sigh. "Heaven knows," he said, "we have done our best. Last year we hired a Moslem doctor to come to Zainabad and lecture on health. But do you think that the people paid any attention? Not a particle; why, they live as badly as ever. The money was wasted. It is my own opinion that these villagers simply do not want to be helped."

I turned the conversation once again to agriculture, hoping that the dewan's momentum would carry him. It did. "Yes," he said, "we have done much for the farmers. Just this week we have applied to the government for a film."

"A film?" I asked.

"Yes," he replied. "A film showing all of the modern methods of farming. It is entitled, *Better Farming for Better Living*. They say it is quite good. You have seen it perhaps?"

I replied that I hadn't. "I'm surprised," said the dewan. "The government praises it very highly. And now that I think of it," he added after a pause, "I believe that it was made in America!"

I tried to look flattered, but I was actually amazed. "Well, that's fine," I said. "But will the people understand it?"

The dewan pulled thoughtfully at his lower lip. "Perhaps not," he reflected. "But I will translate," he smiled.

I objected weakly, "But even with a translator . . . well, after all, Zainabad is not America."

"Ah," the dewan said, "I am a liberal, you see! I want our people to learn from the West!"

I was still trying to rephrase my objection, but he continued, "Some people think only of the old traditions. I believe that India must be willing to change." He smiled shyly. "In my small way I work for that here."

"Alexander Hamilton! Alexander Hamilton!" His mood changed so quickly that I was taken unaware. "That is the sort of man that India needs!" He coughed delicately. "You see, I am a student of history."

He continued, "We have been looking backward too long. History has passed our country by. What we need is a man like Hamilton!" He looked down in his curry as if to find one there.

"Well," I said to relieve my own embarrassment, "I can see that you have the interests of your country at heart." But the dewan was still slumped dramatically in his food, so I went ahead and finished eating my own.

I had hoped to see Khan alone for a few minutes. Our chance came just after lunch when the dewan, who had very kindly offered to provide me with a horse, went off to make the necessary arrangements. Khan and I were left in one of the sitting rooms so I seized on the chance to thank him for his kindness.

"Oh," he protested, "don't thank me. I am glad for the company, and since the government pays my bills, it has cost me nothing."

But what I was thinking about was not just the material help. That had been generous enough, but it was the least Khan had given me. I was thinking rather of the many lessons I had learned during the weeks we had traveled together. When I stopped to think of it I could not really decide what it was precisely that I had learned from Khan; it was more a method than a sum of facts; it was more an outlook than a generalization. Still I felt sure that through some process not unlike osmosis I had absorbed a certain understanding from Khan, and though it was seldom that we had seriously discussed the villages, I realized that it was he who had been my best teacher.

What it was, I decided when I could look back on it later, was that Khan had fitted none of the regular patterns; he was neither the embittered bureaucrat whose whole mind was focused on the faults of his people in softheaded self-pity, nor was he the all too common sentimentalist, overflowing with love and sympathy for the plight of the villager but lacking so totally in any practical faith that he was at a loss to put his good will to use. Since he was a man with a definite job to do he interpreted the villages in the light of that job, sympathetically but realistically, knowing both faults and virtues and feeling bound to conceal neither.

I was brought to take stock of my informants before him. They had fallen into two fantastic categories. There were the rajahs and congressmen who could be grouped together, since both of them were justifying their benevolent despotisms with the usual nonsense about the backwardness of the people and the necessity of their providing a powerful leadership. And on the other hand there were the spokesmen among the villagers themselves who, in contrast to the other, had so completely beguiled me with their talk about the abuses of the government and the authorities and their unspoken assumption of their own complete innocence.

I tried to imagine what it would be like to undertake any real work in the villages holding either extreme viewpoint. It would be clearly impossible, for the one was designed for the palace, the other for Western pulpits. In the drawing room or dharmsala both made good sense, just so long as there was no genuine problem to be faced. But when you were out in the countryside trying to catch an outlaw, you could see the weaknesses of each almost immediately.

What Khan had, essentially, was an animal understanding; I realized this now as I was about to leave him. He was not a thinker. He was a policeman, and his judgment was trued by the most rigid emperical standards. In Bombay, in Jamnagar, you could afford to stretch points, to twist the villages to suit your own theories. But here you could not, and if Khan had tried, he probably would have wound up with a bullet in his head. So it was this, essentially, which had set him apart, which had driven him to a position of such undiluted realism. And it was something of this that he had communicated to me just by allowing me to go with him and to watch him work.

My whole approach to the villages, I realized, had shifted during the four short weeks we spent together, or more accurately perhaps, during those four short weeks I had learned a certain emotional forbearance. It was not that I was less sympathetic before, that I felt less sorry for the individual. It was just that I dimly had begun to sense that the only distinction still worth making was the distinction between the individual and the society, between the people and the civilization.

I had discovered, for example, that it was foolish to talk about the influence of outside forces in the villages; Khan's own statement seemed almost axiomatically true. "In India there are no outside forces." I saw too that it was pointless to blame the government; it was corrupt to uselessness, but that was insignificant, for the villages and the government were sides of the same coin and when you condemned the one you condemned the other. Most of all, I saw the superficiality of my suspicion that the British were somehow responsible for all this. The truth was, the British were never so effective as to have earned much blame, try hard though they did. In the cities where you could see the statues in the parks, the remnants of the empire still seemed very real, but out here it was obvious that their whole period of rule had rolled off India like water off a duck. The cruelties of the empire? They were not even visible to a people adjusted to the Mogul period. The economic exploitation of the country? The poor British were novices in that field compared with the banias. No, the biggest sin of the British raj was that it was a people who knew better playing a filthy game. The rules of the game were not of their making, but had been laid down by India during the years of decline.

So it really was not a matter of blaming anyone. It was just a matter of accepting a fact as a fact, of having enough faith in the villagers themselves to be willing to discern and condemn their faults. It was a matter of seeing caste as it existed, of differentiating between the idealized Hinduism and the real. It was a matter of admitting that the whole village society was old and tired and terribly sick.

"Well, Khan," I said, "I'm grateful anyway." But I didn't explain the reasons for my gratitude for Khan was already beginning to grow nervous. He was anxious to get back on the trail of his outlaw.

Maharashtra

Maharashtra

[24]

LIKE most lines of demarcation in India, the border between the Gujarat and Maharashtra is a vague one. Traditionally the one begins and the other one ends somewhere south of a Portuguese settlement called Daman, about a hundred and fifty miles north of Bombay, not far from where Khan and I parted ways. But actually, such a designation is misleading, for both the Gujarat and Maharashtra are approximate areas; though in the center of each there is a definite core, at the margins their identities intermingle and mix like the eddying backwaters of a lazy stream, in tentative and equivocating explorations.

In general, as you travel south one of the first things to strike you is the increasing fertility of the land, due chiefly, I suppose, to the mountains that rise to the east and send down their soil to the plains. The brown farmland of the north which at one time seemed so rich, gives way to an even more bountiful black loam, and in consonance with this the crops change too, from the jowar and bajri of the Rajputana wastes, through the mug and garlic of the central tracts, to the cash crops of the southern Gujarat coastline, consisting chiefly of castor seed and cotton.

You will notice that the methods of farming change too. The southern Gujrati is an excellent cultivator and since he need not spend much of his time in irrigation, his land is intensively and efficiently worked. The chief improvement to be noticed, perhaps, is in the quality of the southern Gujarat livestock. Here alone, in all of my traveling so far, have I found anything resembling selective breeding. Instead of

147

the animals being permitted to run, in this part of the country they were generally penned, and as a consequence, the villagers were able to maintain two distinct strains of cattle, for working and for milking. To the north, with an almost maddening perversity, only the best and most expensive bulls were tethered so that in practice it was the scrub bulls, whom no one would claim, who were left to the job of siring the herds. The results of course had been all too apparent. In the north the cattle had been pitifully small, nothing like the well-formed Sind strains that were almost the rule in the southern Gujarat.

The villages, too, showed this increased care. As I worked my way south they grew progressively cleaner, and in the place of the century-old patchwork patterns their layouts began to seem almost logical. Best of all, behind each village was a ditch, reserved exclusively for the natural functions, which contributed not only to the aesthetics of the village but to the health of the population as well.

And of course, there were the accompanying changes in the people. In general I noticed that they were increasingly friendly. While their northern cousins had been distant and self-satisfied, the south Gujrati were amiable and quarrelsome. In a sense they were a less responsible people. The percentage of drunkenness, for example, was appalling. When you entered a village after six in the evening it was almost a job to find anyone sober. Moreover, the addiction to opium had increased, and though it was not nearly so general as it had been in Kathiawar, there was a pernicious habit which had developed here of feeding it to adolescents to curb their sex urge. Still, if I had been forced to choose, I think I would have preferred to live in this area which I was entering now, for there was something about the provincialism of the people of the north that made it impossible for me to like them genuinely.

From Zainabad I struck out directly south. I traveled for more than a week without stopping on the exultance of freedom, which was the reaction from the tense, tiring days I had spent with Khan. My horse was a good one, a Kathiawar gelding only about fourteen hands high but hard hoofed and long winded, and in that first burst of energy I was able to cover most of the ground between the state and the borders of Maharashtra. The whole countryside, it seemed, was in consonance with my mood, for its complexion had changed radically since I was last aware of it. There were coconut palms growing wild in the fields and date trees lining the roadways. And in the distance there were the beginnings of the gentle undulations that would eventually swell into the western ghats.

It was just south of Dharampur that I made my first stop; perforce, for I was there overtaken by a storm, an unseasonal thunderhead that blew in from the sea like some dark, angry hawk to pounce on the villages. It struck so suddenly and with such frightening force that I was unable even to get to the nearest village, and I had to lie over in the hut of a farmer, literally helping him hold down his light-thatched roof. For two days and nights the wind continued, but around midnight of the first we lost our battle, for the wind managed to open a door and, with one puff, scatter the roof in all four directions. After that the rains settled in with a vengeance and though we managed to build a wicker lean-to, the mud that we plastered in the chinks soon washed out and we resigned ourselves to being wet and uncomfortable. My position was not nearly so bad as my host's, though, for on the first day the storm carried off his chickens and each hour that it continued the deluge was destroying more of the dikes and channels that he had built through the year. Moreover, when the rains had stopped at last, the majority of his crops had been thoroughly flattened so that, though a few acres of cotton still could be harvested, his cane and castor were a total loss.

It was a mocking touch that when I was able to move on the country looked even more beautiful than ever. On the edges of all of the ruined fields, banks of small propitiatory flowers were blooming.

Farther south I came upon a caravan of Sindhi-Hindus, refugeeing down from Pakistan, a sullen, quiet, sad-eyed people, suspicious of this land through which they were passing and angry with its inhabitants as if they had been tricked into coming. I spent a few days with them, trying to learn something about the persecutions they had been through in the Sind, but they seemed far more critical of the Gujrati-Hindus, who had been kind enough to offer their hospitality, than they were of the Sindhi-Moslems who had driven them out, but who at least were Sindhis like themselves. There was no one in the caravan who spoke Hindustani, but fortunately there was one man who knew a smattering of English, a young city dweller who had a camera shop in Karachi and who had come by caravan so that he could bring his stock with him. When I asked him about the troubles in the north, he told me bitterly that it was the "foreign" Hindus who were all to blame. "These Punjabis were going to attack Pakistan," he confided. "They antagonized our Moslems. That was the trouble." It was a characteristic attitude, it seemed. To the refugees it was the "foreigners" who were responsible for everything; it was clear that their loyalty was not to their race, but simply to the land they had formerly inhabited. Some of the women, I was told, wanted to return to the Sind, preferring the persecutions to the humility of traveling. They could not get the food that they were used to eating. And how could you build a good fire with such wood? I stood it as long as I could, but in the end, my patience exhausted, I parted with the caravan, feeling far less sorry for the Sindhis themselves than the people in whose country they had chosen to settle.

After that I swung inland to by-pass Surat. Here I came upon an interesting series of villages where the remnants of the ancient Dutch colonies in India could still be seen, albeit in poor repair. There was a group of tombs in one village of the unfortunate burghers who had yielded to the climate and the fevers, surrounded by a group of short fat columns like a procession of mourning, forlorn Dutch ghosts. You had only to look at them once to know why the Dutch colonial enterprise had failed. No people capable of an architecture like this could ever have made an impression on Asia. The villagers, even after a lapse of three centuries, would sometimes stand looking at them, scratching their heads. And the Dutchmen in turn would remain aloof, so architecturally self-satisfied and so historically absurd that you began to share the wonder of the villagers and to suspect that no such people had existed.

As I recall, it was in one of these villages too that I began to notice discomforting signs which were the first of increasingly serious indications showing just how badly I had overworked my horse. Until now I had rather taken it for granted that the animal would balk before it was seriously overtaxed, but it was obvious that I had reckoned without the strain of Arabian, which had given him a far greater will than body. He was foundered, it developed, and not long after this he was unable to keep up a practical speed, so, since selling him would only have meant a slower death, I had to shoot him and switch to bullock carts again. At bottom, the loss was more sentimental than practical, since the horse's usefulness soon would have ended anyway, for the western ghats were swinging close to the sea and the country was growing more rugged by the day.

My movements by bullock cart were necessarily much slower. After the previous few weeks they were painfully so, for once again I was dependent upon the whims of others after a tantalizing taste of independence. What made it even worse, for weeks it seemed we were traveling in sight of the Deccan Plateau, which marked the boundary of the Maharashtrian heartland toward which I eagerly had been striving since Zainabad. Strictly speaking, it is not a plateau at all but an enormous fault of some two thousand feet where the level of the land over a majority of South India simply fails to conform with the level of the north. Historically it is important as a natural defense line that halted the rush of a number of invasions. And physically perhaps its foreboding façade is the perfect introduction to the country and its people.

[25]

EVEN physically it is difficult to generalize about Maharashtra. You can't say, for example, that it is fertile or barren as you could in the case of the Kathiawar Peninsula or the cotton belt between Ahmedabad and Baroda. It is an enormous land, the remnant of an empire that was the most recent native dynasty in India, but in almost every hundred miles square there are parcels which would give the lie to any overall description. Maharashtra is a patchwork in every respect, a country not ready for post-mortem judgments, even the terrain reflecting this vital quality in its perplexing and contradictory extremes.

Yet, certain generalizations may still be useful; Maharashtra can be conceived in two large categories—the lowland that lies north or seaward of the plateau, and the broad open plains of the Deccan itself. The lowlands are clearly the richest of the two, but on the seacoast their strips of magnificent fertility are sandwiched in between barren rock ledges insufficient even to support an enterprising goat. The plateau, on the other hand, is fairly uniform from the point of view of the soil and land; here it is the availability of water that determines the productiveness of any given acre. But since the people of both areas are essentially the same, the division is not more than geographically important and even geographically, it would be dangerous to draw conclusions beyond those immediately presented to view.

One of the first things you notice when you enter Maharashtra is the unsettled pattern of its agriculture. There are some villages that are independent and self-sufficient, devoted almost completely to subsistence farming, while there are others, literally within a stone's throw of these, wholly committed to cash crops and to trade with each other. Where there are potentialities for efficient irrigation, wheat and sugar cane seem to dominate the landscape, but in the drier areas, inaccessible to streams, the concentration seems to be on groundnuts and pulses. Moreover, since Maharashtra is in Bombay Presidency, one of the most progressive governmental provinces in India, there even has been a sporadic introduction of machinery where the terrain and the concentration of land permits. In general the results have not been too good, for the subsidy program is riddled with corruption. And in addition, the government, with characteristic bravado, has bought nothing but enormous caterpillar tractors when even the most uninformed common sense would have dictated smaller ones for the two- and three-acre fields that are the rule. Still, the fact that such experiment has been undertaken at all is an encouraging sign for the future. And for that matter, there have been notable successes, chiefly where great landholdings were lying contiguous so that it was profitable for the owners to hire their plowing done by the government even at the prevailing high cost of operations.

In all ways, the influence of the cities is to be noted in the villages of the Maharatha country, for it is one of the few places in India where these cities have an organic connection with the economy and society of the countryside. The largest city, Bombay, is an exception, but places like Poona, Satara, and Sholapur are cultural as well as economic centers and they help tremendously to preserve the sense of unity of the Maharashtrians. Then too, the whole area is crisscrossed with railroads that have given rise to an enormous pilgrim trade, a strange meeting of the old world and the new in which

153

sadhus and penitents from Ahmadnagar and Poona journey to the shrines of Pandharpur and Dharwar on the rigorous timetable of the *Deccan Queen*. Indeed, there is one railroad that depends almost solely on just this modernized religious traffic, a narrow gauge line running from nowhere to nowhere, but passing near a famous Vitoba shrine. Still, this willingness to adapt to modern advantages is a symptom rather than a real difference in itself. To explain it, and to explain the whole temperament of the area, it is necessary to consider its history.

When the British originally landed in India, it was the Maharashtrian empire that, in effect, they were challenging, for though the period was one of political confusion, the Maharathas and their forces were clearly in ascendancy. The weaknesses of the Moguls in the north were apparent, but it was their defeat at Bijapur by the Maharathas which finally made it clear to everyone that the struggle with the west must be waged by them if it was to be waged at all. Under Shivaji, the Maharathas accepted this challenge. By temporizing with the Moguls, who were still nominally a power, they cleared the political debris from underfoot and, by the time the British had become established in Bengal, were ready to meet them with a powerful army. Unfortunately fate prevented a genuine test between Shivaji's empire and the foreign challenger. If there had been such a test, there is little doubt that the ferocious Maharathas would have come out on top. As it happened, however, the Mogul forces in South India were still strong enough to be a deciding factor and if they could not be the rulers of a native India, they were willing to cast their lot with the British. So it was that the Maharathas went down to defeat, a defeat the more bitter for the treachery that made it possible. And so also it was the defeat rather than weakening that strengthened the sense of unity of the vanquished.

But this was not Maharashtra's only cause for bitterness.

Because they already possessed such a well-organized government, the invaders, by seizing just the key positions, were
able to exploit them with an unparalleled efficiency. Elsewhere, the biggest protection of the Indian peoples was the
disorganization of their old traditions, for there the British
were starting from scratch, molding an empire from the very
foundation stones up. Unfortunately this was far from true
in Maharashtra. Here the patterns and institutions were
already developed so that no more was necessary than to
replace the ruler and his top lieutenants with British hire-
lings! In a sense, it would therefore be accurate to say that
the loyalties of the people were used against them so that
their very virtues as an independent nation became, under
subjection, their greatest weakness.

It is not something which the Maharathas have easily forgotten. Rather naturally it has left them with a deep distrust
of the neighbors who failed them in their hour of crisis, and
the foreigners who bled their land so ruthlessly. You sense
this as you travel through their country for the people are
not just passively suspicious like the North Gujrati. They are
eagerly inhospitable and they will literally walk miles for
the chance of snubbing or insulting a foreigner. For the first
time since I had begun my traveling in the villages I was honestly afraid of the people around me, actually so afraid that
on occasions I detoured many miles just to avoid some village
that was notably rabid. Worst of all, I was even denied the
usual consolation of knowing that this enmity stemmed from
sheer ignorance; I always had the feeling that in Maharashtra
the villagers could explain their hatred in the most logical
terms. They were not simply acting on impulse or habit.
They had long experience with people of my color, and on
the basis of that experience they had constructed a philosophy
which I had to admit was entirely logical. Of course there
was still a remnant of that strained respect which the raj had
managed to enforce, but even now, within a year of the de-

parture of the British, it was breaking down with alarming rapidity.

For example, I soon learned not to ask questions. The answers that I got were invariably wrong, and in some cases the farmers would not even answer, but would call their friends to come and witness my confusion.

And yet there were compensations for the uneasiness this caused me. While I had to proceed with an unusual circumspection, I was rewarded with the knowledge that I was at last getting close to the touchy core of village politics. Until now I had felt that I was wandering about in a morass of dead habit and rotting traditions; even in the South Gujarat and the outlaw village of Bursad the rebelliousness was individual and according to the old pattern. But here it was not. There was an early stirring like the flexing muscles of an awakening giant. I could not run away from it. Again and again I had the feeling of some impending crisis around me, and I would take to the road in the misguided hope that by going somewhere else I could leave it behind. But it was as if the whole countryside were breathing in one rhythm, moving together like parts of a body. The giant was indeed beginning to awaken, the giant of Shivaji's slumbering empire!

I had managed the painful trip up the ghats and passed south of Poona over the flat farmlands of the Deccan and arrived at a village called Baramati, situated between Poona and Satara. In the course of my trip I had made a number of stopovers, but until now they had been rather dismal, functional visits, and though I interviewed a number of mamlatdars and learned a few unrelated facts from these administrative officers, I missed the spontaneous friendships which, in other parts of the country, had been so easy to establish.

One of my most serious difficulties arose from my own inability to adjust to the changing conditions. For though the political complexion of the country was different, I was still tempted to think in terms of the north. Here the divisions of popular opinion were more subtle than the pro- or antigovernment factions I was used to. A whole terminology remained to be learned, a whole complexity of political and religious schisms.

For example, it was in a Maharashtrian village that I encountered the first genuinely recognizable Communist, a reformer not just vaguely dissatisfied with the government, but decided on precisely what he wanted to do. Near Poona I spent several days with one such, a practicing barrister from Bombay who spent several days a week in the villages doing party work chiefly and most successfully among cultivators and harijans. His methods had been a revelation in themselves, for though what he preached was far from a classical Marxism, it was equally far from the nebulous humanism into which every position tended to disintegrate farther north. The Brahmins, he argued, (and he was one himself) had gotten control of the Congress Party and were trading on the prestige it had gained through independence to enforce the economic privileges of their class. Did the people expect that Patel and Nehru, both Brahmins, were interested in their standard of living? Was not even Gandhi, he suggested gently, living with Birla, that industrialist? and utterly reactionary? It was not surprising that he was having considerable success, for this line of reasoning appealed to the Maharashtrians, who were sophisticated enough politically to know the accuracy of his facts at least. And look at this village, he insisted. Is caste not just another word for class? The question was being asked to untouchables, chiefly; it is not even necessary to detail their reaction.

Nor were the other parties less articulate here. Until now, the initials R.S.S. had stood for the rather impossible name of a rightist party and not much else. In these villages, however, they became something more concrete; they became hundreds of children drilling in a field, raising their arms in the party salute, and listening to indoctrination lectures. On several occasions I talked with their leaders, chiefly militant Maharashtrian Brahmins dedicated, as was their organization itself, to the preservation of the Hindu "upper middle class." They spoke of the great traditions of India, of the glory of Ashoka and the prowess of Shivaji and, fat old charlatans that they usually were, of the necessity of emulating their spartan traditions. The country had been yielding to the left, they insisted, away from the institutions that had once made her great, and it was the responsibility of the Brahmin caste to lead her back to prosperity and power again. Discipline! That was the thing that was needed. Not this careless talk about democracy and rights! The classical injunctions of Hinduism were clear. They were the intended rulers of the land and its people.

And of course, there were the Socialists, between the two extremes. They were like poor lost lambs deserted by their shepherd, unreconciled as they were to Nehru's decision to stay within the Congress framework. Their policy at the moment was rather inarticulate; chiefly they seemed dedicated to a period of mourning for the erstwhile leader who had withstood the British only to fall victim to the conservatism of the Congress right wing. How could it be, they wondered, that Jawaharlalji had stopped short of the genuine goals of independence, the abolition of the zemindari landlord system, and the destruction of the interests that had supported the British? Their program, and his as he used to express it, turned on just these critical caste and class issues and yet now that Nehru was in a position of power, he was treating them like petitioning poor relations. Was it Gandhi's influence? Had some of his increasing conservatism rubbed off on their former hero? Or was it that Nehru, tired of being on the outside, lacked the energy to break with the Congress machine and take the place to which history had assigned him, as head of the moderate Socialist cause? The Socialists were not bitter, but they were deeply disillusioned and tired by the succession of fresh enemies who opposed them. Gradually they were going the way of their leader, taking refuge in the extremes of the right and the left.

And yet, it was not the individual parties and their programs that interested me most as I traveled through Maharashtra. It was rather the vitality, which they all had in common, the clarity of aim and the conception of purpose. The politics of the countryside had changed overnight from the most rudimentary and instinctive factional grapplings to an incredibly subtle and well-informed competition on the issues that lay behind these factions. In a sense it revealed a new problem to me, contrasting the most backward and the most advanced countrysides as it did, for it made clear that the distance that lay between them had to be measured in years as well as in miles. Still, it was fortunate that I had begun in the north, I decided, for without my grounding in the basic village conflicts I could never have made sense out of the schismatics I met here, the tensions and the intrigues between the castes and the subcastes.

Moreover, I had learned a fluidity of outlook or, more accurately perhaps, a downright opportunism which I had to exercise to the limits of my ability to penetrate the innate hostility of the Maharashtrians. I had learned in the north the absolute necessity of maintaining a noncommittal position while conveying the impression in conversation and acquaintance that I was actually "neutral in favor of" my conversant. Here the technique was even more necessary and useful, for the Maharashtrians were political missionaries by nature. An open mind they could not resist, and it was the one thing in the world I was able to offer.

[26]

WHEN I left Baramati it was with a caravan of Bhavayars, a ragged band of traveling minstrels who had come down from the Gujarat to tour through the Deccan and had stopped in Baramati one night while I was there. There was not much choice. Once again I was stranded, this time by a harvest of canes and pulses which kept all of the farmers busy in their fields, leaving the roads almost wholly deserted. I had seen such troops as this one before, traveling in the north in their bright-colored wagons, and though I had never witnessed one of their shows until now, I knew a little about them from my talks with the villagers.

In most cases they were bands of itinerant actors, local wits who had turned professional, living a hand-to-mouth existence on the charity and gullibility of the admes, as they called them. There were some gypsy caravans, but the majority of them were Hindus who were too lazy to work and too clever to starve, and their performances were usually very slipshod affairs that offered the audiences just a chance to jeer.

Still, I decided that I had nothing to lose by joining this troupe. They were going south as far as Dharwar on a leisurely schedule that suited my purposes, and that would bring me into dozens of villages en route. Accordingly, I sought out the manager of the troupe and explained my proposition to him, and the next morning, when the caravan pulled out of Baramati, I was riding on the tail gate of one of its carts.

This particular caravan was a famous one. It was headed by a man called Swamiji Gopal, who was known throughout the villages of western India, even in places where Nehru himself was unheard of. Accompanying him were the usual jugglers and acrobats, but it was Swamiji who held the troupe together, and after just one performance it was easy to understand, for he had a genius for mimicry that is past description. Very appropriately he traveled in a luxurious cart drawn by no less than four expensive bullocks that on the road served both as vehicle and home, and in villages could be cleared to provide a stage. It was outfitted with every imaginable convenience from an alcohol stove to folding beds; there was even a small closet that swung over one side, providing a private toilet en route. Occasionally some of his entourage twitted him about these luxuries, but Swamiji never felt it necessary to apologize. "Any fool," I once heard him tell a dancer, "can manage to be uncomfortable on the road!"

It was my good fortune to ride with Swamiji. It was an occurrence without precedent, his cohorts assured me, for though there was room for fully half of the troupe in his wagon, ordinarily he was most jealous of his comfort and privacy. It was his custom to sleep through the day while we were traveling, for there was usually a great deal to be done in the evenings, and though Swamiji himself never descended to labor, he complained that the noise always kept him awake. At night he would read after his performance was over, or play solitaire with a deck of grimy cards, or, even more rarely, sit and talk with me in a lisping, unidiomatic, but forceful English.

There were some days too when Swamiji was away. It was his job to arrange the itinerary for the caravan, and about once a week he would ride ahead on his horse to bargain with the villages and arrange for our appearances. He did not trust to luck. His fame was so great that he could usually bully the locals into guaranteeing him a fee, pitting one neighboring village against the other till he brought them all around to his terms. Then, this done, he would come back to the caravan again and relapse into his lazy and comfortable routine. We would get under way, driving hard through the day, each night performing in a different place.

Swamiji himself was a natural comedian. His genius lay not in his prearranged acts but in the byplay which he was able to maintain with his audience, usually to its embarrassment, but always to its delight. In the north, he informed me, he had different routines, but here he specialized in political satires, magnificent imitations of the national leaders, and, when occasion permitted, of local notables. Like so much good comedy, Swamiji's was half bitter and it generally turned against the government bureaucracy which, in spite of the most voluble good will of its leaders, laid such a crushing weight on the people of the countryside. For example, he would frequently impersonate the collectors; much research went into these impersonations, for he would often haunt the district seat for days just to catch a glimpse of his intended victim. But when presented in the villages the imitations justified any amount of effort and time they had cost. Swamiji never needed to announce his subject. He went into his act and his spectators were convulsed.

Invariably these acts were keyed to his audiences. To my knowledge, he had six variations of one, an imitation of Gandhi that he loved to perform in which he portrayed the Mahatma as an inoffensive old fool. In its simplest version he would appear on the stage clad in nothing but the traditional Gujarat dhoti and make well-meaning but inane and pathetic generalizations over a miniature spinning wheel, which never functioned correctly. Increasing complications would finally get him hopelessly tangled in its cotton. As the act proceeded, he became more and more involved in his formless philosophies till in the end he forsook the nonviolence which he was discussing to smash the wheel into a dozen small pieces. The villagers loved it. It was apparent from their reaction that it crystallized some feeling of their own about the Mahatma for often, when Swamiji was through, they would not only applaud but would cry "Yes! Yes!" over and over again.

Then there was an imitation of Patel which Swamiji often

did. This met with considerably less uniform favor and often, when we were stopping in the Brahmin strongholds, it would have to be eliminated from the program entirely. For Patel was the target of an even more vicious satire than Gandhi, who at least was made inoffensive, and since Patel was the patron saint of the Mahasabha, where their forces were strong, he must not be criticized or ridiculed. When he did appear it was as a legalistic sharper who proved, by quotations from the Hindu texts, that black was white, up was down, and any other random proposition suggested by the audience. Once again the reaction of the audience was indicative. From the cultivators and village servants there were exclamations of agreement, while from the petty landlords and the few merchants who were present there were nothing but rather nervous and sour smiles. Swamiji himself enjoyed the characterization and he would often stretch a point in order to perform it. His political acumen was as amazing as his imitations. Though he often came close, he never misjudged.

The rest of the troupe was similarly outstanding. Though they were like satellites revolving around Swamiji's moon, they were all exceptionally good in their fields, jugglers and singers and acrobats alike. The dancing especially interested me once I had seen enough of Swamiji to be able to look past him. There was one couple in particular, a young boy and girl who specialized in dazzling Manipuri routines. What was amazing about them was their virtuosity. To begin with, the dances were gymnastic exercises involving the most phenomenal leaping and pirouetting, and yet somehow never losing their dramatic integrity. There was none of the stiff and labored classicism that confronts the observer of the Western ballet; the wild motions and the violent grimaces of the dancers were like the free and uninhibited expressions of childhood. Yet, the impression was not that of primitivism or again of a self-consciously romantic orgy. The whole thing was so uniformly violent and overdone that it assumed a sort of inverted austerity, like Greek tragedy.

Then there was the fellow who appeared with a pair of trained dogs; it was a step on the program from the sublime to the ridiculous, for one of them was enormous—part shepherd, I think—while the other was a toy not a third his size. The best part of the act was the conclusion, in which the small dog leaped on the back of the larger and rode him around the stage in circles, barking, while the trainer appeared to be trying to catch them. It was riotously received, being even funnier in India than it would have seemed to an American audience, for in India the dog is so generally despised that it was a parallel, to the villagers, to a pair of trained rats.

And of course there were the singers. They completed the program, following Swamiji, when the audiences were sated with laughter. There was one man in particular, with a voice like a woman's, high and clear and full of melancholy, who could invariably reduce his audiences to tears. He sang long, mournful songs that wound, verse after verse, out of an enormous, sad past into an amorphous future, lamenting that life was forever the same, that we were eternally bound to the wheel of karma. It caught the audiences on the rebound from the humor, when they were already predisposed to morbidity and gloom, and they would listen, entranced, the flicker of the lamps picking out their damp eyes and their half-opened mouths. They would sway back and forth in an ecstacy of misery, till at last the performance had come to an end. And even then, they would sit as if hypnotized till the flats were knocked down and the carts reassembled for the road. Only then would they begin scuffling and rising to their feet. Slowly they would file past their self-appointed treasurer, paying their agreed percentage of the fee with coins that clung to their sweaty fingers.

And then, abruptly, the shouts of the drivers would come, and the crack of their whips, the creak of the axles. The caravan would draw out through the narrow streets, leaving the village in quiet darkness again.

[27]

I HAD noticed that Swamiji was avoiding the towns. We had been traveling for three weeks since leaving Baramati and though we had passed close to both Mahableshwar and Bhor, we had detoured around them and had kept to the villages. From conversations with Swamiji I knew that this was not his policy, for he had told me that in just a night in such a town as either of these, he could make more than the profits of a whole week in the countryside, and that with considerably less effort. I asked him about it, but his answer seemed vague, and I was tempted to discount it as an expression of temperament. "The townspeople are uneasy about something," he explained. "I just feel that the villages are safer, somehow."

"Safer?" I laughed.

"I'm serious," he warned. "As a farmer can read the weather in the sky, I can read the reactions of my audience, and I have sensed a very deep unrest in the towns." I led him on. What sort of unrest? He could not be sure, but it was unmistakable. "It is a thing you feel rather than know," he told me. "It is like the tension that preceded the Punjab massacres."

I was listening now. I had considered up to this point that this was simply more of Swamiji's self-dramatization, for experience with him had taught me that he liked to dwell on a sixth sense, which he assured me was what made him the great satirist that he was. He saw I was interested. "Last August," he continued, "the villagers were buzzing with their bloody secret. Of course, it was impossible for an outsider to tell just what it was, but a blind man could have sensed that something was brewing."

"And you think something is brewing now?" I asked.

He replied with disdain, "I know something is brewing."

165

Then he frowned again. "I can't quite—explain. But there is something. Something!" He clapped his palms together.

I was anxious to press for a more definite conjecture, but Swamiji was thinking in personal terms. "Ah, this country is always so uncertain," he pouted. "Some day I will cancel my tour of Maharashtra!"

I tried to draw him back to the subject, telling him how unfavorably the region had impressed me. "After the north," I tried, hoping vaguely to flatter him, "the Maharashtrians seem terribly inhospitable, somehow."

"That's just it," he laughed. "If you had come last month, you might have judged them the most hospitable people on earth. You can never be sure. I have been here a dozen times, and each time the reactions of the villagers have been different. One year they will applaud my parodies of Gandhi. The next they will resent them and remain totally hostile. Why, once, about five years ago, I was turned back at the borders. The villages, all of them, simply refused to have me."

"But there must be some reasons behind this," I objected.

"There are no reasons," he countered in a spasm of petulance. "The Maharashtrians simply don't know their own minds. They are a cliquish people and their cliques change every week." He remained silent for a moment. Then he relented somewhat, and when he spoke, it was with a smile at his own former dogmatism. "Reasons? Oh, of course they have reasons," he said. "But they are certainly hard for a stranger to understand.

"You see," he explained, "almost everywhere else the villages have settled into a traditional routine. There is a working harmony, however grudging, between the cultivators and their landlords, for instance." He sighed. "But not here! Here the cultivators, the landlords, the Brahmins, and the Sudras are still conspiring against each other. Occasionally they compromise, but these compromises mean nothing. No, this country is always in a state of unrest."

I reminded him, "But you think it is worse than usual?"

"Not worse," he answered. "It is different, somehow. It is almost too quiet, in the towns particularly. A few riots or strikes would cheer me considerably." He reminded me, "You have seen the R.S.S. yourself, exercising and training on the village fields. Never before have they been so well organized as this; ordinarily they spend their time giving foolish speeches. It is almost as if they had something in mind, beyond the exhibition of their own fat selves. I don't know exactly what it is all about, but I know when something is wrong, and there is something wrong now."

He relaxed into his reflective mood again. "Almost a year our country has been independent, eh? Well, it is just about time for something to happen, and this is as good a place for it to begin as any! To be truthful, I respect these Maharashtrians in a way. At least they face a problem when a problem exists. They don't hide behind a mystical mumbo jumbo and pretend that everything is just as it was planned. We will all have to come to it sooner or later, I suppose, so we might as well get it over with now. What it is I don't know. But we are close to it here. Something . . . Something! I can feel it in the air."

So we avoided the towns. From Baramati we went westward as far as the edge of the Deccan would permit, swinging down along the lip of the plateau where it breaks into those great chasms that slope down to the sea. For the first few weeks I kept close to Swamiji, for the other performers seemed to resent my presence, but it was not long before the majority had yielded and I was free to come and go among them.

What struck me most was the adjustment they made to the life of perpetual movement which they lived. Swamiji explained that a majority of them had never within memory even known a stationary home. Like him, most of them had been sold to the caravans by parents who were unable to clothe or feed them, and had been trained by the older performers and then made to work out their bond in a long apprenticeship. The whole concept of a home was foreign to them. They became attached to their wagons, their bullocks, instead, and almost all of them had fetishes, little mementoes and charms that represented stability in their unstable worlds. There was one man, for instance, who kept a pair of tamed monkeys. They overran his cart and littered it with refuse. And there was another who was something of a religious fanatic, who carried two huge boxes stuffed with shrines and icons which, whenever we were stopping for an hour or two, he would hastily unpack and set up around him. Even Swamiji was not totally free from this tendency. In his case there was an old portrait of his erstwhile teacher, executed by an unbelievably bad village artist but cherished by Swamiji beyond all measure. When I questioned him about it, he told me that he had not even particularly liked the old teacher who was portrayed. It was the physical object that was important to Swamiji. It was something to cling to, to love, to believe in.

Then there were other adjustments, not so savory; the percentage of homosexuality in the troupe was enormous, for though there were four women dancers who were quite generally available, there were fully two dozen demanding men. The arrangements were taken in stride by everyone, for the Indians are generally quite tolerant of inversions, and it was not at all uncommon to see two men keeping house together and behaving quite like a married couple. Indeed what problems occurred in the caravan as often as not centered around these couples, with sudden hatreds and complex jealousies sometimes following in the wake of their unstable affairs. Even while I was traveling with the caravan there was a knifing of a female dancer by one of the jugglers who had accused her of stealing his lover from him. Fortunately, the wound was no more than a scratch.

But in general the life of the caravan was peaceful. During the days, while we were traveling, I would sometimes borrow the pony which Swamiji tied behind his wagon and go calling on the other performers in their wagons. Almost all of them spoke a little English; they had learned it so they could perform in cantonments and army outposts and, though they would no longer have the chance to use it in this connection, they were glad of the opportunity to keep in practice. The four girls, particularly, were interesting company. This was the first chance I had had to talk freely with women and though they were far from typical village girls, they were able to tell me much about them. Two of them had been sold to the caravan by their parents, into simple whoredom for their earliest years. Then later they had been taught to dance by their masters and occasionally made available to the better-paying customers. Of the other two, one was a temple dancer, a mistress of the priests till she was fifteen or sixteen, having run away, in spite of the warnings of the holy men that she was in the service of God and would be punished. Yet it was the last who had the most exotic story. She had been born into a wealthy Gujrati family, but by the time she was eighteen she had so disgraced them that her ill fame had raised eyebrows for miles around. There was no one who would marry her so, with remarkable candor, her father simply gave her to the first passing caravan. She had known many masters since them, she assured me, but it was better than living with her family, anyway!

There was a juggler, too, whom I would visit occasionally. He was the one who was so preoccupied with his religious relics, an old fake I discovered when I came to know him, for all this religiosity was simply a camouflage. Basically he was no more a Hindu than I was; this was precisely the thing that seemed to torment him, for he had been raised in a strict and orthodox family, yet he could no longer accept the tenets of the old faith. He alternated, therefore, between the most wild debaucheries and equally unreasonable periods of remorse, both of which had achieved a meaning in themselves beyond any valid relationship to his impulses. He was something of an exhibitionist and he once confessed to me in a fit of contrition that he would often heap intentional desecrations on his idols in order to try to free himself from their spell. The details were sordid, tinged with a morbid sexuality, but he would describe them all, reveling in their horror. "Oh, I am wicked. I am terribly wicked," he would moan, panting with a strange vicarious thrill.

The rest of the performers were rather normal souls, within the realm of common perversion at least, dull-eyed men who spent most of their time in gossiping with each other and inventing strange tales. For them the demarcation between fact and fantasy had seemingly ceased to exist long since, for they would slide back and forth with an easy abandon between the half truths of their gossip and the whole cloth of their fictions. Some of the latter were incredibly wild, an outlet for the starved imaginations of the tellers whose lives were actually so dull and uniform that they needed some sort of artificial stimulation. Had I heard that Pakistan was invading India with the help of the British and American armies? Or that Himat, the fellow who was driving the next wagon, had murdered a woman in the village last night? All sorts of precious secrets were brought to me, warnings of plots, advice of counterplots, like the shiny bits of glass that are gathered by some birds and brooded over with an animal ferocity. After a while I learned to fall in with these stories, interpolating and passing them on. It was simply a game that everyone played; when our stories were disproved, we shrugged and forgot them.

That was the one diversion. The only other was the occasional rehearsal of some new routine. About once a week a group of performers would be anxious to try out an act on the rest of us. It was on these occasions that they appeared at their best, for usually they very soon would depart from their plans to embark on a parody of the villagers themselves or on some skit far too subtle for the poor, dulled admes. There was one evening when a dancer did a parody of Swamiji, too complicated for me to follow, but withal effective, for the other performers laughed uproariously, while Swamiji stalked off and sulked for days. Most often, it was Swamiji who did the improvising, mercilessly ridiculing the weak members of the troupe, recalling to each of them his bungled lines, the cues he had missed, or the pins he had dropped. One evening he entertained us for two full hours, by showing us the standard reactions to his act, the bania's hurt dignity, the Brahmin's indignation, and the uncomprehending but enthusiastic response of the Sudra. It was funny, but there was a serious meaning in it too, and it was that which had struck me most powerfully at the time, for in the very perfection of the mimicry there was a comment on the solidity which caste had achieved in this region.

Then there was the take-off which Swamiji once did of me. I had been particularly circumspect, or so I thought, but I was astounded to find how little I had been able to conceal my interests from my observant host. My most casual probings had not escaped him, for all of them were included, embarrassingly magnified, from the oh-so-subtle conversations I had directed to the surreptitious jottings I had made on scraps of paper. By the end of the evening I had been stripped to the skin, all my precious subtleties thrown back in my face, and for days the parody was repeated by the others every time I appeared among them.

Yet, with all this I found that the days passed slowly. Most of the time we were too busy to entertain each other, for during the nights we would be performing or breaking camp, and during the day we would be traveling, each in his own cart. It had been exciting at first, but after a while it fell into a regular and depressing routine of its own, the boredom of movement, the tensions of inbreeding, the regimented hysteria of our nightly performances. I began to think of leaving the caravan. It was convenient of course to continue with them, but I had begun to wonder whether I was not too effectively insulated from all genuine contact with the villagers. It was true that we stopped in a new village each night, but it was also true that we pushed on every morning. The hours between our coming and our going were all too few for any real explorations.

Swamiji must have noticed that I was growing restless. At any rate, the next time he was to ride on ahead, he informed me that if I chose I could borrow a pony from the village where we were stopping and accompany him. The idea appealed to me. In the first place, I did not relish the prospect of staying alone in the wagon, for experience had taught me that things were a little too unsettled, when Swamiji was not present, to keep order in the caravan. More than once in his absences the performers had got drunk and had made themselves so unwelcome in the village where they were staying that the inhabitants descended on the caravan en masse and drove them out on threat of force.

But more important, I was still curious about the uneasiness that Swamiji had claimed to sense in the surrounding regions. He had been reluctant to talk about it beyond our first discussion, but I knew that the thing was still preying on his mind. I wanted to get closer to the villages myself, to see if there was anything which would be noticeable to me, and though he warned me that we would still be pushing on rapidly, I felt that our visits would be less frenzied in any case.

In the end I decided that I would go out with Swamiji, taking all of my kit with me, so that I need not return. Then if we went far enough south and the prospect appealed to me I would be free to cut off and continue on my own. Swamiji agreed that this was a good idea and he offered to be responsible for my horse if I so chose. I said good-by to the others with only a little reluctance and set out on the day that Swamiji appointed.

[28]

FROM Khed, where we left the caravan, we went almost due south along the edge of the Deccan Plateau, following the road that leads down along the ghats from Mahad to Sangameshwar and Derukh. We had picked a bad time to make the trip, for the weather was atrocious, even for South India, and though a few clouds blew in from the west the first day, they seemed only to blanket the damp, hot air. Our horses suffered even more than we did, for they were surrounded by tiny, persistent gnats that clung to their eyelids and swarmed up their nostrils till the poor brutes pawed the dust in their irrational fury. The worst part of it was, we had to press on, riding steadily through the first day and part of the second, till we had left behind us the territory where Swamiji had already arranged the itinerary of the caravan, and got beyond, into virgin land where the route and the compacts had yet to be settled.

The first night out we made camp along the road. Even when darkness was complete, the heat was stifling. Not a breeze was stirring and, in desperation, both Swamiji and I tried dampening our bedding. It was a trick I had learned just a few weeks earlier, advisable only in the most hideous heat when the prospect of lying in a sopping sheet seemed preferable to thrashing in sweaty nightmares. But when we woke up the next morning we were as tired as when we lay down. It was cooler in the morning but a breeze had arisen and caked our bedding with dry yellow dust that crinkled and scratched whenever we turned. We arose and shook the sleep from our eyes, but we were sullen and tired through the morning's riding, and it was long after noon before either of us was wide awake. The dreams and the reality seemed to run together.

To make my misery even more complete, I began to break

out in scabrous sores. I learned later that they had resulted from a deficiency of diet, but at the time I knew only that they burned and stung. In one of the villages I plastered them with cow dung, a poultice which the villager recommended for everything, but it only made my misery more acute, adding a psychic insult to the physical injury. Moreover, I began to notice alarming symptoms, which were later to materialize into amoebic dysentery and about noon of the third day, to my other discomforts, was added an awful burning in my stomach. There were times when I was literally doubled over in my saddle, clinging to the horn to keep my seat, and I felt sure that my trip was to end prematurely in a frantic dash to the cities and to a doctor. But once again I tried a local remedy, this time overripe bananas ground into a paste. Unlike the cow dung, this was quite effective, and in just a matter of hours the symptoms subsided.

On the evening of the third day, we had got as far as Chiplun. It was an incredibly filthy and unpleasant place. After the Gujarat, Chiplun was a decided step backward, almost to the appalling decay of Kathiawar. In a sense it was worse. Kathiawar had been decadent, but that decadence had been kept within natural boundaries. Here, where the people were more imaginative and enlightened, even the very corruption was more ingenious and progressive. Where in the north the villages had been piles of stone, a comfortable anthropological primitivism, here the houses were beamed with old wooden planks and roofed occasionally with rusting oil tins that, however they rotted and fell in disorder, could never blend with the natural rubble. It occurred to me that these were always the first fruits of progress, a higher order of debasement, a mechanized inhumanity. Perhaps, I thought, it spoke well for the future, but in the present it was indescribably ugly and out of place.

We put up in a house of a friend of Swamiji, a compatriot in fact who had migrated from the north and had begun a profitable cattle-trading business which had yielded him enormous riches, by village standards. He was a wealthy man, and he boasted to Swamiji that he had a hundred thousand rupees hidden around the house. It was quite possible, I knew, for cattle trading was lucrative because of the restrictions which most Hindus had to obey.

Still he lived like any villager. His house was rather better, a two-storied wood building in the center of the bazaar with stalls for the cattle and storage place for the grains on the first floor, and on the second five empty living rooms. But it was in virtual ruin and the old fellow confessed that during the monsoons he had to move down with the cattle. The roof leaked badly and with all of his money, he had never quite got around to repairing it.

During the half day we were with him, our host scarcely looked up from the crossword puzzles which he worked at constantly. He did dozens each week and entered his results in a contest sponsored by a Bombay newspaper. But the puzzles were in English and since he knew almost none, his results to date had not been encouraging. He had once got a pen as a consolation prize, but it was broken now, he informed us sadly.

From Chiplun we moved on to Sangameshwar. We left early in the morning while it was relatively cool; for though the worst of the heat was over by now, around noon it was still close to a hundred in the shade. Our horses had been traveling for four days without rest, but we hoped to stop over in Sangameshwar so we pushed them hard through most of the forenoon, putting almost the whole of the distance behind us.

En route we passed through a Brahmin village, the first one I had seen inhabited by just one caste. It was unutterably filthy, for there was no one to see to the thousand petty tasks proscribed to the Brahmins. Its people lived aloof in the most awful squalor rather than lowering themselves to cleaning their own dooryards; and while there were good lands around the village, only about half of them were farmed, and these in an inexpert, desultory fashion. The women were well dressed, and adorned with jewelry, but it was a pretense for their children were spindly and malnourished. It was a dying village, that much was obvious, dying slowly and horribly from the disease of pride.

Then there was the village where we stopped to eat our lunch. It was the most demoralized place that I had ever seen, so demoralized that it went by the government survey number rather than giving itself a chosen name; it was simply Taluka Village Number Nine. We were not welcome, it was clear, for all the while we were there the villagers kept questioning us about our purpose in coming, and assuring us with uneasy repetitiousness that there was no place near where we could spend the night. They most probably were convinced we were spies for the police come to investigate some forgotten crime; it was only when we left that they showed any friendliness. Then they lined the roadway and waved good-by.

But then even Sangameshwar was not much better. Its surroundings were pleasant, but the village was not, for there was about it the same air of dilapidation which had so depressed me in Chiplun. It was really more a town than a village, but the difference was entirely a matter of size, longer rows of houses, greater numbers of people, proportionately greater filth and squalor. I could not help thinking, as we rode into the place, how much it resembled some enormous junk yard, strewn with cast-off and broken things, recognizable but entirely useless, apparently. The whole village had a deceptive temporary appearance, as if its inhabitants were making-do through some short-term emergency, perhaps an earthquake or a recent fire, which had deprived them of a more suitable standard of living.

Even the people themselves seemed vaguely surprised by the awful conditions under which they lived; there was never the pathetic, oxlike resignation which I had come to expect during my travels in the north. They avoided the rubble in the streets rather than making repairs, but they always seemed aware of and disgusted by the ruins. They were like the careful housekeeper who has inherited a dirty kitchen but has not yet had time to clean it to her liking.

As we were entering, Swamiji reined his horse in suddenly, so suddenly that it caused me a momentary fright. "Can't you see it? Can't you feel it?" he said with excitement. He looked at me helplessly, knowing I could not.

He explained. "I have only to come into a village to know what the people are feeling, thinking. Here," he said, looking around as he spoke, "I can tell that this place is unsettled, somehow."

"You understand?" I didn't, yet, and Swamiji shook his head, incredulous. Then he rode off, rather piqued at my stupidity, and we set about arranging for our lodgings in Sangameshwar.

[29]

ONCE again we stayed with a friend of Swamiji. This time it was an erstwhile itinerate mendicant, a charming old faker who sold Ayurvedic medicines, such exotic preparations as tiger bone and cow's urine. He had known Swamiji for a great many years, since they had traveled together with a village medicine show, and it was by the merest chance that we met in the town square where we were busy making arrangements for the quartering of our horses. But the two friends spied each other and fell into an embrace, calling each other fond, vile names. And after that, of course, there was nothing we could do but stay with the old fellow for as long as we were in Sangameshwar.

The house where he lived was a fantastic place. It was like a museum, littered with all manner of rare herbs gathered by our host at great trouble and expense and all possessing the most magical qualities. Here, for instance, was the shin bone of a monkey, just a rub of which would cure syphilis unfailingly. And there, the testicles of a panther which, when pulverized, would restore an old man to his youthful vigor. But apparently our host took his calling none too seriously, for Swamiji twitted him unmercifully about it. "Ah, yes," he agreed. "It is an undignified living, but for a man of my years, there is nothing else!"

The first night in Sangameshwar was spent in reminiscence, the two friends recalling their years together. I tried to sleep, since they spoke in Gujarati, but they would awaken me periodically and translate some anecdote. As a result, we were all quite tired the next day, so Swamiji and the old mendicant slept most of the morning. I set out nevertheless to explore the town, hoping at least to learn its general layout.

My reactions to Sangameshwar were varied at first glance. It was a strange combination of the old and the new; there were several large government offices, for example, with freshly painted signs advising of their functions. But as usual, the modernity ended at this, for these offices were peopled with harried babus who were far too preoccupied with the complexities of their reports to concern themselves with anything else. A few of them were gracious enough to talk with me, but the talks were uniformly and consistently unprofitable, for they were unable to discuss the jobs of their departments except in terms of their personal problems. Once again it was "these people" who were responsible for everything; they kept the words in front of them like a shield. It was obvious that they felt sure they held the country together with their paper clips and staples.

I visited the local bank as well. Here the conflict of customs was even more apparent, the exigencies of modern bookkeeping faring badly in the immutable traditions of the village. It was a "half holiday" I discovered, a religious festival which necessitated the blessing of everything imaginable, and when I entered, bank clerks were busily daubing the premises with a varicolored paste. The rite was explained to me by one of the officers; he was a Christian and "above this sort of thing," as he put it. He grumbled that he would have to spend the next two weeks removing the paste from his ledgers and files. And indeed he would, for the place was a shambles. An old holy man had been secured to add tone to the proceedings and, not appreciating the intricacies of double-entry bookkeeping, he had scattered colored water through most of the accounts. The officer was quite unreconciled to the business, and I could not help laughing at his ineffectual anger. "Really, this is quite impossible," he told me, turning away so that he would see no more of the debacle.

There was also a government refugee camp in Sangameshwar. I visited it on the second day of our stay. It had been established, according to the official in charge, to house refugees from the Bijapur famine district. But now, he told me, it was quite deserted, all the refugees having gone back to Bijapur again as they did every year, in the hope that it would be better and that they would be able to raise a decent crop. They would be back in a month or two, he told me, for these hoped-for crops invariably failed. For years this pathetic cycle had persisted, but the Bijapuris would never give up hope for their own lands. To me the situation seemed infinitely tragic, but to the officer it served only to illustrate a point. "The government has given them the camp—" he complained—"but they refuse to stay and farm this land.

"You see," he began, but I interrupted him. I knew the argument all too well—the stupidity of the villagers, the progressiveness of the government, the truth and error so tragically interwoven. I excused myself and struck out on my own again to see what else I could learn about Sangameshwar. Anything seemed better than staying here and hearing the old refrain again.

Yet, the more I saw of Sangameshwar, the less I liked it. I had never been very favorably impressed by the place, but at the beginning I had noticed only the obvious disorganization, the physical squalor in which the people were living. After two days of exploration, however, I found far more cogent reasons for my uneasiness, and I began to understand just how wrong I had been to compare it to villages I had seen before.

To begin with, Sangameshwar was a "strong Brahmin town." I had heard of them before, but this was the first I had seen where the rule of the higher castes was anything more than a default on the part of the cultivators, at bottom. In Kathiawar, in the Gujarat, there were as serious abuses, but the tragedy there was that the people had accepted them. Not so in Sangameshwar. There was no question of acceptance when the Mahasabha and the Rastraya Swayamsevak Sangh were in force.

I had gone out to the gymkhana on the day after my arrival. The Sangh was there going through its maneuvers, making passionate declarations of Hindu solidarity and fanatically offering up its clenched-fist salute. From the military point of view its maneuvers were childish, for it was armed with nothing but pointed sticks, but the spirit of the occasion was terrifying to anyone equipped to draw parallels with recent European history.

The drill field itself was about a quarter of a mile square. At one end was a wooden tower about fifteen feet high, draped not only in the tricolored Indian flag, but in various emblems of Hindu fanaticism. The inscriptions were in Maharatha and I was unable to read them, but I learned later that they were the usual props to self-hypnosis, with such meaningless but apparently inspiring slogans as "In Strength There Is Victory" and "Hinduism Is Life!" But the most awful thing was the earnestness of the participants; mostly they were children from ten to fifteen, but when I arrived they were being taught to make lathi charges against sandbags that had been denominated enemies of the order. They rushed at these enemies with teeth clenched and eyes sparkling while the others encouraged them with party slogans, striking and ripping and gouging with a vengeance till The Threat was averted and The State was safe. Finally they closed in formation again and listened to a few inspiring words from their leader. Then they sang an anthem, or more accurately, a recessional, and giving the salute, disbanded till the next afternoon.

I must admit that the ceremony was highly impressive. Indeed, in this impressiveness lay much of its point, for it largely seemed to be the theory of the Sangh that a show of strength was all that was needed for its purpose. The fact is, they are a small minority in numbers, and they could scarcely afford to provoke real violence, but they are right in assuming that their very organization would serve to intimidate the diffused majorities. While I was watching their demonstration I noticed the people around me. They were open mouthed, appalled at the ferocity of the display, a fact which the squad leaders of the Sangh seemed aware of, for several times they set out to reinforce the lesson. They would march their troops obliquely across the field till they were passing quite close to a knot of villagers. Then suddenly with a right wheel they would bear directly down on them, forcing them to scatter in embarrassment and surprise. I was half tempted to stand my ground on one such occasion, just to see how the young soldiers reacted to the surprise. That I did not, I realized later, was simply because at bottom I was honestly afraid to do so.

Yet it was not true that the lower castes were wholly intimidated. It was because they were not that these demonstrations continued, for it was the very existence of a powerful resistance which drove the Sangh to such energetic extremes. But the opposition was more subtle in its devices. For example, there were four or five local curd sellers who went about the village crying their wares and improvising little songs in the manner of minstrels. They were a village tradition, and I had heard them often, but usually these songs were simply humorous or obscene. Here in Sangameshwar, in Maharashtra generally, they almost always had a strong political flavor.

For example, Swamiji translated this one for me:

> *I have a cow; she gives me milk.*
> *In return I give her hay and shelter.*
> *I have a Brahmin; I give him my earnings.*
> *But what does he give me?*

And another, equally direct and bitter, which a betel-nut vendor sang occasionally:

> *The Brahmins, they say, are the chosen of God.*
> *Chosen to own and to rule the land.*
> *And I, lucky fellow, am the chosen of the Brahmin.*
> *Chosen to support him in luxury and idleness.*

Nor were all the songs and slogans half humorous. "We have a saying," my host informed me one day, "if you see a snake and a Brahmin, kill them both. If you can only kill one, kill the Brahmin."

A few months before I would have dismissed such a saying as in keeping with the whole tradition of caste, a part of the habitual complaining which is allowed, even encouraged, as an outlet for all the latent discontents. Yet somehow I knew it was different now. To begin with, these slogans and songs were spontaneous; they showed that the people were genuinely bitter, that they were not simply repeating the words of their fathers. And of course, there was the reaction of the Brahmins themselves. Their feeling of insecurity was the greatest proof that a discontent was rising in the people which had to be countered with banners and with the threat of clubs.

"Then you see it now?" Swamiji asked me when I was discussing my reactions to all this with him.

"I am beginning to see it," I answered cautiously. And indeed, beginning was just the word.

[30]

SINCE my arrival in Sangameshwar, I had grown increasingly preoccupied with the activities of the R.S.S. I had spent many hours on the edge of their parade ground, watching their cadets march up and down, and several evenings Swamiji and I had devoted to discussions of the principles and aims which they professed. It is hard to explain; what interested me particularly was not anything strange or unreasonable about the group, but on the contrary, its very familiarity and, in another sense, its inevitability. For it was an organization that had to exist, and like the astronomer who discovers a new star without seeing it just by observing its effects on the known constellations, so I realized I had long anticipated the R.S.S. It was like an electrical connection. Things suddenly made sense which before had seemed so entirely impossible, and I realized belatedly how obvious it was that the life-and-death conflicts which exist in the village should eventually be translated through such a group as this into the power politics of Delhi. I had known the Sangh before, I realized, in every bania and Brahmin-ridden village. Wherever there was a remnant of the decadent old order, there was the Sangh, though as yet unnamed.

I decided that somehow I must meet the Sangh leaders. It would not be easy, for the R.S.S. is as suspicious of outsiders as it has a right to be, and I knew I would gain nothing by approaching directly. Nevertheless, I developed a careful strategy, avoiding any overt interest in the Sangh, relying on the strangeness of my own position to interest the R.S.S. in me. The strategy worked. On my fourth day in town a delegation from the Sangh paid me a call, ostensibly to bid me a welcome to Sangameshwar, but actually of course, to learn just who I was. I was perfectly candid. I had come, I said, as a part of a general tour of the villages, and I was anxious to stay in Sangameshwar for a few days just to learn something of the life and manners of its people. As I expected, the Sanghamites tried to dissuade me; Sangameshwar was just another little town, they told me. I would see nothing here to interest me. I might far better go south to Derukh or Sangli. But I was adamant, and when they discovered that I would not take their advice, they decided to do the next best thing; all at once they grew enormously interested in my project and volunteered to plan my program for me.

That was just what I wanted. I knew that I would learn little or nothing about Sangameshwar in the company of the Sangh, but I hoped that through the medium of this conducted tour I would be able to learn something about the Sangh itself. So it was arranged that my studies would begin the next day with a visit to one of the local temples. An old Brahmin clerk was assigned as my guide and the delegation departed only moderately uneasy.

It was significant that my tour should begin with the temples. Anything else would have been very unlike the Sangh, for it is the habit of the group to conceive of the future in terms of what they call "the glorious Hindu past," and it was only natural that my indoctrination should begin with some founding in that glorious past. Of the four days that were to be allotted to my touring of Sangameshwar, fully the first two and a half were spent at the temples, hearing endless stories of the exploits of the gods, all calculated to imbue me with the proper respect.

Unfortunately, however, my reactions were all wrong. I had approached the temple with a certain respect, but the longer I spent in conversation with the priests, the harder it became to retain that respect. It may have been a prejudice occasioned by what they said, but the priests themselves seemed hopeless degenerates, lacking completely in all those virtues and disciplines about which they talked so long and loudly. They spoke of the ablutions prescribed by their religion, taking time off between their words to blow their noses between their fingers, and they documented their arguments about Hindu culture by inaccurate quotations from the Vedas and Upanishads. They were men of great learning, my guide assured me, yet he trusted them with no deference at all himself. It was obvious that in effect they were expensive antiques, kept up by the Sangh for their symbolic importance.

As translated, their orations led up to one thing; the foundation of India's greatness was caste. "Caste is Hinduism and Hinduism is Caste!" The proposition was as simple as that, I was told.

I objected weakly. Wasn't it true, I asked, that caste was a later innovation in Hinduism? I knew perfectly well that it was.

"Oh, no," the priests answered. "Caste a new thing? Oh, no." They smiled together at my naïveté.

They set out to elaborate, but my guide raised his hand. He had decided to explain it himself. "You see," he told me, "we Hindus believe—" the phrasing was a concession to my own unenlightenment—"we Hindus believe that the soul goes on, that it does not live or die with one man or animal. This soul is rewarded or punished in the next life for the way it behaves in this. So you see—" he groped for some modest statement—"we Brahmins have earned our privileged position. In ages past, in other bodies, our souls have been proven worthy of this.

"You pity the lower castes, perhaps. It is only because you do not understand. The Sudras, the untouchables are being punished in this life for sins they committed in previous incarnations. Who knows? The cultivator who starves in Bijapur may have been a dacoit his last time on earth. At any rate, we know that Brahma is just and that he would not make one suffer if he did not deserve it." He folded his hands comfortably across his chest, inclined his head, and beamed his satisfaction.

It was an argument to which there seemed to be no answer, no answer at any rate short of a denial of all Hinduism, for religion and politics had been tied together so neatly that no one could tear them apart. It occurred to me to wonder how orthodox was this connection, but I decided that such a question was neither here nor there, for Hinduism is as Hinduism does regardless of how the ancients might react to the present. It is certainly no comfort to the cultivator, I realized, when he is suffering under the tyranny of caste as it is practiced, to know that the abuses are utterly without sanction, to be able to say, "You can't do this to me." The fact seemed to be that it was being done, that religion had become a political weapon, with the entire force of tradition and orthodoxy being called in to witness for the established powers.

My guide continued, "From our point of view, every living thing has a soul of its own, so that the body in which it finds itself at the moment may be an animal's or an insect's as well as a man's. And therefore the relation of a Brahmin to a Sudra is precisely the same as a Sudra to a dog. It is all a matter of dharma, duty, and of the merit which has been earned in previous lives.

"Indeed—" he laughed, to set himself apart from them— "there are some who say that we must show no mercy to the lower castes, that it is a part of God's plan that they should suffer in this life and that we are thwarting His will if we better their condition. But I do not subscribe to this. The Sangh maintains that each caste is responsible for those below it, that it is the sacred duty of the Brahmin, for example, to see to the welfare of everyone else."

He assumed a careful air of weariness. "It is a great responsibility, you may be sure. Yes, the burden that has been laid upon us is enormous. No one ought to envy the Brahmin, dear sir!"

"But you spoke of privileges too," I reminded him.

"Oh, to be sure," he agreed, "there are compensations. But then, when it is God Himself who has rewarded us, who can begrudge us our few indulgences? It is only right that in return for our labors we should be given a certain respect and deference. You are an outsider or these things would be obvious to you. Our own people are perfectly willing."

"But then what is the purpose of the Sangh," I asked. "Isn't it to strengthen the power of the Brahmin caste?"

My guide assured me that such was not the case. "Why," he said, "no one questions the supremacy of the Brahmin.

"No, you must not be misled by radicals," he assured me. "All Hindus everywhere are in accord with us." Then, deciding that he was perhaps a little too vulnerable, he added, "All but a few malcontents, anyway.

"In India, as you realize, we have a one-party system. It is not like the West, with its endless squabbling. You will pardon me, dear sir, but we are above this sort of thing. Our people are perhaps wiser and more humble than yours."

He considered for a moment, then he continued, "There are perhaps some minor disagreements over ways and means. But Hinduism is united in its realization that we must recapture our great past, for the good of the whole world."

I objected. "But even the Congress party," I pointed out, "isn't above a certain factionalism. There is the Forward Bloc, on the left, for example, and the Mahasabha and the R.S.S. on the right."

"Oh, but factions is too strong a word," my guide laughed. "The Forward Bloc, I grant is a dangerous clique, but it is no more than a clique. And as for the Mahasabha and the Sangh . . . why, we are just a sort of inner circle of the party.

"You must consider it this way; our own group is composed of the more advanced and patriotic members of Congress. There are some men who are temporarily—confused, we might say, but never fear, our own band will bring them to their senses. Narain, for example. He is not a bad man, but he is dangerous, because he tries to mislead the masses. He is entirely concerned with the physical, the material! The tragedy is, he forgets the soul."

"The soul?" I began to feel that the conversation was once again slipping beyond my grasp. It was like a stream that runs along the surface for a while only to dive into some subterranean cavern again.

"Of course," my guide said with growing warmth. "What does it matter how the body lives on this earth? It is a place of bitter unhappiness for all of us, in which our souls are seeking release into limbo.

"I have to laugh. You Westerners rush about, all excited about the circumstances in which you live, struggling for this, demanding that as if in the end these things were important. Ah, I tell you, you will all find out eventually that your struggles and your demands avail you nothing. The meaning of this life lies not in idle wishes but in the acceptance of what it has pleased the gods to give you. It is the duty of the rich to accept their position with no feelings of arrogance or pride. And it is the duty of the poor to accept their poverty as the design of the universe, and to ask no more."

He sighed. "What does it matter, this life we live here? We are born in pain and we die in pain. Duty. Virtue. Humility. Passivity. These are the things that go down through time. You must not judge our people by the standards of your own. We do not want wealth, or happiness in your sense. If our people are unsettled, it is only because they have departed from the age-old traditions of Hinduism.

"See the stars," cried my guide. I looked up, but it was noon and the stars were invisible. But his eyes were closed. "They have always been there and they always will be whatever we do. We cannot change that."

I was about to suggest that I didn't want to change it, but he was by now in the midst of a religious ecstasy, the palms of his hands pressing together between his knees and his body swaying in an alarming manner.

188

Finally he recovered himself enough to conclude. "What are the great traditions of this country? They are not mob rule, democracy, if you wish. Equality of the good and the bad is not among them. They are traditions of holiness, acquiescence in duty, concern with the spirit rather than with the flesh. Yes, these are the traditions of Old India, my friend. And it is time, past time that we returned to them."

As I thought of it later, I was a little confused. I realized that any pretense of tolerance was useless, for I hated the principles which my guide had argued as the rationalizations of an ugly theocracy. Was one bound, I wondered, to accept every injustice that was able to claim the sanctions of tradition? Was the tolerant man condemned to the acceptance of any unspeakable viciousness that called God as its witness?

It was a critical question, for I had promised myself earlier that I would not commit that cardinal error of judging one society by the standards of another. And yet now it seemed that I must either do that or lose myself in a mystical morass where the most awful oppressions and debasements of the individual were somehow transformed into new, bizarre virtues. In the end, of course, my emotions tipped the scale. It was foolish to pretend that I could suspend my judgment. I had judged already, and I had judged against that brand of Hinduism which is preached by the Sangh, which has as its goal the return to a period of complete and total religious feudalism. If it were narrow-mindedness to judge a system on the realization which it allows the individual, then I was wholly committed to this narrowness by instinct, and it was just as well to admit it now.

And admit it I did, as early as the next day. We had finally left the temples and gone on to Sangh headquarters. But it was no more than a change of scenery, of course, and once again my "touring" was to bog down in talk. This time my host was one of the local leaders, a retired government servant holding the title of Rao Bahadur, one of the many dispensed by the British raj in wholesale lots to its loyal clerks and bookkeepers. The whole atmosphere at Sangh headquarters was strangely unreal; the Rao Bahadur and the others talked frantically about all sorts of wholly imaginary problems till it was apparent that they were trying to draw attention from the real ones. Poverty? Disease? Famine? These they chose to brush aside as crassly material, preferring to hold forth on such fascinating intangibles as "the corruption of the masses" and the "decline of piety." I stood it stoically for several hours, but I realized that my caution was serving no purpose. It was obvious that the Sangh was fencing with me now, keeping me at a distance and tiring me out.

"All right," I said finally, throwing caution aside. "If the aims of the Sangh are spiritual as you say, then what is the purpose behind all of this drilling that goes on every evening at the Gymkhana field?"

There was a general consternation and a few vague protests, but the Rao Bahadur was master of the situation. "I repeat," he warned, "our program is of the spirit. If we discipline our bodies, it is only to transcend them."

I felt I was clawing my way through cotton wool, but I was determined at least to embarrass my hosts. "I don't understand that," I insisted doggedly. "What do you mean, you discipline your bodies to transcend them?"

The Rao Bahadur sighed in a superior way. "I suppose it is hard for a Westerner to understand, but this subjugation of the body is a tradition of Hinduism; to be precise, it is a teaching of Karma Yoga. You see, we believe that to attain to the spirit, we must first gain absolute control of the body, so we put our youths through this program of training in order to encourage their physical self-mastery. It is a subtle distinction—" he smiled to suggest that it was perhaps even too subtle for me to understand— "but we emphasize the physical because we consider it unimportant, because we are anxious to have done with it, to put it behind us."

It was a good answer, but by now I had nothing to lose. I could sense that I had already revealed my hostility. "And is that why," I asked with a certain bitterness, "they spend their time in military maneuvers?" Once again there was a menacing undertone of Maharashtrian, but I pressed the advantage I felt I had gained. "Is it a concern for the spirit that makes your cadets learn the techniques of lathi charges and hand-to-hand fighting?"

And I *had* gained the advantage. The undertone had stopped, and everyone waited for the Rao Bahadur to speak. He smiled, and made a few ineffective gestures. "No," he said finally. "That is something else." He shifted his bulk uncomfortably in the chair, looked at me for a moment in undisguised appraisal. The realization seemed to flash between us that now we both understood the other's position.

"This is a difficult period for our country," he said finally. His whole manner and approach seemed suddenly to have changed. "This is a difficult period for India. You agree?" I nodded my head, but I kept my silence.

"I felt you would not be interested in these things. They are side issues. I have been talking about the fundamentals, but like most Westerners you seize on what seems most dramatic. All right," he laughed. "You shall have it. You shall have it.

"We are training our young men because we have no choice." He paused. "You know what has happened in the Punjab? Hundreds of thousands of Hindus have been killed, slaughtered in their homes by the Moslems. I repeat, it is a side issue. It has nothing to do with the ultimate aims of the R.S.S., but before we can begin our rebuilding of Hinduism, we must make it safe from the threat of Islam.

"Unfortunately, there is but one way to deal with the Musselmen, and that way is through simple, unrelenting force. The whole history of our country is one long proof that it is impossible to live beside them in peace. Even now they are scheming to overthrow our government. They are all the same; there is no use making distinctions. We can't

191

argue with them. We can't bargain or extract promises. We have got to mobilize and throw them out."

It was a reply I had expected. But I was not convinced. Was the Rao Bahadur so naïve, I wondered, as to seriously consider that the Moslem minority constituted a serious threat to the state?

He must have sensed that I was still suspicious, for he decided to make still another concession. "And of course—" he continued—"it is not only the Moslems. We cannot be too careful at a time like this."

"Then who else?" I asked, continuing on the offensive.

The Rao Bahadur scowled and looked around him suspiciously. He made a gesture that spoke eloquently of the need for caution. "We have many enemies," he said enigmatically.

He leaned forward. "You would be surprised to know," he whispered, "how powerful the Communists are in these sections." I was not at all surprised, considering the alternatives, but I assumed an expression of understanding and sympathy. "Malcontents!" spat the Rao Bahadur. "They have no program but a program of destruction and waste. Everything that in the past has made India great they would trade for this ridiculous 'equality' of theirs, an equality which levels the good and the bad, the honorable and dishonorable, the virtuous and the wicked!"

"But surely you aren't worried about them," I said. "After all, you say that Hinduism is united against these threats from the outside world."

The Rao Bahadur replied, "That is true, we are united—basically. But there is a limit to how far we can trust the mass, isn't there?"

"Is there?" I asked.

"Of course," he insisted. "The majority is always vaguely dissatisfied. In their ignorance they are quite capable of doing infinite harm. It is always necessary to protect them from themselves!"

I concluded, "And this is the job of the Sangh?"

"It is the job of the Brahmins," the Rao Bahadur corrected me. "The Sangh is just trying, in its modest way, to reawaken the caste to its responsibilities. Don't misunderstand me. I don't blame the cultivator who listens to the idle talk of the troublemakers. It is our own fault, the fault of the traditional leaders who have been too weak to enforce what is for the good of the order. If we tolerate the irresponsible elements about, they are bound to corrupt a certain number. The blame must be shouldered by the authorities themselves who have allowed them to spread their dangerous theories.

"I repeat, our program is a program of self-discipline, a rallying of the traditions of the upper castes. It is the aim of the Sangh to lead the people of India back to the values of their glorious past."

And it was on this note that the day's discussion ended. As for myself, I was far from satisfied with it, for though one level of pretense had been stripped away, I wondered whether we had yet got down to the truth. It was not a question of whether I believed in the program of the Sangh as outlined by the Rao Bahadur. It was a question of whether even he believed in it, whether it was indeed a rationalization of his position or more simply, just a blind to mislead me.

Since the first day I had met them, I had been increasingly suspicious of the studied stupidity of the members of the Sangh. Perhaps it was because they had overplayed the part of indolent, ineffective, fumbling old men. There was such a striking contrast between their avowed confusion and the precision of their internal organization, such a significant difference between their vagueness in discussion and their sense of direction in practical matters. Were my guides really trying to indoctrinate me, I wondered, or were they trying only to impress me as harmless old fools? Were they arguing a position which they felt to be valid, or were they simply diverting my attention with platitudes? I felt rather like a bull in the bullring, charging after one brightly colored generalization after the other, tearing and thrusting and tiring myself out without ever catching a glimpse of my real target.

I remembered Swamiji's original suspicion that the people of Sangameshwar were uneasy about something; I could understand now; they had a right to be uneasy when the lions had so suddenly lain down with the lambs. If only my guide and the Rao Bahadur had bragged of the strength and power of the Sangh; that would have been quite in keeping with their position and could have been readily discounted as pompous wishful thinking. But they had not. They had talked rather of their own share of guilt and of their interest in the welfare of the lower castes. It was as if their power were a foregone conclusion and they were seeking only justification now!

Duty and Virtue and Humility indeed! They were strange words to come from the practical men who had directed the training of the cadets at the drill field, who had written the hypnotic slogans that they chanted. The evidence and the explanations just didn't seem to jibe. If I had met the Sangh under different circumstances, I would have been willing to accept it at face value, to say that it was a collection of tired reactionaries who were yearning for a return to "the good old days." But now I had the uncomfortable feeling that perhaps the stupidities of the Sangh were quite intentional, that while I was laughing at their arguments, the Rao Bahadur and my guides were laughing even harder at me. Swamiji's suspicions came back to me again. Yes, I too could sense a certain uneasiness.

I went home and retired, still wondering what it was.

And I awoke with the answer ringing in my ears!

[31]

"GANDHI is dead!"

The words came as a wail, distant and far off, to intrude on my sleep, breaking the deep, early-morning silence only recently come to the streets of Sangameshwar.

"Gandhi is dead!"

I pushed my face into my pillow and caught at the vanishing sense of oblivion, drawing my coverlet tighter around me to ward off the chill of the morning air.

"Gandhi is dead!" It was repeated at intervals, a long arching cry of indescribable sadness, as lonely and as inhuman as the voice of a coyote baying out his animal grief to the moon.

"Gandhi is dead." I was coming awake slowly, fumbling on the floor for my snake boots now, fumbling as well with a disorganized consciousness that seemed as alien and disordered as this strange room I was in. I edged cautiously past the two or three chairs in the room and stumbled to the small square of window opposite. It commanded a view of the town square of Sangameshwar and I stared out, trying to blink the sleep from my eyes.

In the middle of the broad space there was just one lone figure, kneeling in the dirt and sobbing to himself. It was an old man and I could see that between his long cries he was convulsed with the most awful physical grief. It was like a pain in his stomach, for it doubled him up and rocked him back and forth, clutching at his viscera, his face twisted into that grotesque broad grin that comes with the most violent and unrestrained sobbing. I looked around at the other windows, but there was no one. I listened, but I could hear no other sound. Even the sobbing and the crying seemed formal and unreal, the versicle and response in some litany of misery. I went back to the bed where Swamiji was lying and tried to wake him, but he only grunted; like all villagers he was accustomed to sleeping amidst noises, and would not be disturbed by one random sound now.

"Swamiji!" I whispered, gripping him by the shoulder. "There's something wrong . . . someone in the square . . ." But he groaned again and pulled the blanket over his head. He muttered from its depths, "It is nothing . . . nothing."

I went back to the window. The old man was still there, sobbing to himself and crying out at intervals. And still there was no other sound in the village, no movement but the swirling of dust in the street. I was bewildered, and chilled through. I went back to my bed and lay down again to wait for the dawn. And slowly, as if I had never been awake, I drifted back into a deep and abandoned sleep.

Gandhi is dead! It is hard to describe my feelings upon re-awakening that morning. I did not have to be told that the news was true; I suppose I had known it, even at the first. The sensation was one of appalling numbness, an inability to concentrate either my feelings or my thoughts, as if I were still in the grip of some awful nightmare that would go away when I was more fully awake.

Somehow I knew without being told that Gandhi was not dead of natural causes. He was an old man, and he was weak, so this should have seemed quite possible, and yet somehow it never even entered my mind. There are certain men who seem born to be martyred and though I had never considered it in a logical way, I realized that I felt that Gandhi was one of them. The question in my mind was not how, but by whom.

I had plenty of time to search for the answer. Swamiji and our host had gone out without waking me, and they returned after a while to say that they had been visiting a friend who owned one of the few radios in Sangameshwar. But they knew no more than I did, it seemed, for the announcers were as uncommunicative as the old man I had heard. They too only repeated in undisguised astonishment that Gandhi was dead.

It is a strange thing to be presented with a fact like this, with no explanation, no particulars at all. The mind works best with details and pictures; without them it bogs down, or runs in circles. As I recall, the news made no single impression on me. It filled me, rather, with an awful foreboding, a vague, ill-defined, unreasonable fear, a suspicion of everything and everyone about me. Gandhi was dead. Was it the beginning or the end? Was I to grieve or to hate or to nod my head wisely? Was it a tragedy or a crime or an inevitability? It had elements, I felt sure, of each.

Apparently the villagers were as bewildered as I was. The first day the streets seemed wholly deserted. The bazaars had not been unshuttered since night and the plows stood alone in their empty furrows. I went out expecting to see knots of people gathered together at the square, mourning or arguing, but there was no one at all but a few old women who were going to the well with pots on their heads. Even they seemed to avoid each other's eyes, as if each had suffered some personal bereavement. I went back to the house and spoke to Swamiji, but it was obvious that he was not inclined to talk. There was nowhere I could go with my excitement and curiosity; I had been left, apparently, to my own resources.

I began at the beginning. Who might have killed Gandhi? No one, I decided. No one but a madman. But it was no more than the reverence of the moment, of course; the question was not too hard, but too easy to answer. In a way, it was Gandhi's personal integrity which made him a target for so many criticisms, for a man cannot be a friend to everyone without also being in one sense an enemy of all. It was necessary to make the distinction, I saw, between Gandhi the symbol and Gandhi the man, for while the one was universally loved and respected, the other was subject to the most deadly hatreds.

I suspected, as the majority of villagers did, that Gandhi

was most probably killed by a Moslem, by some misguided zealot who was striking a blow at the Mahatma as the living emblem of Hinduism. Islam would not be quick to forget the millions of believers who were slaughtered in the Punjab, and though Gandhi himself had fasted for peace, that was the sort of detail which could easily be forgotten. And then, at least this much could be said for those Musselmen who considered the Mahatma an enemy of theirs; he was the leader of a Hindu renaissance to which he had given far more impetus than he could ever give direction. I could easily imagine some distraught, maddened refugee rejecting his efforts to disclaim the tragedy, insisting that the uprisings of the Punjab were a logical and foreseeable result of Hindu nationalism. Indeed, I had come near making the charge myself, of blaming Gandhi for the most costly unrealism, and though under the circumstances I felt vaguely ashamed of myself, I could not wholly deny the suspicion, even now.

Then there was the strong possibility that a Hindu was responsible; there was nothing unreasonable about this, even on the face of it, for I had met many who had a curious gift of loving and hating Gandhi simultaneously. I recalled Swamiji's own parody of him and of the reception which it had usually received in the villages. It seemed to prove that there was a certain vein of bitterness beneath the habitual adulation. There were many who would remember that one of Gandhi's first acts was to call off a strike of cultivators against their landlords and that one of his last had been to abolish rationing, which had already resulted in widespread famine. There were some with even better memories who remembered his noncommittal stand on caste issues, who were aware that he was the focus of the theocratic state which others were finding it so easy to misuse. Yes, there were Hindus too who felt Gandhi was dangerous, to whom the most sincere self-sacrifice was not quite enough, who demanded of their saints something more than virtue, who wanted revolutionary leadership as well.

And finally, of course, there were the Mahasabha and the Sangh. Their grievances were perhaps most recent and to the point for they attacked the Mahatma from the opposite direction; according to their creed he was dangerously radical. And like everyone else, they were partially right, for while Gandhi had never spoken of abolishing caste, he had argued repeatedly for its relaxation, for such heretical doctrines as association and intermarriage. At one time, they felt, he had been doctrinally sound, or at any rate, at one time they had overlooked his liberalism, yet now that India was their own to rule, they had taken a far more critical view. It was the upper castes, their reasoning said, who had financed and led the struggle for independence, who had suffered most seriously for their opposition to the raj, while the mute majority had barely acquiesced. And now their position of authority was being questioned. The very foundation of their system was threatened. Were they to countenance the gradual dissolution of the old order by someone who pretended to be one of them?

No, it was not hard to say who might have killed Gandhi. It was hard to say who might *not* have killed him. And it was hard to say, in the absence of that knowledge, just what it was that his death really meant.

[32]

TO THE people of Sangameshwar it meant many things. The initial effect there had been one of shock; for the whole of the first day and a part of the second, there seemed nothing but a dull and oxlike incomprehension. I had walked through the streets completely a stranger, alone in a town of some eight thousand people, separated by my own inability to grieve in the simple, direct manner of those about me. But gradually this stupor was beginning to wear off, to be supplanted by a more natural and conventional sorrow. The sense of outrage and incredulity was passing and the loud and heavy lamentations were beginning.

Quite early on the morning of the day following the tragedy I watched an old woman at the well drawing water; as she was setting her clay pot on the ground, it slipped and dashed into pieces against the stoning of the well. The accident seemed to touch some hidden spring, for when she stooped to collect the pieces she collapsed, first to her knees, then on all fours, and finally to lie sobbing, prone on the ground. I thought she had surely been taken ill suddenly. But she had not. For a whole day she had contained her sorrow and now it had suddenly released in such a flood that there was nothing she could seem to do to control it. And it was this way with most. They were going through the habitual motions of their day, dry eyed and entranced, when suddenly in the middle of whatever they were doing, they would seem to awake to the reality of their loss. The numbness would drain from their minds all at once and the tragedy would make its first real impact. They would look about them, almost in surprise, and then flee into their houses or clasp at each other.

People in grief, like people in joy, seem almost instinctively drawn together, the sadness of the individual joining the sadness of the group and somehow becoming a corporeal thing. In the afternoon a strange thing happened; a hysteria, almost a riot of grief developed, a frightening thing for one who stood as completely outside it as I did. It began, they say, when a young girl broke into uncontrollable sobbing in the main street of the town, apparently simply losing possession of her body and stumbling back and forth, blinded by tears. Several other women rushed out of their houses to quiet her and to lead her home, but she would not be quieted, and with these extra attentions, her sobbing turned into an incoherent screaming. For a while the others continued trying to help, but gradually they too were sucked into the vortex till there were twenty or thirty, all clutching at each other and shouting in chorus that they wanted to die.

The men rushed out of their houses to stop it, but the women turned on them, scratching and biting, as if their attempt to interfere somehow placed them automatically in the ranks of the conspirators against Gandhi. They retreated, bewildered, and for perhaps half an hour the women continued their hysterical crying, biting, and spitting at anyone who attempted to quiet them or to quell the disturbance.

And then as suddenly as it had begun the whole thing ended; the women all at once grew quiet and ashamed. They joined their husbands and families and went home, rather dazed at their sudden unexplainable performance.

After that the village seemed calmer for a while. The stiff, unnatural tension had vanished and Sangameshwar began to resemble what it was, a town in deep mourning for a well-loved leader. There were a few exceptions, two old brothers, for example, who insisted on fasting beyond their powers and after four full days without food of any kind, expired together, within an hour of each other. But the penances of the majority were less strained and disastrous. Life was inevitably beginning to win out over death. Slowly the silence of disbelief and horror was giving way to the articulate cries of grief.

"You see," Swamiji explained to me later, "we are not simply mourning for a political leader. Gandhi's death is a tragedy to each individual, as if a member of his immediate family had died. I know it is hard for an outsider to understand, and I'm not even sure I can explain it myself, but to us this is not just the death of a man. It is a blow to our faith, to our way of life."

I had not pressed Swamiji for this explanation, but nevertheless I was glad he was offering it now, for as he suggested, in spite of my own sympathy for Gandhi, I lately had felt very much estranged from them all. What had bothered me particularly was Swamiji's own reaction, for cynical old sophisticate that he pretended to be, the impact of the news of Gandhi's death had been as great upon him as upon the simplest villager. For twenty-four hours he had taken no food, observing all that time an almost ritual silence. For twenty-four hours whatever it was that we had in common simply disappeared. And so now it seemed that some dam had broken, releasing all the stopped-up words and phrases, beginning as a trickle, rising in a flood, and finally rushing out in an emotional torrent.

"Gandhi . . ." he began. He stopped and shook his head. "It is so terribly hard to explain," he sighed. "It seems all of our feelings about Gandhi are bound up with our feelings about ourselves, about our history as a people. But this you must see. In spite of what errors the Mahatma might have made in his political career, he has given us more than he could ever take away. He has given us our pride as a nation again!"

He continued, "You've got to think of what India was in order to appreciate how we feel; you've got to remember that prior to Gandhi we were like a whole race of people ashamed of themselves. The worst crime of our conquerors was not that they stole the country's resources or the wealth of our princes. They robbed our people of their self-respect. This was the most awful thing of all. When Gandhi came we were embarrassed and abject before the superiority of the British raj. As fast as they could, our leaders were becoming more British than the men who ruled the country!"

He was deeply moved now. "You cannot imagine it, but we felt out of place. In our own country out of place! As if all of our traditions, our very religion were a series of errors which the English could correct. 'We must make you ready for self-government,' they told us. But what they meant was 'We must make you exactly like ourselves. We must give you our accent, we must give you our outlook, and when your skins turn white, perhaps you will be ready!' And what fools our national leaders were! They agreed, and even when they fought the British it was in striped pants and long coats, in parliamentary debates. They had surrendered their cause in the act of defending it! No wonder we felt ashamed of ourselves. No wonder we tried to learn the foreigners' language. Whole generations of our people grew up convinced our own was gibberish because our conquerors told us that. They sent politicians to change our government, missionaries to teach us whom we must worship. And so convinced were they of their superiority that gradually we began to believe in it too. Our clothes were wrong? Then we would dress like the Englishman, even if he laughed at us and thought we were foolish. Our foods were barbaric. Even our rajahs and durbars took to eating boiled fish and puddings. But it was never right. When we lived our own lives we were subjects of pity and condescension. And when we tried to adapt it was just as bad, for we were never more than a poor imitation.

"And then Gandhi came! You cannot understand. . . . Then Gandhi came, and overnight this changed. He did not go to the British in the coats and trousers. They came to him, and he received them in his dhoti! But the best thing about it was that Gandhi had been one of them. He had gone to their schools and practiced in their courts. He had all that the West could offer our country, and he returned it and said it was not enough! Not enough. For years, generations, the white man had been almost a god to the people of Asia. And now Gandhi had said it was not enough and had given them back the whole culture of the West.

"Well, my God! . . . Once again we could hold up our heads; we could worship our gods without feeling ashamed. We could aspire to something greater and more decent than being highly paid servants of a foreign government."

He paused. "You see, Gandhi was not a politician. He was a spiritual leader, a father of his people. And the very measure of his greatness was that they were willing to follow him even when they knew he was wrong. We followed him out of love, not conviction, really. We followed him, tolerant of his temporal blunders, because we knew that without him we would not even be men, but 'coolies' and 'natives' with no choice at all.

"It surprises you apparently that I can attack him as a politician and love him very much in spite of this! But do you hate your father who has given you life because you see that he sometimes makes serious mistakes? No, my friend, the thing is bigger than just the agreement with a man or the disagreement. Only an Indian who has been through it can ever know what Gandhi has meant to the people of this country."

Now Swamiji leaned back and was silent for a moment. It was as if, with this speech, he was utterly spent, for he stared pitifully down at the backs of his hands, breathing hard and frowning to himself. When he looked up it was with a sudden change of expression and an undisguised note of weariness in his voice. "What will happen to our people, my friend?" It was obvious that he felt it was the end of everything.

[33]

AND yet in reality, of course, it was not the end. Even as Swamiji was asking this question his mind, like the minds of all the villagers, was steeling itself to accept the inevitable. The resilience of the human spirit is great; it had suffered a blow but it was recovering already. Gradually the village was straightening its back, raising its head, and blinking its eyes.

And yet, even in this there were certain dangers. During the two days that followed the death of Gandhi an overwhelming sadness had settled on Sangameshwar, leaving no room at all for other feelings. For two days at least all suspicions were forgotten, everything that separated one man from another. In the depths of a sadness as great as this, all the traditional hatreds and the divisions were lost. Yet with a return to reason there is a return to unreason. Detached as I was, my own reactions had been quicker and more perceptive than the reactions of the majority, but I could see that they were not substantially different. At first I had been stunned as they were stunned. And then I had grieved. They were grieving now. But inevitably I had begun to ask questions, to accuse. And just as inevitably, the villagers would do this.

Already the attention had begun shifting to the tea stall. There was a radio there that had been lent by a cloth merchant and the third day it was tuned loudly to All India Radio with its sketchy, disorganized sequence of news broadcasts. A crowd had collected, just a handful at first, standing sullen and dry eyed, whispering together, drawing patterns in the dust with their calloused feet as they waited for the details that were not to come. They heard Nehru speak, and Patel, and Narain, but all of them talked in generalities, repeating the same unnecessary elegiacs and pathetically cautioning their countrymen to be calm. As time went by I was increasingly sure that the government was fearful of wholesale reprisals, for nothing else, I felt, could explain its reluctance to make the particulars of the killing known. And apparently there was good reason for the grisly suspicions, for though there was no wild talk, or threats of violence, it seemed evident that the excitement which had been so long building up needed only an object to turn it to fury. Already I had sensed a shift of emphasis. The talk was no longer of Gandhi the man. The villagers were preoccupied with his death as an event, with the act of violence, the killing itself. It was almost as if they hoped it was a Moslem so that they would have someone to blame, some outlet for their feelings. And what a shock it would be, I decided, if they discovered that it was one of their own who was guilty instead.

The strain was beginning to tell on all of us. The crowd dispersed slowly, that second night. As for myself, I went home feeling almost disappointed that something had not happened to break the spell.

But Swamiji was more like himself that evening. Like the rest of us he had shrugged and put off his surprise, and though his sense of humor seemed a bit restrained, he was obviously in a far better mood than I was.

"This waiting is getting on my nerves," I told him. "Aren't you curious yourself to know who killed Gandhi?"

"Curious?" he asked, with a grave expression. "No, I'm not. You see, I know who killed Gandhi."

I was almost as shocked as by the original announcement. "You know who killed Gandhi?" I repeated slowly.

He nodded his head and smiled grimly. "It was your friends in the R.S.S.," he said.

I was bewildered. "But I have heard nothing!" I protested. "No news has come over All India Radio from Delhi."

Swamiji shrugged. "What has that to do with it? Those Delhi babus will be the last to know." He paused. "You remember when we came to this place I told you that something was in the air?" I nodded. "Well, I am telling you now that the Sangh planned this killing and in time you will learn that I am right again."

"But how do you know these things?" I demanded.

"In this case," he said, "even you should have seen it. On the very day that Gandhi was killed, the members of the Sangh were distributing sweets."

I was revolted. "You mean they were celebrating?"

Swamiji smiled grimly. "More or less," he replied. "In this country we distribute sweets as a gesture to show thanks to the gods for favors granted."

"But even so—" I protested—"we might know they would rejoice! But is that a proof that they were responsible, I wonder?"

"Well, it is," he said, raising his voice quite suddenly, "when they do it before the death is announced!"

He relaxed again and drew his pose around him. "And where do you suppose they have gone so suddenly?"

"Gone?" I asked.

"Yes, gone," he replied. "The whole Brahmin section is virtually deserted!"

"But just the day before this happened . . ." I reflected.

"Yes, the day before you were talking to the Rao Bahadur. And the next day, where was the Rao Bahadur? Probably in Poona or Sholapur. Not here, I can tell you!"

I felt tired and confused. I remembered the long conversations I had with the members of the Sangh. I knew that in my moments of greatest suspicion I had never considered them capable of this.

"What a completely senseless waste!" I exploded. "Gandhi, killed by these foolish, old clowns. . . ."

"No! Don't make that mistake," Swamiji cautioned. "They are not as dumb as they like to appear. They are like lizards that change their color to hide. The stupid babu is a common type, eh? Well, these fellows can be stupid too, when they wish. But never underestimate the R.S.S."

He explained. "The Sangh is not a collection of crackpots who decided to kill Gandhi as a gesture or a threat. They are the dagger arm of a well-established group, established in government as well as in the villages. They are few themselves, but their actual membership is just a quarter or a tenth of their actual strength. The Sangh—you could squash it as you would squash a dung beetle, but the trouble is, it would mean no more, either.

"Once the babus had decided that Gandhi was more of an enemy to their class than he was an ally, his death was virtually inevitable, and apprehending one group of plotters would not have stopped it. You have spent enough time in the villages to see how powerful the banias and Brahmins are! Can you dismiss a group as strong as this with such careless words as 'foolish clowns'?"

"But not all banias and Brahmins are Sanghamites," I objected.

"If they are not it is because they do not have to be," he replied. "Where their power is not challenged, of course they are peaceful. But where it is—well, look around you, my friend."

I argued, "But Swamiji, if this is so obvious, then why haven't the other villagers seen it? The majority, I'm convinced, think a Moslem killed Gandhi. They aren't even considering the R.S.S."

Swamiji sighed. "That's true, I'm afraid, but it's only because they have been fooled by Congress with its ridiculous doctrine that the country is united on all of the serious, fundamental issues. It's a leftover from the days of the British, I suppose, for then it was true that we wanted the same thing. We wanted independence, and that's as far as it went. Now we see independence meant something different to each of us. Of course the villagers think a Moslem killed Gandhi. He is the very symbol of unity of all Hindus. But now the symbol, like the unity, is no more. Perhaps it will bring the people to their senses!"

"Well, if it does," I insisted, "then the Sangh will have miscalculated."

"Yes," he replied. "That is the risk they have taken. But they have apparently decided that it is no longer necessary to placate the liberals and the lower castes. For a long time their clique has made use of the Mahatma. There was much in what he stood for that supported their position. His religiosity, that was easy to use. And his muddled economics were cut to order. Most of all, the Mahatma was forever cautioning against violence regardless of the justice of the cause. Better far to live virtuous and poor, he told us, than to seize what is ours by using force. According to Gandhi we were to get what we wanted by appealing to the better nature of those in power. Ah! How the banias seized on this doctrine. It was a better protection that cannons would have been!"

I was confused. "You make it seem," I insisted, "that Gandhi was actually on the side of the Sangh!"

"No," Swamiji corrected me, "he was not on their side, but he was on the side of nonviolence and it amounted to the same thing.

"As you know, the upper castes are already in power. All they have to do is retain their position, so anyone who opposes a violent change is defending them whether he wants to or not. Of course, Gandhi wanted to bring about a change; he wanted to give the cultivator his rights. But he wanted to do it through moral persuasion, and all the banias had to do was not be persuaded."

But I was still dissatisfied. "Then why," I asked, "should the Sangh ever have decided to kill Gandhi? I should think that if all that you say is true they would have had most to lose by his death."

Swamiji smiled. "A few years ago what you say would have been entirely right," he agreed. "That is exactly why Gandhi's death is important. It proves that the Sangh has come into its own. You see, now the Sanghamites are not going to be satisfied to assert the rights they already have. They are actually anxious to strengthen their positions, to press their abuses even further than before. They feel they are strong enough to do this now, and they feel they have enough backing in the government. Believe me, the meaning of Gandhi's death is that the traditional powers are taking the offensive."

It was a bewildering idea to me, I must confess. As much as I had recently learned about the Sangh, I would never have been ready to say this myself, or to accept it without some further thought. And yet wasn't it really quite logical, I wondered, that with the advent of independence this should happen, that the millions of petty village rulers should make their bid to capture the country?

There has always been an integral connection, I knew, between the countryside and national politics. Almost every leader of importance beside Nehru had come originally from the villages. The issues in Delhi were the village issues, tax collection and land-tenure legislation. And it was inevitable, I saw, that this being the case, the real struggle for power must take place in the villages.

I reflected on all that I had learned already about the relationship of the upper and lower castes, and upon my naïve assumption that in the course of time this master-servant relationship must break down. It was not at all inevitable, I realized. A political vacuum existed in Delhi, but it was all too likely that this vacuum would be filled by the inrushing force of the privileged classes. The whole machinery of government had been built up to serve the will of some vested interest. Well, vested interests there were in plenty, and now it was obvious they were making their bid. The death of Gandhi? It suddenly paled into the insignificant event that it actually was, just one small move on the master plan that had been carefully worked out by the Mahasabha and the Sangh. Yes, as Swamiji said, Gandhi's death was inevitable once we posited the existence of the Sangh. And the existence of the Sangh was just as inevitable in the light of the inflexible caste structure in the villages. I began to see that the relaxation of caste might simply be a part of the breakdown of India, a function of her decadence of the last few centuries rather than a result of any progress or enlightenment. And if that were the case, it followed all too logically that with the rejuvenation of the country, caste would be rejuvenated. Certainly there were those who were willing to fight for it, and apparently they were growing bolder by the hour.

I had come full circle. Once again I saw that there were no missing pieces in this jigsaw puzzle. The Sangh, Gandhi's death, the state of the villagers fitted together all too neatly. Of course one fact might seem more newsworthy than another; a murder is always more dramatic than habitual abuses. And yet one man's death could never be more than a minor part of the historical tragedy. No, if Gandhi's death meant anything at all, it was simply because of the symbolism which it suggested, because through that death the world might learn of the terror and brutality which the villager knows so well. The murder of Gandhi was a part of the Indian scene, just as were the Mahatma's life and teachings; the wise old guru was a tradition in Asia, but so was the slaughter of political rivals. It was the best of India being pitted against the worst, the most sincere self-sacrifice against the most brutal self-interest. And it was not a fight to be won with one blow, or with four bullets through the body of a frail little man.

I thought of the thousands of tiny villages where I had seen precisely the same struggle enacted, Brahmin against Sudra, bania against harijan, tradition against justice, might against right. And gradually the immediate scene seemed to fade. It had happened before and it was happening again. Sangameshwar, Swamiji, the murder of Gandhi all began taking their place in the historical perspective.

[34]

IT WAS in this frame of mind that I decided to leave. It was not as abrupt a decision as it seemed, for with this sudden access of understanding, my motives for staying in Sangameshwar seemed to vanish. I had been waiting for something; what was it, I wondered? I had been waiting for a logical time to depart, waiting for a conclusion, an end to the episode, as if history ran in convenient cycles. And now, of course, I realized how foolish it was to visualize the thing in these terms. It was the fate of any wanderer, I knew, to see many beginnings but never an end.

When I spoke to Swamiji he tried to dissuade me. He apparently had grown used to my company by now, for he protested, assuring me that much would be happening and that I would be missing a great deal by going just now. But I would miss many things if I stayed as well, for one village was far from the whole of India, and already I had begun to hunger after miles, to covet new friends, to thirst for new villages. Nevertheless, I must confess that I wavered in my decision; several times I delayed my departure a few days on the ill-advised theory that there would come some one day when it would be easier to leave than it had been before. For example, once I stayed to watch a riot which Swamiji had predicted in glowing terms, and once again to watch the lower-caste villagers burn several houses in the Brahmin quarter. But after each of these episodes I felt just as dissatisfied; I was unable to see either as a neat conclusion, perhaps because the villagers themselves were unaware of any real sense of accomplishment.

And so it was that I was forced to admit that whenever I left I would be "leaving in the middle," that the rush of events was steady and relentless, not geared to the schedule of a casual wanderer. It was as if I had only begun to see that I was traveling through time as well as through space; it was a thing which one easily forgot in the Gujarat, but it was not so easy to forget it here.

Moreover, in Sangameshwar one was not so isolated from news of the outside as in most towns I had seen, and for the last few days there were exciting reports of trouble on the Hyderabad border, and in the south. I knew that I could not be everywhere at once, but this was the temptation I was under now, for having decided to leave I could not leave fast enough, nor encompass enough country to satisfy my greed. Accordingly I repacked my gear for the trip and asserted myself against Swamiji's blandishments. When he saw that I was serious and would not be dissuaded, he helped me to make my final plans.

From Sangameshwar I would go south, we decided between us, taking the horse that Swamiji had borrowed for me at

Khed. I could leave compensation for its owner with Swamiji and thereby expedite the first leg of my trip. It was an important caution, he assured me, for I would be traveling through rather hostile country as far as Hubli and it would be better if I had not to risk my usual impromptu arrangements till I was south of there. Below Hubli, of course, the horse would be useless, for there the mountains and the jungle begin. But by that time it was safe to expect that I would be able to find guides and carts to take me farther. It was possible, Swamiji suggested, that I might choose to strike directly out toward the coast from Hubli, which would mean negotiating the Mysore forests, but would also save me a considerable detour. The possibility was a thrilling one of course, and mentally I already had committed myself to it, but at Swamiji's suggestion I agreed to leave this decision to the moment when I had to make it.

Just two days were spent in this planning and refitting, for I was determined that this time there should be no delays. And so, on the appointed morning I rode out of Sangameshwar and turned south toward the jungles of Mysore.

Kanara

Kanara

[35]

THE country did not change much south of Sangameshwar. I followed the edge of the highlands as planned, detouring inland just once or twice, and then shortly, with the object of asserting my new freedom. The land was not universally barren, but there was a universal carelessness in the way it was farmed so that even in the midst of some rich, fertile tract, there might be two or three farms that would be lying idle. Once again, the villages seemed to follow no pattern, for while one would be rich, the next would be poor; while one would be peopled by alert, clever farmers who kept their homes in reasonable repair, another, perhaps less than a mile away, would be literally falling about the ears of its inhabitants. But since I moved along rapidly I saw nothing too closely. Traveling by night and stopping by day, in less than a week of my departure from Sangameshwar, I had got as far south as Belgaum and Saundatti.

It was here that the actual jungles began. Riding along the lip of the western ghats, I began to notice the smooth plains below me giving way to a dense and heavy scrub growth. At first it was only the eroded gulleys that were choked with thistles and advancing brush, but by the end of the day when I had watched these beginnings, I had entered a land of fantastic fertility.

I knew from the maps that the forests of Mysore are all that remains of the enormous tangle of teak and bamboo that in the days of the Vedas covered the whole of India from Cape Comorin to the Narbada. In form, they comprise a narrow

217

strip perhaps two hundred miles wide and five hundred miles long, sweeping in from the coast and assaulting the steep ridges and fissures of the Deccan Plateau itself, creeping and crawling up its barren rock slopes like some subtle and malignant marine invasion. To the south, where the barrier is less high and forbidding, they achieve their goal and spread out on the highlands, annexing the whole of the Nilgiri Mountains and extending at least halfway across the peninsula. But for all their fertility they are an unhealthy area, so unhealthy indeed that they are almost uninhabited, at least in the lowland coastal regions where cerebral malaria is particularly rife. On the slopes of the mountains there are a number of tribes living, but they are seminomadic and utterly tribal, appearing and disappearing from time to time and clad only in green leaves worn over their noses. Withal they are a timid and friendly people who come and go like ineffectual wraiths, and while the idea of their presence might cause me some discomfort, I knew that these tribes themselves were no danger. The real problems were natural ones, the denseness of the jungle and the scarcity of water, the herds of wild elephants and the occasional rogues, and the king cobra which I discovered was native to these forests. Nevertheless I had already made my decision and I was too stubborn to change it in the light of this new knowledge, so swinging east to Dharwar to hire a guide, I struck out toward Karwar directly through the forest.

The first day in particular I shall never forget. It was a nightmare; we rose by the gray light of dawn and by the time the sun was visible on the horizon we were already on the slopes of the forested cliffs. I had expected some hills, but nothing like this, for it was mountain climbing and forestry in equal proportions, a scrambling up and down from tree to tree, swinging from roots and dropping from branches. The slope in some places was so steep that the brake grew out on a thirty degree angle from it, digging its roots into crannies and cracks in the sharp and treacherous rock. By the end of the day I was bruised and bleeding from slipping and scrambling for holds, but my condition was nothing compared with the condition of my guide; his bare feet left a trail of blood on the stones.

Several times that first day I saw evidence of snakes, discarded skins and, once, a few eggs, but my guide assured me that they were no danger to us, that the avalanche of small stones which preceded us would warn them. Later, he agreed, we would have to be more careful, when we had got to the damp floor of the forest below. There, he suggested with a pointed glance, it was necessary for the one with shoes to go first.

That night we camped in the bowl of a great tree, building a fire in the small clearing directly below it. The heat was uncomfortable, but I slept almost on top of it, while king cobras chased pit vipers round and round in my dreams.

The next morning I woke slowly. It was as if I had been drugged and had slept in one position for a week at least; the first thing I remember is a consciousness of pains, even before my eyes opened or I tried to move. I blinked. My lids were like heavy shutters sliding back and forth on an unoiled hinge. I moved my fingers. They were lumpy and swollen. I closed my eyes and lay still again. When I was able to raise my head a little and survey my body at full length I felt worse, for every scratch of the day before was a livid welt, puffy with infection. I rolled my head to look at my guide. He was busy on himself with a piece of sharp flint, squeezing and lancing with a methodical air, as if this were a part of crossing a jungle. When he saw I was awake, he smiled broadly; he offered me his flint but I declined politely, preferring a dirty razor blade from my pack.

But once under way, the going was better. In the first place, we established an easier pace than the day before when I suspect that my guide was half fearful I might choose to turn around and go back. He had wrapped his feet in an old rag which he carried, clotted with the blood of previous expeditions, but even with that it seemed necessary for him to feel his way gingerly along from one rock to another. Moreover, the slope grew gentler through the morning and by noon it was no worse than thirty degrees. It was clear that we were nearing the floor of the valley, and the end of the most painful part of the crossing.

As we continued, the vegetation grew increasingly dense. In part, the gentler slope explained this, but equally it was due to the fact that the bare rock was now interspersed with patches of soil. A scrubby cactus began to appear, then an occasional clump of parched desert grass, until finally even the rock began to show green where forest mosses were creeping across it.

That afternoon we came upon a tiger drinking from a rill not a hundred feet from us, but there was something so essentially peaceful in the scene that I had not even the slightest momentary fear. He looked up at us slowly and licked his whiskers, his expression being that of a benevolent old grandfather, wizened and tired and yet calmly alert. He resumed his drinking when we went on our way. Sometime later we flushed a family of peacock. They were rarer here than they were in the north, but accordingly these were beautiful birds rather than the scabrous specimens one sees in Kathiawar. The *pater familias* spread his great tail, like a curtain with a hundred eyes peering through it, but when he found that we did not frighten as easily as he hoped, he herded his hen and his chicks away.

Now the vegetation itself began to change. On the slopes of the ghats the trees had been enormous, venerable old peepuls and massive banyans established in the rocks in centuries gone by. But as the land leveled off a scrub brush took over; here the struggle for life was more subtle, adapted to creeping vines and a stunted brake that were less demanding than the trees. A majority of these forms were thorny, it seemed; one cut or was cut, tore or was torn, and our progress

—which through most of the day had been good—was slowed to a dogged and bitter pace. The sun was sinking, but we fought our way forward, for my guide insisted we should not stop here. There was only a belt of this brake, he said, and soon we would enter the jungle proper. I confess I grew panicky when the darkness began falling and we were still clawing our way through the thorn and brush, nor was I reassured when, in explaining his haste, my guide admitted it was full of snakes. At last, however, it came to an end, opening out into a broad and rocky plain. Beyond that, I could see, the real jungles began with great teaks and neem trees dominating the skyline.

We continued till we had come to a clump of mimosa, yellow with flowers and sweet to smell. It was mossy and cool, soft underfoot, and we decided that here we would camp for the night. I declared a veritable feast of thanksgiving, opening two days' rations and sharing them with my guide. Then both of us cut wattles to serve as our mattress and fell immediately into a deep and abandoned sleep.

[36]

AFTER that, our traveling was a matter of routine. Ordinarily we would break camp around six in the morning in order to get most of our walking behind us before the sun had penetrated the jungle. We averaged about twenty-five miles a day, which was not bad considering the problems of terrain, and that we did not go farther was only the result of the wretched state which my feet had reached. In general we kept to the elephant trails, great tracks of ruin hewn out of the jungle where the wild herds in their habitual coursing had raged up and down like whimsical cyclones. The paths that they left were broad and clear, only the sturdiest trees being enough to deflect them, and we were particularly lucky in striking one soon, which ran directly east in the direction we were going.

For about two days the country continued uneven, stretching before us in great fertile undulations, virginal and lonely and faintly malicious with its poisonous berries and its nests of vipers. After that there was a stretch of level jungle, but it came as no relief for it was accordingly more dense. Here even our elephant track was wiped out by the overnight growth of bamboo and cactus. The worst problem of all was the insects. In this section the mosquitoes were particularly bad, and though I felt reasonably sure they could not be malarious, the nearest village being many miles away, still they dealt with us hideously as we pushed along, stripped to the waist and sweating profusely. Moreover, there was a sort of prickly caterpillar just the touch of whose fur caused an acute irritation; one day when the breeze shook the treetops above us they rained down on our bodies like droplets of fire. But eventually this level stretch ended too, and with it the plague of our fellow travelers. Once more we were in a genuinely mountainous terrain, confronted by the accustomed inanimate obstacles.

It was shortly after that we came upon a village, the only one we found in the interior of the forests. It was a settlement of a strange aboriginal people whom my guide referred to as Siddhis. What was peculiar about them was the obvious fact that they were not Indians at all, but Africans by race, a startling discovery, but one more than proven by their gutteral language and their physical proportions. They were Moslems it seemed, of a foreign sect that looked like a mixture of orthodoxy and voodoo, a fanatical wailing having replaced the loud but emotionally restrained prayers of Indian Islam. Moreover, their clothes, while Indianized considerably, bore obvious signs of a foreign influence, and most conclusive of all, a few of the elders had tatooed their bodies in the African fashion.

After an involved line of questioning through a chain of

interpreters, I discovered that the Siddhis are a mystery to themselves, for though there are, apparently, some myths explaining their origins, the majority are unaware of their strange situation. The truth seems to be that they came from Africa either as coastal traders or as refugees originally, only to be driven on the rocks of the Kanara Coast and gradually forced back into the bordering jungles. There they have settled glumly into their tribal pattern, adapting to the minor change in their surroundings, rearing their children in the old tradition, and perpetuating their religion and their language.

Since they were an unfriendly people, we did not stay with them, but for three days we camped in the bush nearby, journeying into their village during the day occasionally on the pretense of buying supplies from the people. Eventually I found a few old heads who had learned some Urdu from the local Moslems and I was able to establish a halting contact with them, enough to learn the bare facts of their life. But my interest soon waned for it seemed that the Siddhis were gradually losing their independent existence. The tribe was dispersing, the young men going coastward where they could make a good living by lumbering or fishing. The few who were left were a dying remnant, riddled with malaria and amoebic fevers, and I was only too anxious to leave them behind and get back on the trail toward the sea again.

Still, the time had not been entirely wasted, for I hired one Siddhi to serve as a porter, a young man who was joining his brother on the coast and was anxious to earn a few rupees while traveling. He was sullen and unreliable, but as strong as an ox and I did not regret my decision to take him, for in addition to carrying the large part of our load, he suggested a number of shortcuts to my guide.

From the village we swung almost directly north to intersect a stream that wound out toward the sea. It involved a detour but our porter suggested it since it eliminated a rather difficult stretch of climbing. Probably he was right; from my point of view, though, nothing could have been harder or less pleasant than this detour, for the stream was nothing but a stagnant ditch that wound its way sluggishly between sheer walls of rock. For miles we waded along its slippery bottom, breaking the scum before us as we went, only occasionally finding some treacherous path that clung to the bank for a few hundred yards. Two nights we spent in the jaws of this canyon, clinging to sloping and uncomfortable campsites. Happily, on the third morning, the banks leveled out and we were able to ascend them and continue through the wood.

Near the coast, the vegetation was once more very lush. It was perhaps less densely treed than it had been, but where the interior had been too dry to support much underbrush, the slope of the land having been constantly seaward, the region just behind the last range of hills was dank and steamy and correspondingly thick. Here a whole new flora began to appear, more strictly tropical than anything I had seen, huge elephant ears and philodendron twining around stumps and the corpses of dead trees, orchids growing out of fallen logs, and exotic mushrooms and toadstools everywhere. Some of the trees bore enormous blossoms literally a foot or a foot and a half across. Others had wonderful varicolored leaves, red and gold in a streaked effect. Even at night the jungle was bright with the insidious luminescent parasitic growths, balls of fire in rotting stumps and patches of bright slime that winked at one startlingly. Yet all of this fertility was faintly malicious. It seemed to press about one's throat. Everywhere there was the subtle violence of the jungle, its slow strangulation, its brilliant decay.

Moreover, this was the snake region. Naturally enough they thrived in the steamy and oppressive atmosphere. Nests of adders were all about and frequently we saw the great king cobra itself. Once I nearly stepped on a slow form that was making its way casually across the path in front of me. It was a banded krait, one of the most deadly of snakes, though no more than a couple of feet in length. At night we slept in a carefully cleared triangle with a fire built up on each of the corners. I say slept, but in my case I use the word loosely, for I twisted and turned in an agony of discomfort.

But snakes were not the only fauna. In addition to numerous sambar and nilgai, we also would catch sight of the barking deer, a pretty little animal about the size of a goat. These deer were apparently of a curious disposition, for they often would approach us, yipping like small dogs. But they were incredibly fast; when one turned to confront them, they disappeared so quickly the eye could not follow. Even more secretive, it seemed, were the numerous jackal, for all during our trip we never caught sight of them, though every night they would begin howling in concert, screaming and raging like lost souls in hell. After a while we learned how to start them ourselves and we would pass boring hours in barking and howling. When we began to ascend the last line of the ghats, though, the jackals dropped behind to the jungle proper.

It was here that we noticed the first signs of man's presence. On the far side of the hills the whole slope was crisscrossed with paths which, according to my companions, had been made by the lumber scouts in their search for new timber. Soon after, we began to encounter tree stumps and whole areas which seemed to be entirely logged out, and finally, when we were only about sixty miles from the coast, we began to find the camps of the timber crews themselves. We stayed for a day in one of the largest to rest for the final leg of our trip, but by now we were close enough to the sea itself that it acted as a magnet, drawing us onward.

The last day of our trip we rose long before dawn. We had determined to reach the coast that evening, for the lumbermen assured us it had been done before, and we felt confident that few others had been so eager as we were. Accordingly we burned all of our bridges behind us; we took only enough water for twenty-four hours, jettisoning the extra along with the rice, which until now we had carried as an emergency food ration. I had soaked my feet in brine for several hours, insisting that my companions do the same. Then I greased all present with tallow, to prevent chafing, and we set out, happy in our ignorance of what was before us.

That final day was certainly the worst that we had experienced since beginning our whole trip through the jungles; though the conditions were unfavorable, my guide and I estimated that we covered almost forty miles in twelve hours. It was a fantastic ordeal and we could never have made it had it not become an obsession near the end, for all of us were walking on the sides of our feet, stumbling along half blinded by the pain. By noon we were so tired that none of us could eat, though we were scarcely halfway to the coast by then. By six in the evening we had exhausted our water and all of us had almost ceased to sweat. The Siddhi boy was crying to himself; his feet were in the worst condition of all. Even my Kanarese guide was trying to blame me for this foolish attempt, though it had been his own idea. We were walking in a daze for the last two hours, scarcely daring to think of our destination, heads down, eyes closed, lips thick with thirst, moving one foot after the other, and grunting at each step.

And then, there was the ocean. It came so suddenly that we could do nothing but look at each other and groan. All at once we were standing on the edge of a bluff and there it was spread out before us. There it was, the curve of sand, reaching gracefully out to north and south. There it was, a windy infinity of sky and water, blending in the sunset. We sank down to our knees with surprise and relief, but the very sight was new energy and strength, and the next thing we knew we were rushing down the slope, oblivious to the blisters and the raw flesh of our feet. As we ran we discarded our packs and our clothing, littering the beach behind us in our haste. Then together we plunged into the great lazy waves, touching, tasting, bathing in our triumph! The salt stung our bodies and burned in our wounds, but we laughed and screamed and cried like madmen. We threw water in the air and ran it through our fingers. The beach! The ocean! The Arabian Sea!

[37]

THE Kanara Coast. If you find it on a map, you will discover that it lies on the west side of the peninsula about halfway down from Bombay toward Cape Comorin where the Indian Ocean becomes the Arabian Sea. As one might expect, it is rich and lovely, a land of broad beaches and blinding white sand. And yet, without seeing it, it is impossible to imagine the beauty and spaciousness which it actually possesses.

Any description of Kanara must begin with the mountains. They are the backdrop that lends depth and dimensionality; one seldom really sees or thinks about them, but they are always present—in substance and in spirit. Beyond these mountains lies the rest of India, as beyond the sea lie Africa and Arabia, and yet, both are symbols of a distant possibility; the sand, and the sun, and the palm trees are reality.

The beach itself is of an incredible whiteness. All colors are heightened by the brilliance of the sun; the sea is the most amazing cobalt hue, the line of the palm trees the liveliest deep brown. And yet over it all, like a silver wash, there is the dazzling brightness of the atmosphere itself that is all but blinding to a dweller in darkness from the bleak northern latitudes or the inland provinces.

The Kanarese people are in harmony with their surroundings. After the villagers of the Deccan they seem almost like gods for they are strong and tall with gleaming white teeth that show almost constantly in their black, laughing faces. The children are particularly beautiful to watch, for they gambol in the surf like playful minnows, splashing water around them like handfuls of diamonds, and leaping, glistening themselves, in the sunlight.

The villages in Kanara generally are built just behind the first line of palm trees, near the sea, the beach itself serving as a village common where the inhabitants come to gossip and to stroll. But actually, the division into villages is misleading, for the whole coast is really like one great community, no hard and fast distinctions being made between the property of one and the property of its neighbor. Moreover, these villages are transient themselves, the houses being woven of coconut fiber which, each year before the monsoons begin, are torn down and rebuilt to withstand the rains. It is hard to separate cause from effect, but a whole different atmosphere prevails along with this; for without the architectural reminders of the past, the present and the future assume their proper importance. One notices, for example, that caste is less important than almost anywhere else in the Indian peninsula and that the whole dogma of Hinduism as evidenced here is lightened by a sense of humor and perspective. The people eat fish in enormous quantities, hence their otherwise unaccountable good health, and experience has even taught them that if the children are fed sharks' livers, they grow much faster and are less susceptible to disease. Mostly, this unparalleled liberality is due to the simple physical circumstances of the Kanara district, but in part it can be traced to the social heritage, in which these villages have been almost equally lucky.

From the earliest history the Kanarese people have been a cosmopolitan seafaring race. The majority, of course, in every period have been simple fishermen who stayed close to land, but always among them there have been those brave souls who have dared to sail out of sight of their shores, bringing back when they came the fish nets of China, the dates of Persia, and stories from everywhere. Like most coastal peoples they are outgoing and experienced, aware of a world much wider than their horizons, tolerant of strangers and foreign viewpoints, and anxious to learn from whomever can teach them.

It is a matter of record that there is a large intermixture of European blood in the Kanarese peoples, and as you travel down the coast you see signs of it yet in an occasional villager who has far more the appearance of a Portuguese or Spanish trader than of an Indian. There are whole villages, one finds, quite jealous of their blood which, to judge from appearances, must be a quarter European and, as always, this intermixture seems to have produced a type far superior to either of the parent stocks.

The thing that is apt to strike one most quickly is the spontaneous, friendly manner of these people. There is no need here for introductions or for the subterfuge which I had often found necessary in other parts of India, for every family holds perpetual open house. For example, when a fisherman is detained away from home, he simply puts in at the nearest village where, with no talk of payment or even of thanks, he is kept as long as he wishes to stay. It is a tradition, but it is a great deal more than a tradition, for there is nothing grudging about this hospitality. Rather it is a simple reflection of the unstudied kindness and good will of the Kanarese villagers. In all of the time that I spent on the coast, I was never in want of food or lodging, nor was I ever allowed to repay my hosts, though on a number of occasions I felt compelled to try. The possessions of the villagers are simply numbered, their clothes, their houses, and the day's catch of fish, but they are as prodigal with these as millionaires, and any man is welcome to share them.

As I recall, I spent less than a month in Kanara. Yet it might have been a year without my being aware of it, for there is about the whole place a sense of well being that seems to deny the existence of time. At one's back lie the mountains, dark and inscrutable, shutting out all thought of anything beyond, while on the hard sand beach the waves roll in as if all the world converged on this spot. It is with the greatest difficulty that one can bring himself to believe in, much less to think of an outside world. To me, the Kanara Coast was not a place so much as a state of mind.

[38]

MY TREK down the coast began from a point about ten miles south of the port of Karwar, at a small fishing village called Binge not far from the place where my guides and I emerged from the forest. At Binge we had lain over for almost a week, recouping the strength that the crossing had cost us, but inevitably the sores and the blisters all healed, and I had no excuse for further delays. My first inclination had been to take my guide with me to serve as an interpreter and general intermediary, but I eventually decided against this course and resolved to continue alone instead.

The weather was deceptively mild when I set out. There was a steady light breeze that flew in from the sea that made walking seem almost dangerously easy and that tempted one to ignore the intensity of the sun. For the first two days I was susceptible to the temptation and pushed myself far beyond a reasonable limit with the result that my arms and my neck were burned so badly that I could scarcely go on the next morning. But probably I was lucky to have got the warning, for if I had continued, things might have been considerably worse; hereafter I was able to plan my schedule more cautiously, avoiding the hot noon hours.

As amended, my regime was roughly this: I would start out around six in the morning from the village where I slept, continuing till nine or ten, when the sun rose over the top of the hills. Wherever I was I would stop for lunch, begging fish or prawns from the willing villagers, occasionally partaking of those enormous village feasts which the Kanarese get together on the spur of the moment. In any case the food would be tasty and plentiful; nowhere in India had I seen anything to compare with it. Both seafood and vegetables were apparently quite cheap and the cookery of the Kanarese is the best in India. Fruit would be served in ridiculous abundance—mangoes, custard apples, papaya, pineapple, cashew, jack fruit, guava, and sweet limes being piled on plantain leaves in front of the guest. After lunch I would rest for an hour or two, perhaps talking with someone who knew a little Hindustani. Then, depending on the impression that I had received of the village, I would push on until sundown or rest for the night.

My first real stop was at a village called Shadur, about ten or fifteen miles north of Kumta. Like all of the settlements that front on the beach it was a gentle, quiet, lazy little place that dozed in peace through the hot part of the day, coming to life in the morning and evening when the fishing fleet was putting out to sea or returning again. It was as unobtrusive as a village could be; from the sea, the only evidence of its existence was a neat row of boats drawn up on the sand and an occasional net spread out in the sun for drying or for mending by the village women.

When I arrived in Shadur I was welcomed profusely by the head of one of the fishing co-operatives, a veteran of some vague and menial service with the American Army in India during the war, an old fellow who went about in a loincloth, the prerogative of the oldest males in Kanara, but who addressed me as though we were fellow countrymen in a dialect English that was bristling with Americanisms. Udi was his name, but he remembered wistfully that the G.I.s had called him "something like Muck . . ." I told him that Udi was simple enough for me and moved into his hut for the duration of my stay.

Udi's house was the typical Kanarese villager's. It was a dramatically simple and functional place, just a low thatch roof supported on poles and a few sections of siding that had been woven from palm fronds. It was set in a grove of similar houses well spaced in the shade of a peepul grove and in front of each one there was a baked-mud courtyard edged by a low curb to keep out the sand. It was obvious that the division between indoors and outdoors was not an important one to the people of Shadur, for during the day they all seemed to live in these courtyards and even at night a majority slept there. The houses were simply a concession to the monsoons when the rain would force them to move inside. Now a number of them even had their walls taken down so that they were not much more than open-air pavilions.

At one end of the grove there was a large stone building. I asked Udi about it the day after my arrival and learned that it belonged to his fishing co-operative and provided a storehouse for nets and equipment. In another direction there was a two-story smokehouse, efficiently designed and carefully built. Like the storehouse opposite, it was community property, once again belonging to the fishing co-operative.

These co-operatives themselves were interesting. I had heard of them before while I was traveling on the coast, but until now I had never fully realized the importance they played in the life of the Kanarese. In Shadur alone there were four of them, existing in a state of friendly rivalry. They had begun long ago when numbers of families had pooled their man power so that they could sail larger boats. Since then they had grown into enormous organizations, for no single fisherman could possibly compete with them. Now they had assumed a multitude of functions, becoming governments within governments, villages within villages.

I learned that these co-operatives practiced two kinds of fishing. In the first place they set the usual gill nets in deep water, but what interested me most was what Udi called "school fishing," a seining of mackerel that was practiced in the shallows. I had noticed that in front of a majority of the villages there would be two or three men sitting back near the palms, staring at the water with fixed intensity and rotating their heads from side to side. Now I discovered they were "fish watchers," men stationed near the beach to be alert for signs of these offshore schools. It seemed incredible, but they were able to tell when a school was near by the color that the water assumed. One would give the alarm and signal his cohorts, banging a brass gong that was hung from a tree. This established the school as the property of his co-operative, so it was only natural that the fish watcher was a valuable man.

Still, the deep-water fishing was interesting in its way. Every morning the large boats would push out from shore loaded with nets which they would drag between them or plant in the water just beyond the shoals. These boats sometimes would be out for several days, depending on the way that the fish were running, for if one of them returned with less than a full load, it was considered a disgrace on the fishermen and their co-operative. Whenever a boat landed, the whole village would come down to see what the fortunes of the sea had been, praising the catch if the ship were their own, deprecating its size if it belonged to a competitor.

Ordinarily it was not necessary for Udi to sail, for his job as head of the co-operative was largely administrative, involving chiefly the keeping of accounts and the settlement of disputes between members of his group. Several times while I was staying in Shadur, however, he did go out for extraordinary reasons, and in each case I went with him, for it was the best chance I had to meet the sailors under casual conditions. The boats themselves were surprisingly large. They were perhaps forty feet long and ten feet wide, with a draft of from ten to fifteen feet, flexible old scows roped together with rattan, giving and bending with every swell, spitting their calking at every good roll. They were sailed with a modified lanteen rig, the picturesque triangular sails of the travelogues, but when light there was nothing picturesque about them at all, for they were driven within inches of their weary old lives.

233

At sea the sailors were excellent companions. During the day they lounged on the deck of the boat or spent their time in telling stories to each other, long improvised ballads in which they were the heroes, stories of their conquests of foreign women, and stories of their travels in distant countries. Most of them, of course, had never sailed for more than a few hundred miles from home; but then, nobody took these tales seriously anyway; they were just long, drawn-out daydreams, dreamed out loud.

I remember one fellow in particular, a singer who, when we were standing on the shore in the evening, would sing the strange half-caste folk songs of the Kanarese fishermen, fluting little tunes neither European nor Asiatic. His voice was as high and as weak as a woman's but it was lovely and everyone would sit quietly when he sang, so that there would be not a sound but his thin, reedy tones and the groaning of the rigging under the weight of its draft. Then there was an old man who specialized in horror stories, of enchanted ships, and of two-headed sea monsters. These he told with symbolic gestures, contorting his own face into hideous and appropriate shapes. It wasn't that the others actually believed him but that they pretended to; belief was their part in the play. It was as if these stories and songs supplied some stimulation that was lacking in their humdrum lives.

Onshore, unfortunately, they were far less tractable. They drank heavily and most of them grew surly when drunk, uncovering an almost sadistic streak which their wives and families knew all too well. They were men of surprisingly violent emotion, perhaps because of the even lives they led, and there was scarcely a night during my week in Shadur that I was not awakened by some drunken brawl. These fights were never over anything serious; like the stories I had heard they were largely fictitious, fomented as a salutary form of exercise, as an outlet for energies too long pent up. Frequently the adversaries would fight for a few minutes and then, unable to take the thing seriously any longer, clasp each other in gales of laughter and lie down to sleep in a drunken embrace.

Yet in other spheres they were quite sober and capable. The business meetings of the co-operative, for example, showed a side of the villagers that was revealed nowhere else, and demonstrated perhaps those qualities which made them essentially different from the inland peoples. For the fishermen of Shadur judged nothing by tradition. Their standards were empirical, their decisions reasoned, and the competition between the neighboring co-operatives drove them to the most candid and blunt self-analysis. These meetings were correspondingly spirited and exciting; it was all Udi could do to keep them in hand. If there was any official who was shirking in his job, he would be denounced in the most direct and colorful prose.

At one meeting that I attended the villagers were discussing a new motor vessel which they were proposing to build in co-operation with all the other co-operatives in the hope of carrying fish to the Bombay markets. They had apparently had a bitter experience before. A similar vessel had been sabotaged by its pilot, a member of one of the rival organizations who had been bought out by one of the large Bombay buyers. As Udi explained the situation to me, the markets in Bombay had things just as they wanted them and if they could continue to buy fish under monopoly conditions they could keep the price down to a quarter of what it should be. Shadur had dared to challenge the cartel, which was controlled by what Udi called "the Bombay banias," and the banias had managed to buy the loyalty of the Shadur boat's pilot who put sand in the oil. The proposal now was to build a new boat, the main issue being whether the same thing could happen again. It was Udi's argument which carried the day. If it did, he shouted, they would build still another.

It was this spirit about the people of Shadur that I admired. It was evidenced not only in their co-operatives but in their whole lives. Everything they did they did for a reason, never simply because convention decreed it. Their houses they patterned after the conditions of their lives, not after the plans of forgotten builders, and their social code was inspired by at least a rough concept of justice instead of by dead habit. Unlike their inland cousins they did not automatically bow to the weight of tradition. They did not begin with the abject assumption that the heavens were on the side of the established powers.

Of course they had sacrificed much to utility. They could not afford the time and the money that were devoted to the building of shrines in some sections, and the architecture of Kanara was correspondingly barren. To the traveler, the coast was far less picturesque than the depths of the country where Hinduism prevailed, for here there were none of the exotic shrines which had been erected to commemorate man's slavery to the past. Yet, if there were any place in India where there seemed a hope for the future, it was here in Shadur and the villages like it, and when I left after only a week or so it was with the feeling that in one sense I had seen the best. There were no temples to Vishnu, no altars to Siva, no hint at all of "the beauties of antiquity." But there were two things in Shadur that I had missed everywhere else. There was freedom, and there was self-respect.

On the day I was leaving I got the best proof of this. Udi had asked me to talk to a meeting of untouchables, an organization which he had helped to found for the education of the casteless Hindus of Shadur. It was the first time I had ever seen anything like it; ordinarily the harijans were so abjectly humble that the very idea of improving their lot could never penetrate the depths of their misery. But here was a whole untouchable community that met together to do precisely this, and not only did they discuss new methods in their crafts, but they even studied the Vedas and the Upanishads.

At Udi's suggestion my talk, which he translated, was little more than an exhortation in praise of the fine spirit which the group had shown and a suggestion to the members that they work even harder. But at the end of the meeting the head of the group approached me with a grimy piece of paper in his hand. It had obviously been torn out of a ledger and to judge from its appearance its preparation had been a labor of many hours. It was the thanks of the group for the talk I had given, written in a bewildering and pitiful English, but it was also a sort of credo for the group, a statement of the philosophy which had brought them together.

In a halting hand and through a welter of erasures, this is what I was able to make out:

An humble address—

It is a greatest pleasure to us that the supreme soul of America, a country thousands of miles away from this country, has arrived to our place presumably in our community which is most backward in all respects of human civilization. The supreme soul though born in America and fully studied each and every heart of his country is not satisfied of it, because in my humble opinion one who is born in this world, would have his motto that he is born for the goodness of others accordingly, the supreme soul who has done his sacred duties in his country, has decided himself that his duties in his own country is not worth considerable when there is a biggest part of the world outside his country, and hence it is his bounden duty to serve for other countries in the world.

I on behalf of our community, humbly offer my hearty thanks to the supreme soul of America for having arrived amidst us a poorest and backward community to study the pitiable conditions of the community. This institution has to learn many more things. I humbly thank the supreme soul of America for offering his valuable advices to us.

Yours most obediently
P. D. Kundulkar
President

I must confess that I read it with mixed emotions. There was the peculiar phraseology and the awkward grammar, and in spite of the fact that all eyes were upon me, it was all I could do to restrain a smile. And yet, as I read further I began to realize that this was not just an experiment in pidgin English but an experiment in another respect as well, an experiment in a new and foreign kind of thinking. It was the earliest and most inexpert attempt of a people to grasp the strange idea of equality, the ludicrous, pitiful, wonderful first effort of the untouchables of Shadur to assert their humanity. Couched though it was in terms of humility, this was essentially a demand for recognition, and for all of the confusion in the run-on sentences, there was an unquestionable seriousness and integrity here. When I finished reading I began to feel sorry for the condescending and self-satisfied tone of my speech. If the truth be known, the supreme soul of America was perhaps just a little ashamed of himself.

[39]

"A SHIP!"

It was early in the morning when the watchers on the beach first cried the sail of the trader that plies up and down the Kanara Coast bringing fishhooks and cloth and bangles from Trivandrum. The beach was crowded, for the arrival of the trader is always an important event in Shadur. But this morning it was important for me as well, for I had decided to ship south rather than continuing by myself.

Standing from the shore, the ship seemed enormous; actually it was no heavier than the local country craft, but I learned later that the trader was a converted Arab dow and that it loomed large because of its ungainly lines. It was built for hard use in inadequate ports and at the moment it was driving through the heavy surf where it would be run aground at the flow of the tide to be left high and dry at the ebb. After a few hours of trading on its sloping decks the sea would come in to float it again and, its business completed, the trader would sail on to another village and another high tide.

Udi had promised that he would be able to arrange my passage. The captain, he told me, was a friend of his and there would be no trouble at all in getting me aboard for a very moderate sum. The ship would be touching at almost every small village, so progress would be exceedingly slow, he warned me. But the prospect nevertheless appealed to me and I hoped there would be no objection from the captain of the trader.

There wasn't. Within an hour of the time the ship grounded, Udi had completed all the necessary arrangements and I had collected my clothes and my few possessions and loaded them into one of the holds of the ship. I knew that I would have to live on deck since there were no quarters at all for crew or captain, but the prospect of this did not seem so bad, so when the trader left Shadur I was ensconced on the foredeck.

I discovered that traveling by country craft could be quite pleasant. For the first day the sea continued relatively calm and by trimming the sail till the ship heeled well over, we were able to beat a fast course down the coast. Since we were homeward bound there were not so many stops as Udi had feared and I had hoped; and on the average we put in just once a day, and then for a matter of a half hour or an hour.

The commerce of the trader was largely in cloth. At each village that we touched we were swarmed by the women, for this was the one commodity that could not be made locally, though in general the Kanarese were self-sufficient. By order the ship would also secure certain chemicals that were used in the staining of nets. Chief among them was something that looked like tanbark; a whole afterhatch was loaded with this. In each village, of course, the children were irrepressible.

239

They would swim out to the ship while it was miles offshore so that by the time we were near enough to hail the land, they were swarming in the masts and rigging like ships' rats. On the beach, our arrival was a signal for festivities only barely falling short of a religious fair, for the trader was the only link of these villages with the interior of the country and the news from there.

What was most interesting was that overseas news came first. Africa and Arabia, even Europe and America seemed somehow to be closer than Delhi and Mussoorie to the average coastal villager. I commented on this to the captain, I remember, but he saw nothing peculiar at all about it. "After all," he told me, "they are connected by water. The inland is separated by miles of land."

Ordinarily in each village we would be served tea and sweets. The relationship between the crew members and the villagers was good and it was not unusual for the whole ship's company to be invited ashore for a village feast. But it was seldom that we could take advantage of these offers, for the schedule of the tides was firm and inflexible and unless we wished to lay over a whole day, we had to be off when they gave the word.

Yet even at sea I found conditions quite pleasant. I discovered on the first day that in addition to me there were three other passengers who were sharing the deck space, two Maharashtrian nuns from a South Indian convent and an old Belgian priest, all bound for Calicut. We were a peculiar company, but the monsoons were nearing and the coastwise steamers had suspended their schedules. Apparently the nuns and the priest, like myself, were accustomed to whatever transportation was available.

The old priest was a veritable religious patriarch. Beneath a classic head of white hair, his face was the face of a fourth-century saint, as gnarled and seamed as the bole of an old thorn tree. His chin jutted out at a dramatic angle and his mouth was sunk in, for he had no teeth, and when he opened his lips to speak, it was as though the words echoed out of a wind-hollowed cave. Three times, the nuns told me, his order had appropriated funds so that he could have a denture made. But three times he had found better uses for the money—some charity that needed the precise amount. He was reserved and distant when I first approached him; our racial kinship impressed him not at all. But eventually, by dint of a labored campaign, I managed to establish a friendly footing. I discovered then that he was not at all what he seemed, for actually he had a subtle and delightful sense of humor. Nor was he overly impressed by the dignity of his office; even I was occasionally surprised by his sallies. I remember one morning when the sea was running high and the nuns were unable to keep down their breakfasts. By turns they were telling their rosaries, sucking on limes, and turning to vomit over the stern. The incongruous process amused Father Leonard. Reclining on my bedding he turned to remark, "Ach! Poor women. They cannot stay well, even with the help of three sweet limes and the Virgin Mary."

Most often his conversation was serious. Father Leonard's humor was of the deep, sustaining kind and he did not spend it lavishly in light conversation when it was so essential to his philosophy and to the work he was doing. He was a Jesuit, I discovered, and most of his life had been spent in organizing churches in South India, though he was now retired to a school for young priests where he was a teacher and a counselor. He talked almost constantly of his village parishes and of the troubles he had encountered in his work among them; it was clear that he was far from reconciled to the life of relative inactivity on a South Indian mountaintop. When he found I was not unsympathetic he even discussed the more personal aspects of his work—doubts he had felt in his younger years and his growing impatience with Hinduism. I could not help comparing him in my mind to those missionaries whom I had met occasionally in my own travels. Being a Protestant, the comparison was embarrassing I felt, for Father

241

Leonard was so completely and unreservedly dedicated. I had never been very much impressed to date by the sacrifice the members of my own church were making, for their isolation was a rather precious thing replete with jeeps and electric refrigerators, to say nothing of their jaunts to the hills during the hot season when their parishes agonized on the boiling plains. Father Leonard was obviously a different type; he was his own monument to years of unflagging service, for though the lines of pain were etched deep in his features, he had the enthusiasm and the strength of a man of thirty.

Many days we spent in talking together, while the hours and the miles slipped quietly past, all sense of time and distance seeming dulled by the lovely monotony of ship-board life. From some chips of wood that I found on the deck I managed to carve out a rude set of chess men. After that we spent a good deal of time in an inexpert competition that amused the sailors.

And yet time was passing. Once in a while, at night, I would lie awake listening to the waves on our hull and reflect that in just a matter of days we would be putting into Calicut. Calicut as a place was not important to me, but it was the end of this lazy and relaxed existence, the beginning once more of riding in carts and drinking bad water and frying in the heat. Until now I had never felt sorry for myself, but I suspected I was close to that state of mind, for the prospect of returning to the inland villages gave me a frightened feeling, and I tried not to think of it. Until now I had been able to travel on my nerves, eager for anything that presented itself. What was it, I wondered, that made me feel now so tired and hesitant about continuing through Tamilnad?

I took stock of myself. Physically I was all right, though the strain had been more than I ever anticipated. I had lost weight, perhaps twenty or twenty-five pounds, and I had suffered from the usual tropical complaints. Often these nights I felt a tautness in my stomach and running my fingers over the margin of the abdomen I would wince with the sudden pain that it caused, but then I had known long ago that I had contracted amoebic dysentery. It was surprising what a dispassionate view I could take. Somehow I judged everything in terms of my plans, and sickness was now no cause for personal alarm. It was just a question of how long the machinery would hold out.

My nerves were perhaps in less perfect condition. I had noticed that the isolation had taken its toll. I had been too long living under the strain of a foreign language, of a foreign culture, of foreign viewpoints. For one thing, I knew that I laughed too easily and that after laughing I often had to hold back the tears, for all my emotions seemed to run together into strange spasms of feeling, undifferentiated and meaningless. Father Leonard had noticed it too and once, when I laughed too hard at a quip of his, he laid his hand on my shoulder, and smiling, said, "One has to learn to relax in this country."

Yet the problem was still there. What was it, I wondered, that I dreaded so to face at Calicut? It was not just the heat or the dusty roads, or more contaminated food or questionable water, nor was it returning to the discomforts of day-to-day living among a people to whom, in the last analysis, I was alien.

No, the truth, I decided, was that I dreaded once more becoming emotionally involved in the villagers' problems. I dreaded the large-scale feelings which one is able to avoid so successfully in a more modern society. From the beginning I had been entirely unable to maintain a self-possessed attitude, to stand outside of the things I had seen and study all with a cold, detached gaze. I had been drawn, again and again, into the vortex of hates and loves and sympathies and fears; in my own small way I had recapitulated too closely the primitive sensations of my primitive environment.

Now my fears became tangible, for I had accurately diagnosed them, and I wondered if I must actually go through

243

it again, detesting the bania, sympathizing with the cultivator, sorrowing for the woman who dies in childbirth. You
were spared nothing in Asia. That was the trouble. You lived
knee deep in life's most horrid realities. Oppression was not
a word that was used by union men living in inadequate
two-bedroom houses. It was the right of life and death over
the villagers that is exercised by some hereditary zemindars.
It was famines and leprosy and inhuman wickedness. It was
blood and death and violence.

In the night when I would think of this I would toss on
my bedroll and shut my eyes, hoping for sleep. But it was
as if the shore were reaching out to meet me, for the presence
of it all became almost palpable.

Yet, I was not even tempted to run away, to flee to the
cities, to abandon this last journey. The fact was, there were
conflicting feelings about it all, and among them there was
some intangible compulsion to go on. To begin with, this
compulsion seemed as vague as my fears, like some dim and
intuitional migratory instinct, yet it too had its logical explanation and was founded in the experiences I had already
had.

Most important, there were questions that I still wanted
answered. If I could have asked the questions that would
have served just as well, for in this case, formulating the problem was almost equivalent to finding the solution for it.
Questions and answers, problems and solutions, hatred and
anger and fear and affection. If only I could leave them all
alone and stay on this boat where everything was simple!

My feelings were not new ones. As a matter of fact, they
were virtually indistinguishable from that universal desire
to retreat from all of the unpleasantness of life and see only
that which is cheerful and encouraging. No, my feelings were
not new. They were as old as the wish to run away from
what we cannot solve. They were simply the temptation to
flee from a situation that tested the value of my basic optimism. For somehow I knew that South India was the arena

where all the forces of history would be brought together, the spirit of tradition and the spirit of change appearing in their most dramatic and most violent contrast. Even now I could feel a tightening of the diaphragm, a visceral dread that I had known before. My sleep was light and I would awake at a sound with all my senses poised for some emergency. As the days went by it even became harder for me to concentrate on my chess playing or my talks with Father Leonard, for more and more I was lapsing into a protective silence, creating a defensive shell around myself.

Yet there was a sadness, too, a sadness that I must leave the beauty and the peace of the coastal section, for though I had just come to realize it, the whole month that I spent there had been a vacation from the physical and emotional rigors of traveling through the inland regions. The climate had been cool and the scenery beautiful, but more than that the people had been happy and there had not been the constant demands on my sympathy that every day in Kathiawar or Maharashtra had presented.

I realized this especially on the day that we landed. It was all I could do to leave the beach. I remembered the struggle that had been necessary to reach it and I hated even to think of turning inland again. I knew that once there I would be eager enough, but even knowing that did not help me to shake off the torpor, and though I cursed myself for a sentimentalist, still I lingered on the beach almost the whole afternoon.

In the evening I went back for one last look. It was the time of day that I had first seen the sea and as on that first day, the oblique rays of the sunset were turning its surface to a gold lamé. It was a deserted section of beach I had chosen. Just one old man was fishing in the surf, standing knee deep in the water, and clad only in the customary little pouch. Slowly and evenly he was casting his net and drawing it to him with quick, strong motions. The whole process seemed more like some ritual dance than a realistic attempt at netting fish. I would have sworn he had not seen me, and yet suddenly he turned and came walking back to the water's edge, holding before him a large, fat mahseer, leaping and glistening in his net. As he showed it to me he did not say a word; it was as if he sensed the mood of the moment. Then he stepped around me and walked up the beach to disappear in the darkness behind the palm trees.

I cannot say why, but this simple action filled me with a sudden and almost painful sorrow, a peculiar blending of beauty and misery that I was entirely at a loss to understand. But I turned and followed the fisherman's footprints. The sun was almost completely down now and I knew it would be many months before I would look at the Arabian Sea again.

Tamilnad

Tamilnad

[40]

THE term "South India" is a misleading one. It is the name that is used in casual conversation to indicate the whole of Tamil India, from the borders of Hyderabad to the tip of the peninsula. It is misleading because it seems to suggest something as simple and clear as a geographic division, while anyone who has ever traveled in South India knows that that area is a great deal more than that.

Accurately considered, South India is not simply or even primarily a matter of boundaries. It is a separate culture from the rest of India, a different race, a distinct set of languages. In a nation in which regional pride is common, the pride of the Tamil in Tamilnad is uncommon, for to him the whole population of the country north of the Kistna River consists of interlopers.

Strictly speaking, there is no early history of the Tamils. Researchers have shown them to be the land's first inhabitants, but the period of their tenure is so incredibly ancient that even its approximate dates are hard to establish. It is known that their ancestors, the ancient Dravidians, roamed the country as far north as Rajputana and from the ruins that they left at Mohenjo-Dero, it can be deduced that they were far from a primitive people. But even the present Tamils, their pure descendants, can add little to the incomplete picture of their rule, for the very definition of that early society seems to permit no inquiry; it is the "pre-Sanskrit India."

Racially, the people of South India are Dravidians. The origins of their group can only be guessed at, but the guesses that have been made by the best-informed anthropologist suggest that they were once closely allied to the Africans. At some early period, these scientists claim, the parent stock came down from the Near East in a great migration that divided at the Red Sea, one half populating Africa, the other half India. There are some obvious physiological arguments for this theory in the broad noses and lips of the present South Indians. And while there has been some intermixture and pollution from the north, the majority of the Tamils are dark and curly haired.

The Tamil language is an anomaly too. Unlike almost all of the languages to the north, it dates much further back than Sanskrit itself, the basis for Hindustani, and most of the others. There is one offshoot of it in Malayalum, but both languages are still very closely identified, possessing a grammar and a pronunciation that are extremely difficult for a Westerner to master. It has been argued that Tamil is the world's oldest language, but it disputes this distinction with the Near Eastern tongues. How old it is can nevertheless be appreciated from the fact that it predates even the oldest Hindu scripture. Of early Aryan history there are at least the poetic and questionable accounts of the Vedas and the Upanishads, but of the Dravidian people even those early texts can only speculate on ancient beginnings.

However, in later years, the history of the Dravidians is all too clear and definite, for it is a history of decline from a ruling power to virtual exile in one corner of their early domain. As successive invasions entered India from the north, the Dravidians were driven ever farther south, and even later, when the rest of India was assimilating, they were still barricaded and hostile behind the Kistna River. Today South India is no longer hostile, but she is conscious of her separate history and traditions. Nor is it easy for anyone who visits South India to forget that here is a separate nation.

Even the most casual observer will notice immediately the cultural differences between south and north. In Tamilnad there is an entirely different tradition in temple architecture and in the other arts. Nor is this the subtle difference that one is apt to find from one area in the north to another next to it. It is a complete and striking cultural disconformity, an enormous block fault of philosophy and aesthetics. It is in the south, for example, that you see those temples which in the West are considered typical of all India, hundreds of feet high and built of solid rock, intricately carved over every square inch. They are monuments to slave labor, but they are magnificently done, for the South Indian gods are real fire-eating dragons, entirely unlike the overly refined Sivas and Vishnus of farther north. There is something terrifying about a South Indian temple, a fanaticism which frightens the unbeliever. It is decadent perhaps, but there is a frantic quality which makes the conventionalities of the north seem trivial. The temples at Madura and Rameswaram are enormous pylons crawling with life, their gods killing and wooing, copulating and dying in monstrous heaps of frenzied stone. A Gujarat friend once confessed to me that even he felt ill at ease in these South Indian temples, where the gods of plague and smallpox were worshipped and where the bloody Kali was ensconced in majesty. The whole temper of the religion was different here. There was something threatening and moody about it, as if some ghost of the old Dravidian society were haunting the temples and mixing with the priesthood.

In the countryside, there are differences of religion too. For one thing, the taboos against meat were not observed as rigorously as they were in the north, except of course in the case of the Brahmin caste. At one of the first villages I visited in Tamilnad a cultivator was blessing a well he had just built by tearing off the head of a chicken with his hands and rubbing the bloody neck along the pivot. It was a thing which could not have happened in Maharashtra, where the protection of life is the duty of all castes, but here it was countenanced by the very priesthood, representatives of which were taking part in the ceremony. I was later to discover that throughout South India there is a large element of superstition mixed in with religion, the temple priests doing a land-office business in magic talismans and secret potions. In Virudhunagar I visited a temple where one priest sold an ointment to enlarge the linga while another, even more ambitious it seemed, sold a draught which would enable one to live forever.

But these are only the most dramatic cases. What was more typical of Tamilnad was the constant presence of a degenerate priesthood that begged alms for spells and incantations, a company of metaphysical odd-jobs men. The status of most of them was extremely doubtful, but then the definitions of priesthood are so loose and indefinite that even though few of them could write their own names, the villagers were afraid to deny their claims.

These parasites were everywhere, dressed in the saffron garments which apparently gave them the right to defecate anywhere, to sit in the bazaar idly scratching their testicles or searching for fleas in their pubic hair. They were as ill kempt as animals, their hair being matted into greasy plaits literally inches thick, and yet they claimed the most fantastic privileges from the villagers and, worse to say, got them. It was a religion gone mad that these wanderers exemplified, a religion devoid of rules or reason where the dogma had become so blind and unquestioning that anything that was claimed was automatically yielded. There was resentment against the ignorant old fakirs and even the legitimate priesthood spoke mildly against them. Yet it was not safe to encourage too critical an attitude, for the Brahmins well realized this might lead anywhere. It was better for them to offer their protection to anything that claimed the sanction of religion than to start a chain of reasoning which, once begun, might even undermine their own position. The result of this was all too clear. The distinction between the real and the spurious had broken down, with no one willing to draw

a line and say that this was orthodox and that was not. Senya-
sis, fakirs, religious pilgrims, all of them claimed something
of the status of the priesthood, and because they were so
numerous and had so much influence, no one would dare
to deny them.

I could not help thinking of the statues of Ganesh, the elephant god who rides upon a mouse. What a perfect parallel
it was to the conditions that exist today in the Hinduism of
Tamilnad!

Yet the tragedy is, the abuse does not stop at the level of
the Senyasi and the itinerate fakir. It continues, politically
and economically, through the intricate and inflexible caste
structure. Nowhere in India does caste have such importance
as it does through the villages of Tamilnad, for the relaxation that has been noticed in the north and west has simply
not begun in the south.

In the south, it is still the law of the village that an untouchable may not enter the Brahmin section unless he has
been sent on some specific errand, and even then he is bound
to keep to the roadway. Under no circumstances can he enter
the house or even the courtyard of a Brahmin home. All
intercourse between the two extremes must be carried on by
a representative from the intermediary castes. The temples
themselves are closed to harijans, though by law this exclusion is not permitted; since private temples are excluded
from the regulation, a great many of the South Indian temples have become "private."

But the untouchables are few. What is even more dramatic
is the total subjection of the Sudra caste. This is the lowest
caste that is actually recognized, for the untouchables are
considered not to exist. The majority of the Sudras are tenant
farmers, working for a quarter or a third of their crop, the
majority of it going to the Brahmin zemindar or to the bania
who happens to own the land. The society is therefore almost
entirely feudal and in practice it is the habit of the banias
and zemindars to speak casually among themselves of "my

villages" and to refer to the people who live there as "my cultivators." It is not a careless form of speech at all. The fact is, the landowner exercises precisely the same rights as the landowner in tenth- or eleventh-century France, whatever the government or its leaders may say. Since the Brahmins control all the petty courts there is no recourse at all for a recalcitrant Sudra, for to be accused by a Brahmin is almost to be convicted of any crime regardless of evidence. Moreover, since the very livelihood of the Sudra depends on employment by one or another landowner, he often submits to fantastic punishments rather than face the loss of his employment and his house. In the paddy fields in upper Madras the flogging of workmen is not unheard of; though such a thing is clearly "illegal," legalities mean little to a starving villager. It is not that the villagers are wholly intimidated. It is rather that there is no reasonable outlet for their frustrations—a Brahmin house burned, an overseer killed, these are the forms that their protest must take.

Yet it is precisely this that makes South India both the center of orthodoxy and the center of rebellion. Everywhere else there are certain social "safety valves" but here the safety valves have all been tied down. There is a tension and uneasiness that one is able to sense beneath the external peace of this section, a presence of fierce hatreds, a capacity for violence that exceeds that of any other people in India. Even as early as my first few weeks in Tamilnad I knew that if there were ever any large-scale revolution, it would not take place in the Gujarat or in Maharashtra. It would originate here among the harijans and Sudras. It was incredible, but the Brahmins never seemed to realize this. They spoke often to me of the happiness of their cultivators, citing it as a proof that "the old order" was best, that the radicalism of the north could lead only to misery. I asked once or twice whether these same Brahmins had not noticed the hammer and sickles that were chalked in their courtyards. Invariably they would laugh and say it was just a joke. And I really think they believed that it was.

Yet communism in South India is not a joke. To the government in Delhi it is a serious enough matter to justify the imprisonment of thousands of villagers who have been accused of organizing riots and strikes. The Socialists too have a strong following in the south and their sign, a cane knife crossed over a cogwheel, is displayed in every town in Tamilnad and in at least a third of the villages as well. It is not really that the South Indians are so politically conscious. They are conscious only of their own grinding poverty and of the system of organized exploitation that prevents them from ever rising above it. But they are willing to listen to anyone who offers a realistic program of land reform and they are willing to call themselves members of any party that sponsors the overthrow of the zemindar class. So far, communism has been more urban than rural, Madura being the scene of its greatest successes, but it is inevitable that the token organization of the Communists should be able to serve the villagers too. Essentially their successes have consisted of giving a name to a faction already in existence and in providing a rationale of revolution to a revolution already in prospect. Yet the effect is the same. Throughout South India the best young minds are being tempted by communism because it is almost the only political doctrine that stands for equal rights for all castes. It is not that they have actually chosen communism, but that every other party has simply ignored them or offered them nothing but sentimental platitudes as reasonable and as unsatisfactory as those of the British. The last straw, perhaps, was when Nehru abandoned the Socialist cause when he came to power. Until then he had been almost an idol to the villagers. It was a disillusionment of major proportions. This disillusionment was not peculiar to South India; it had caused unrest in every section, but its political importance was magnified here where there was already such an enormous social maladjustment.

255

Yet this talk of revolutions could possibly be misleading. Actually there were no obvious signs at all, but that was just the trouble; the status quo was so entirely inflexible that there was no room for adjustments. In Maharashtra the balance of power could shift and it did, from day to day in each village. But here the social system had been deadlocked for generations on precisely the same terms. I had the feeling that if anything changed, everything must, that if one cultivator in one village managed to obtain a concession, that event would immediately disturb the scale and unbalance the whole economy of the countryside.

I had not been wrong when I had anticipated that in Tamilnad the problems which are common to all of India would be presented in an appreciably sharper focus, the forces better defined, the issues clearer. Getting from one place to another was easy; everyone travels by bullock cart in the south, but there were other problems less easily surmounted than finding transportation, I now discovered.

For one thing, I found that in South India it is harder to walk into a village unknown and unexpected and strike up an acquaintance with the local patel and beg food and lodging from him. The Tamil villagers are a little more suspicious and, while they can be pleasant enough when they conclude one is harmless, a great many fears seem to go through their minds before they are willing to arrive at that conclusion. It is natural, I suppose. At any rate it is in keeping with the general suspense and uneasiness of the region, but nevertheless it made it extremely difficult for me to get more than a passing knowledge of most villages.

The language problem was less serious than I had expected. Hindustani was virtually useless in the south, but in about two out of every three villages that I visited I found officials or ex-soldiers who spoke surprisingly good English. A greater difficulty lay in convincing the Tamils that I was not a spy for the Brahmins or zemindars, for my race, of course, made me suspect from the first and the questions that I asked only completed the picture.

One of the first things I discovered was that I could not associate both with the landowning class and with the cultivators themselves. If I so much as asked directions at a zemindar's estate, I was marked automatically as an agent of his. Inversely, if I traveled in a Sudra's cart, I was dependent on this caste for all of my needs, for the news of my associations would have gone before me and spoiled my chances with the higher castes. In practice, however, this did not make much difference, for as a foreigner and non-Hindu I was unclean in any case, and even on those rare occasions when I was entertained in a Brahmin house I would be fed on the veranda. After a few such experiences I avoided the Brahmins and kept as much to the villagers as possible, but this did not work any great hardship on me, for it was the latter who interested me most anyway.

[41]

ONCE again from Calicut I traveled by bullock cart, this time with a caravan of jute farmers and traders who had brought a cargo to the port a few days earlier and were now returning to Pahghat and Trichur. Our course wound roughly in a southeastern direction, following the pass over the Nilgiri foothills, through paddy and cane, jute and gram that grew in abundance to the edges of the roadway.

The beauty of this country rose from its very order. There was nothing of the wild and natural scenery that I had encountered on my trip through the Mysore forests; just the opposite, here there was an air of discipline as if even the seasons were kept to their schedule. The holdings were either very small or very large, depending on whether they were tenant or farmer owned, but there was a certain uniform standard of efficiency that seemed to suggest some master plan. From the occasional low rise one was able to view the highly intricate and elaborate system of wells and reservoirs, chutes and spillways that directed the water on its complicated course. Moreover, there seemed to be no fallow land, no forgotten corners or intentional pathways. The ground was laid out with the precision of a checkerboard, one crop growing directly up against the next.

I was pleasantly surprised. After Kanara I had expected that any landscape would seem barren and depressing, particularly the south, where I knew from my reading that the standard of living was abysmally low. Yet, however poor the cultivators might have been, I was first of all impressed by the richness of the land, for it was apparent that whatever poverty might exist would not be the result of a poverty of the soil. Instead of the sandy plains of the north, the ground sloped away in almost constant greenery, a few bare patches that had been recently plowed presenting a moist and rich brown loam. Almost all the roads were lined with trees, neems, and peepuls, and the fragrant tamarinds, so that traveling was almost cool and comfortable, even at noon and in the hottest hours.

The whole atmosphere of the country was different because of this. In the north, the picture that one was apt to get was of a landscape overpopulated and yet somehow still wild, crawling with life yet paradoxically primitive. Here, on the other hand, there was a sense of order, not just of the land but of the very people on it, the evidence of a system and a social discipline which, however unjust, was striking in itself. I noticed that wherever there were contiguous small holdings there would usually be just one well to irrigate several fields, with some co-operative system for drawing the water that saved time and expense for all concerned. Frequently too there would be some community provision for the thrashing of all of the various grain crops, one central pit where the whole thing could be done rather than in the dooryard of each farmer's house. On the large estates things had progressed even further and once or twice I noticed electric well pumps. But here I had a harder time working up enthusiasm, for these estates rested virtually on a foundation of slavery.

But that was precisely the paradox of the south. It seemed the richest and most efficiently farmed land in India and yet the people that it supported had less to eat than even the tribesmen of the Kathiawar wastes. The whole picture was different. This was not marginal land; even its dense population it could easily support if the division of its yield had been anything like equal or if the inequalities had simply been less. Yet the poverty of the people had taken a terrible toll. For generations this whole segment of the human race had been bred to the most atrociously substandard conditions until now, like white mice, they were accommodating to it. I have literally measured the girth of my arm and compared it to the thigh of Madrasi farmers. In almost every case my arm was bigger, sometimes by a matter of two or three inches.

The average pay for field labor in Madras is eight annas, sixteen cents a day, and since it is seasonal work, at every zemindar's village you see dozens, sometimes hundreds, fighting for this wage. The food of the South Indian is generally rice and pepper water; in good times some dal, a mashed pulse, is added, but to counteract this there are months in the year when famine can be expected almost regularly.

While I was talking with some of the caravan drivers, I learned that we were in the midst of a famine now. "Not a big famine when everyone dies," they explained, "but a little one that kills children and weak old men."

They pointed out its more obvious effects, the sunken eyes and the swollen bellies, the children and the old women lying by the roadway, too listless to brush the flies from their lips. In one village particularly the ravages were terrible. The worst effects were to be noticed in the children. One woman brought a sick baby for me to look at that was swollen with malnutrition till her flesh was like putty. I pressed my finger into the skin of her ankle and the impression stayed there for nearly five minutes. There was nothing much that could be done at this stage, but I gave her some milk powder that had been lying in my pack. Peculiarly enough the same woman had a son of about two years who seemed perfectly healthy. It was not hard to see that she had been forced to make a conscious choice between the two children. The drivers agreed that this was the case when I asked them about it, and they went further than that. "It is the sensible thing to do," they agreed. "Better lose the girl than lose them both."

Yet in general they were quite dispassionate about the whole thing. I was surprised that they did not show more concern for these starving villagers, whose fate they might share if something should happen to cut their small wage. But I suppose they had seen too much of starvation to be seriously impressed by it in a strange community. Almost all of them had lost two or three children of their own of "the usual things that children die of."

As we worked farther inland, conditions seemed worse. As my drivers had explained, this was not "a big famine." It was almost a regular yearly affair and could be discounted by them without much thought. But each night when we stopped, the local villagers would gather silently about our caravan, standing at a distance while the drivers cooked their food, then approaching abjectly when we had finished eating. They did not seem even particularly excited or distraught. They were like the lean and servile village pye-dogs who come slinking up with their tails between their legs only to turn and run if you made a move toward them. Mostly there were old men with the bandy legs and the swollen little bellies of the constantly underfed, at once aloof and distinguishable from the professional beggars who would crowd about us clawing at our clothing. Usually when the plates had all been scraped out they would be invited to come and eat what they could find, but even then they would approach more timidly than hungrily to divide a half chapatty or a smear of dal.

One of the most surprising things I noticed in these villages was that there were so few outward signs that a famine was in progress. In the bazaars the shops were stacked with food, and sticky sweets were being sold on every corner. The contrast between the castes was enormous, of course. In the Brahmin section there was no misery at all; there life was carried on as serenely as ever without a doubt or a suspicion of guilt. In the temple grounds foods were left as offerings, as usual, before the gods. In some villages these foods were later distributed, but in many they were simply thrown away.

Yet if there were signs of resentment or threats of rebellion I must confess that my eye was not sharp enough to catch them, for instead of any organized, responsible protest, the energies of the rebellious seemed dissipated in petty thefts. Every once in a while a zemindar's house would be broken into and its storeroom ransacked, or a shop in the bazaar would have its padlocks smashed and a few maunds of grain would be missing the next morning. But in general this violence was so scattered and misdirected that the authorities simply branded it the work of dacoits and, while a few hungry villagers might have food the next day, no essential difference in their position resulted.

I wondered then and I have wondered later what it was that prevented a more wholesale outbreak. After all, it would be the easiest thing in the world to take the entire bazaar by storm. For that matter, even violence would not be necessary if the cultivators of the section simply declared their independence, for the whole Indian Army would not be foolish enough to march on such a mob, let alone the police.

And yet they preferred to starve, not for want of food, for food there was in great abundance, but simply for want of the money to buy what would otherwise be shipped somewhere else and sold. It was incredible. A whole country intimidated by tradition, emasculated by a twisted religious law, deprived of its very will to live by an elaborately rotten social code. It was like Gulliver staked out on the ground by Lilliputians, his body crisscrossed by thousands of threads, yet it was even more fantastic because in Gulliver's case the threads had been real while these were imaginary.

Rather it was a phenomenon of mass hypnosis, perpetrated on a whole class over a period of generations, a constant suggestion of inferiority and guilt that had worked its way deep into the subconscious of a nation. I wondered where one would draw the line between the religious and secular aspects of village life. Any distinction at all would be purely imaginary for the very word *secular* has no meaning in India. The whole thing was an enormous Gordian knot, the strands all woven inextricably together. Perhaps, I thought, Alexander had been right. Perhaps the sword was the only solution.

At any rate I was glad that I wasn't in a position where I might be expected to offer a reasonable alternative. It was much easier, I decided, to by-pass these issues and concentrate on the problems of my day-to-day traveling.

[42]

MY MOST immediate problem was finding a new means of transportation from a village called Devikolam. It was here, after about two hundred miles of traveling, that the caravan had finally come to a halt. It was early May but already the monsoons were beginning to blow in from the Arabian Sea, and I knew that I had only a month at best before the rains began with a vengeance.

Outside of Devikolam I made contact with a band of pilgrims bound for the Madura temples. All roads in South India seem to lead to Madura; though officially Madras is the headquarters of the Presidency, it is Madura that was the seat of the Dravidian kingdoms and the holy city of the Tamil Hindu. It is one of those Indian towns that seem to have escaped the advances of Western civilization, but whether for reasons of convenience or in obedience to the traditions, the British never were very much in evidence here. Like Surat in the Gujarat and Satara in Maharashtra, Madura is wholly an Indian city, which is to say, it is not a city at all, but an enormous, sprawling, oversized village.

In May the great pilgrimage is well under way. From every village and town in South India a stream of sadhus and religious penitents is pouring over the roads toward the Meenakshi temple. Brahmins and untouchables, rich men and poor, the stumbling blind and the withered sick, take to the roads that lead to Madura as if impelled by some curious migratory instinct. In later years a few weak souls have begun to travel by bus or train, but since this violates all of the religious laws, the traditional majority will have nothing to do with them. On these pilgrimages even the Brahmins must walk, begging their food from the villages they pass through, for the pilgrimage is intended as a humiliating experience and it is from this that its spiritual good derives. In practice, caste is still strongly observed, for a Brahmin inevitably will beg only from Brahmins, but even as a bare nod in the direction of equality, the pilgrimages are uniquely democratic in Hinduism.

The group that I joined was from the Malabar Coast. The majority of its members were Brahmins and Vaisyas, but they were accompanied by a retinue of lower-caste villagers who, for all practical purposes, had come as servants. The leader of the caravan was an old senyasi, a priest retired to the life of contemplation, but since his resources were entirely of the spiritual sort, two young brothers had taken charge of the more practical problems. The band had already been traveling for two weeks and it was still seventy or eighty miles from Madura, but the morale seemed to be breaking down so rapidly that I was in doubt whether we would ever reach it as a group. For one thing, the senyasi had laid down a series of far too rigid dietary laws so that everyone, including the old man himself, was forced into violating them secretly.

But still worse, the pilgrimage seemed to be composed of the most hopelessly antipathetic types possible, including everything from orthodox old banias to younger men of the most heretical disposition. There was scarcely a day that we did not have an argument over some obscure point of Hindu law, and unfortunately the senyasi himself was of such a peaceful disposition that he invariably fled from these wranglings.

I spent most of my time with one of the two brothers. He was a graduate of Benares Hindu University, who had recently come home after two years in the north and was making this trip to please his father. His heart didn't seem to be in the project, for to him it was just a long and rather boring walk, yet I owed him a great deal for it was through his good offices that I was permitted to join the band in the first place.

From Devikolam the pilgrimage worked gradually eastward, following the banks of the Vaigai River. At this time of year the river was no more than a trickle, cutting its course across the broad, sandy bed, but the Vaigai was no less holy for all this and several times a day we would stop to bathe. Moreover, occasionally we would detour inland to visit some notable village shrine, so it was not strange that with these various delays our progress seemed uncomfortably slow to me.

The countryside here was surprisingly dry. No rains had yet fallen and the soil was parched, the reserves having given out some time ago, leaving the crops in this section to wither. A few of the zemindars' wells were deep enough to permit at least some small-scale irrigation but the independent ryot, the community of cultivators, seemed once again on the verge of famine. Occasionally now we would meet on the road the desolate caravans from farther south. Word had come up of mass starvation in Tinnevelly and these were apparently the refugees from that area. Their clothes were gray with the dust of the roads and they were lame and blistered from the long trek they had made, but there was nothing here, no food or work, and so they would continue wandering vaguely to the north. As we passed them, they moved off to the side of the roads as befitted those of humbler caste, but there was no mistaking the enmity in their faces as they watched the well-fed "penitents" go by. In the whiteness of the sun their faces were like masks, shadows making deep wells of the eyes, but they were masks of a bitter and dissatisfied people and I always felt a little uncomfortable when we met them.

The local villagers were not much better off. In addition to their poverty and the extended drought, I learned that a number of local moneylenders had managed to buy up almost the entire rice crop. They were holding it, they said, against bad times to come, but just what constituted bad times was hard to decide when already there were thousands on the point of starvation and millions only a handful of grain away from it. In every village we would see the women scraping through the sand of the threshing floors, hoping to gather enough for a meal from the husks and the chaff that were mixed in with it. In one town I saw something even more dramatic, a single episode which symbolized the whole plight. A baby had crawled into the mouth of a rice jar that had been turned over on its side for the last few grains. She was crying there, and in the mouth of the jar her sobs were turned into something weird and terrible. Even the Brahmin pilgrims seemed a little unsettled by the strange booming cries of hunger and pain.

Near Madura conditions were a little bit better. Here there was more of a cash economy, for a number of families had sons in the mills who were able to send home a few rupees each month. Moreover, the mills had bought up much land, turning it back to the ryot at a nominal rent as a bribe for the cultivators' support and to provide a sort of "fire line" against the spread of communism.

Yet, paradoxically enough, it was near Madura that I first came in contact with village communism in force. There was even one whole village that had been won to the cause and had hoisted a red flag from its desecrated temple. The sight of it sent a chill down my back, not so much out of simple fear of revolution, for revolution by this time seemed a longed-for thing. It was the thought that the revolution was adopting these symbols.

With increasing frequency as we approached the city we found the hammer and sickle chalked on rocks; it was apparently not just a symbol of protest but a genuine assertion of Communist strength. In the villages a favorite place for it to appear was on the walls of the temples, or on the bodies of the gods. From the artistic point of view this was a sad desecration, but politically the challenge could not have been better placed.

Indeed, it was perfectly clear to me now that this was precisely the form that the struggle was assuming, religion, tradition, authority on one side, dissatisfaction, bitterness, and revolt on the other. It was fitting that it should be approaching its climax in Madura, the seat of the old South Indian kingdom. Its fortress had withstood a great many invasions. I wondered if it would be able to withstand the newest.

[43]

THE fact is, I was never to reach Madura. When we were less than two days' travel from the city I first got the news from the village grapevine that blasted all of my established plans. It had finally happened; about a hundred miles north a whole section of the countryside had revolted against the zemindars, and now one phrase was blowing south like the sparks of a forest fire: "Tanjore has struck!"

I made a quick calculation. It was about twenty-five miles

from our present location to Madura. From there it would be seventy or eighty more to the southern borders of the Tanjore district. By passing Madura I would save twenty miles, by traveling alone I would make far better time, so with no warning to anyone I dropped out of the pilgrimage and began scrambling around for some means of transportation.

This proved to be a harder job than I expected. In the first place, all normal transportation was suspended; the roads to the north were almost totally deserted with the carts and the caravans pinned down where they were. I tried to rent a pair of bullocks, but this seemed almost equally difficult, for as soon as I admitted I was heading for Tanjore, all my potential renters simply laughed and shook their heads. At last I went to a large jute plantation and bought two animals and a light traveling cart. Then recruiting the services of a local cultivator, I set out the day after the pilgrims had moved on.

The Tanjore district lies south of Madras about a hundred and fifty miles down the east coast. It is some thirty miles from the sea itself, not far from the mouth of the Coleroon River. Immensely wealthy in terms of land, it is a district that is controlled very largely by the zemindars, only a few handfuls of men owning all of the farms that it takes literally hundreds of thousands to work. The story was not clear but this much seemed definite: at the very moment when the crop was ripe the cultivators announced that it would rot in the fields if they did not receive half of everything that they harvested.

The daring of this strike was almost incredible, for to the zemindars one year's crop was just interest on an investment. To the cultivators themselves it was a whole year's food. They were literally gambling death by starvation. The entire countryside seemed to be holding its breath at the temerity which the cultivators of Tanjore had shown, and it was ob-

267

vious that their interest was more than academic. In an important sense, this was a test case.

My progress was slower than I had hoped it would be. I discovered after just a few hours on the road that the bullocks I had bought were old and weak and that it would be at least four days before I could get to Tanjore. I had no way of knowing whether this would be fast enough. I doubted that it would, for it seemed impossible that the cultivators could hold out even this length of time against all of the mobilized forces of the zemindars. It was maddening to plod along the roads at a pace much slower than I could have walked, but it was far too hot now for a long forced march, so I seemed to have no alternative course.

Now I noticed that the cultivators were interested in my presence. In each village I passed through I was an object of curiosity, for it was strange that I should be heading toward Tanjore. Ordinarily it was necessary for me to stop each evening to get grain and hay and to water the bullocks. Before, I had been dutifully ignored in the bazaars but now I was the center of raucous attention. I tried my best not to say too much, for I could already foresee a great many problems and I was anxious not to compound them by taking sides and incurring the wrath of one group or the other.

The fact is, even a hundred miles south of Tanjore the repercussions of the strike were readily felt. All the village police were alerted and in uniform, and almost every zemindar had hired guards. But try as I might I found it impossible to maintain my noncommittal position, for the villagers were unwilling even to give me water before ascertaining that I was not from the government. They were careful never to refuse directly, but in each village I found myself frustrated and confused till I finally sought out the village headman and explained to him that I was in sympathy with the strikers.

Still, my most difficult problem involved the police. I was about two days from Tanjore when the order went out that all traffic moving over the roads toward the town was to be stopped and rerouted around it. The government had apparently been taken unaware, but it was mobilizing its forces with remarkable speed, placing itself, as governments must, on the side of law and order, on the side of the zemindars. For a day and a half of my now-precious time I was detained at a village called Muttukotai, before I finally succeeded in bribing the police officer and insinuating myself behind the government blockade.

Once past the blockade the temper of the people was obviously and decisively different. Here the zemindars, rather than making a show of force, were trying to make themselves as inconspicuous as possible. The whole balance of power was different. The support of the strikers was no longer tacit. Every village was hung with bright red streamers and collections of grain were being taken in the bazaars. I confess I began to be a little bit nervous, for the whole area was in a state of anarchy and while there was little violence there was even less assurance that the whole countryside would not suddenly go up in smoke.

The rumors kept filtering in. The government was preparing to send in troops. The strike had been won, the strike had been lost. The Communists had seized control of the town. Actually remarkably little had changed. This disruption was almost entirely psychological, but that was precisely the most dangerous kind of disruption in a country in such a delicate balance as South India. What had happened really was that a handful of farmers had dared defy the traditional powers, yet the effect of that upon the people who heard of it was almost equivalent to a declaration of war.

I could understand why the government was so concerned with keeping the uprisings generally secret. It was the idea itself that was the greatest danger, regardless of the outcome of this particular strike. Guns you could seize and men you could arrest, but something more important than either was involved in this case. The whole idea of the immutability of

269

the old order had been called into question by the strikers at Tanjore.

The chain of events had already begun. There was no reason why, coincidental with the strike, there should be uprisings in many of the surrounding villages, yet as I neared Tanjore these uprisings were beginning. Whole estates were turning on their zemindars and driving them off of their land with hoes and shovels. Even the police were keeping very largely to their houses, for they knew they were powerless if they provoked the issue. There was very little rioting on a wholesale scale, but it was clear that the cultivators were ruling the district. Probably things would have been considerably more exciting if anyone had been fool enough to challenge that rule.

Just outside of Tanjore I was stopped again. This time it was by an informal militia of the Kisans, the leftist organization that had organized the strike. This time bribery was no solution. Technically there was no breach of the peace in Tanjore but, once again, this was no more than a convenient fiction, for it was the Kisans who roamed through the town at will and the police who functioned only at their sufferance. Of the four men who stopped me only one was armed, and I must admit that there was no suggestion of force, but this was in keeping with the spirit of this ghost uprising; the sides were so uneven that there was no question of resistance. I was taken to a nearby village and interned until the local Kisan leadership could talk with me. Under the circumstances it occurred to me that I ought to be frightened, but I discovered that for some reason I wasn't in the least.

[44]

MY BILLET was on the first floor of a deserted mill shed. After I was escorted there by the group that had stopped me, I was invited to make myself comfortable until morning when it would be possible to "arrange for my safe departure." I apparently presented quite a problem to my captors for they didn't know what attitude they ought to take, so I tried to make things as easy as possible by construing my detention as a sort of protective arrest. The four villagers were only too willing to fall in with this and very quickly their original hostility dissolved.

As it developed, I didn't have to wait until morning. Around midnight a young man came to talk with me. As soon as the Kisans had been advised about me they assigned one of their workers to an immediate investigation. When he arrived, their man was all apprehension, apparently envisaging an international incident and even before he appeared to make his apologies I could hear him berating his subordinates outside. He was enormously relieved to find me quite comfortable and ready to dismiss my temporary inconvenience, and understandably so since if I had chosen to do so I could have caused the whole Kisan movement embarrassment.

Actually, things could not have worked out more fortunately. Ever since starting for Tanjore I had wondered how I would make contact with the Kisan leadership and demonstrate my sympathy for the cause of the cultivators. And now suddenly both of our roles were reversed. The organization itself was on the defensive. I had only to be generous and understanding to win at least a measure of trust and good will.

We talked most of the night, the young organizer and I. He was a Brahmin himself, I learned during the conversa-

271

tion, but he had studied in the north and on returning home had found himself unable to fit into the community. Visvanathan was his name. He was about thirty years old but he had a boyish face that made him look less in spite of the fact that his head was half shaven, the remainder of his hair growing long and being knotted at the back. He had joined the Kisans about two years earlier after breaking with his father, a petty zemindar. Since then he had been organizing in the villages of Madras—a thankless job until now, apparently.

But I was far more interested in the Kisans than in Visvanathan and as rapidly as I could I steered our talk toward that subject. I had no idea how long my luck would hold and I intended to exploit it as long as I could. What interested me most was the true relationship between these two words, Kisan and Communist, for in one sentence Visvanathan seemed to imply that they were the same thing and in the next he would speak of them as separate organizations.

When I asked him he explained that actually the Kisans were not affiliated with the Communist Party. In fact, he even expressed some fear at the extent to which his group was being swallowed by the Communists.

"But," he explained, "there seems nothing we can do about it. We know that we can count on the Communists for support, so whenever it comes to some practical issue we must accept their help whether we want it or not."

I asked him what this meant in the case of the Tanjore strike. It was a case in point, he insisted. For more than four years the Kisans had been trying to organize the cultivators for such an effort as this, but they were short of funds, they lacked trained leaders; all of their efforts to date had been abortive. "The Communists have a better organization," he explained. "For years they have been working to develop it in the villages. They have not been seeking mass following as we have but slowly they have been forming a corps of leadership, just one or two men in each community."

I wondered what use they had made of this leadership. Visvanathan said none; they had been gathering strength on the theory that the mass would choose its own time and that they would be there with weapons and slogans. "You see," he explained, "they make us come to them. That way they assume no part of the blame. If a strike like this fails and the strikers starve, why it is the Kisans who are responsible, not the Communists. If it succeeds, it is still their men who are in command and we are bound all the more closely to the party.

"But," he cautioned, "I don't mean that they were sacrificing our interests, for at this stage our interests and theirs are the same. The whole problem in Tanjore is as simple as this: shall the cultivators get a full 50 per cent of the crop? Ten years from now we may be ready to debate the fine points of distinction between our parties. But now there is really only room for two, the prozemindari and the antizemindari."

I asked Visvanathan whether the Communists had formed the same sort of coalition with other parties. He told me that they had; as a matter of fact, their forces were available for almost any peoples' cause. This seemed like excellent strategy to me, for in effect the Communists were making themselves indispensable without ever calling on the people to make a conscious choice whether to support them or not. In very few cases, Visvanathan told me, had they ever argued a program of their own. It had served their purposes far better, apparently, to solicit a practical, undefined good will.

I could see the effect that this was beginning to have. Even Visvanathan, who was relatively sophisticated, tended to speak of the Kisans and the Communists in one breath as if they were factions of one party. How much harder it must be for the average cultivator to make any kind of significant distinction between the men who helped him and called themselves Kisans and those who helped him and called themselves Communists. Gradually, by lending the resources of the party to all the many splinter groups, the Communists were contriving to soak them up the way a dry sponge soaks up water. Nor was their strategy complicated by the fact that the zemindars called everyone who opposed them categorically a Communist. This was the final proof to the untutored ryot that their choice was between supporting the landowners or the party.

And yet I had noticed that Visvanathan, in spite of his lapses, did speak of the Kisans as a separate and distinct group. I asked him to explain why if he consistently worked with them he didn't call himself a Communist and be done with it.

The distinction, he said, was chiefly in the future. He added a great deal that I already knew, that the Communists were working for more than certain changes, that they were anxious ultimately to gain control of the government. "The Kisans," he said, "have no such program. We are interested in improving the conditions of the villager but as long as the government lets us alone we will pick no quarrel with its principles and methods."

"But in practice," I asked, "does it let you alone?"

"No," Visvanathan admitted. "In practice it treats us precisely as it treats the Communist party so that most of the time we must work underground." He cited this strike as an example. "Now that we have made a display of force, the police will not bother us, but if they had been able to apprehend us in the planning stage we all would have been thrown in jail."

He added, "But at least our major interest is not in gaining power for our party. That is why we are willing to use the Communist machinery as long as we can profitably do so."

This seemed like a full stop. I could not imagine anyone speaking seriously of "using" the Communists, but in a sense this was my introduction to Indian communism and I didn't dare assume too definite a position. Instead of arguing the point any further, I asked Visvanathan about this particular strike, for most of what I had heard to date had been little more than rumor, far removed from the source.

Yet my previous understanding had been largely correct. In Tanjore, the traditional crop division had always called for three quarters of the yield to go to the zemindar, one quarter to the farmer. There had been some agitation in previous years but the greatest concession that had ever been wrung was when the Kisans, by themselves, had secured for a minority of their membership something like a third of the crop.

But two months ago the Kisans and the Communists had begun to mobilize for a general strike, not advising the cultivators of their plans till it was nearly time to harvest the crop. In a matter of days the word had gone out through the party organization that a stand was to be made. And even Visvanathan admitted that he had been surprised by the large percentage of agreement it had found.

"Probably," he suggested, "the fact that this was supposed to be a bad year anyway had something to do with it. The conventional 25 or 30 per cent would not have gone far, to judge from the fields. I think it was just a question of starving for something rather than starving for nothing. Anyway that was the slogan that the Communists used and their success has been phenomenal."

I asked Visvanathan how the Kisans were organized. He said that here they were divided into cells, each area being under the supervision of one villager who was responsible for the discipline and morale of his group. Ordinarily there was not much trouble, he said, but it was impossible for the leaders to be everywhere and occasionally, if a strike were long drawn out, there was much bitterness and a certain amount of violence. Already in Tanjore two zemindars had been killed. Visvanathan insisted that they had brought it upon themselves; in both cases they had hired local "goondas" to drive the striking cultivators from their villages. Ordinarily violence was not necessary, however, for organized, the power of the ryot was tremendous and it was seldom that a zemindar was foolish enough to back them into a corner. "Unfortunately," he said, "they usually realize that time is always in their favor. As for the Kisans, we must win a strike immediately if at all; the people do not have staying power."

I asked Visvanathan what he meant by this and he explained that since they had no reserves of food they had to depend on what the neighboring districts could spare from their supply and smuggle in to the strikers. "The trouble," he said, "is that the villager by nature does not see very far beyond the boundaries of his own village. It is hard to convince the headmen that it is to their interests to support a strike in another district."

"But what about the Kisan membership?" I asked.

"It changes overnight," Visvanathan lamented. "While we are striking here the cultivators are loyal, even to the point of risking starvation, but when we are striking somewhere else their interest fails. There is not enough sense of broad unity among us."

I told Visvanathan that this sounded pessimistic. "Don't you think that the strike will succeed?" I asked.

"A single strike never succeeds," he replied. "The best we can do is get some temporary concessions. You see, the ryot suffers for years to get these specific improvements, and then as soon as they are achieved the whole movement falls apart and we have to start over again five years later." What he really hoped for, Visvanathan explained, was the development of confidence on the part of the villagers. When this was established over a wide enough area some significant and permanent improvements could be managed. I wondered, however, whether when such a time came it would be the Kisans who were in the best position to profit. I didn't say it, but it seemed to me that this was the same development for which the Communists were waiting.

I had been bothered all along by Visvanathan's assumption

that the Kisans could take the Communists or let them alone. Actually they were like the man who rode the tiger; everything was all right till he tried to get off. Still I didn't feel that I was yet in a position where I could argue the point without jeopardizing my position, for I knew that whatever Visvanathan said, the Communists were the dominant strength in this area.

Accordingly I raised the practical question; would I be permitted by the Kisans to spend some time in Tanjore? In spite of the friendliness that Visvanathan had shown, he wasn't entirely sure at first. I pressed the advantage that I felt I had gained, citing the fact that I had proved my good faith by dismissing the circumstances of my extraordinary arrest and detention here by the Kisan irregulars. Visvanathan seemed to feel a little uncomfortable but he agreed to plead my case with his superiors, reflecting, I suspect, as I intended that he should, that it was still not too late for me to cause the Kisans trouble. We would proceed to the headquarters in the morning, he decided, and present my petition to those in authority, but I suspect that Visvanathan himself was on my side, for he hinted that I should repeat my strategy there.

[45]

ACTUALLY there was no need for strategy the next day. Like Visvanathan, the men at the Kisan party headquarters were too relieved to feel anything but gratitude and embarrassment when they learned that I did not take my detention seriously. At the time I could not understand all this apprehension but Visvanathan explained to me sometime later that when the report had come in that a European had been detained at the borders, all assumed it was part of the strategy of the zemindars. On arrival, we were the center of excited attention, all present asking nervous questions of Visvanathan, but as soon as he assured them of my sympathy for their cause their anxiety found an outlet in effusive hospitality. It was decided in a brief consultation of the whole group that I should be allowed to spend the next three days in the district, the time being fixed as a matter of necessity since Visvanathan himself could be spared for no longer. Things were sufficiently upset, all present agreed, so that it would not be wise for me to travel by myself, but Visvanathan himself was the first to insist that it be I who plan the entire itinerary.

In a sense I was encouraged by what I saw in Tanjore. That same afternoon we left town and in my bullock cart headed north toward the section of rich paddy land that lies between the Coleroon and its largest tributary. It was here that the bulk of the zemindari estates lay and I was anxious to visit a few of the villages to talk, with Visvanathan acting as interpreter, to the striking cultivators and their families.

The villages generally were on a rather small scale. On our way we passed through a number of them that could not have housed more than a dozen families, just a few huts clustered together on the edges of fields. The zemindars discouraged large concentrations, partly because less time was lost in reaching the fields, but equally because in smaller groups, the cultivators developed less of a corporate identity. Visvanathan explained that the Kisans were always strongest in the traditional villages, much larger than these, where with a hundred or two hundred families there was always a certain sense of community. And indeed, we could notice the difference at once. Unlike Tanjore, in these smaller settlements our reception was grudging and there was no sign at all of enthusiasm and confidence. Several times the cultivators crowded around our cart, glad of the chance to criticize someone, asking Visvanathan when the strike was to be settled and why the Kisans were taking so long. It was clear that these people did not trust anyone, and that they felt they were doing the movement a favor. Visvanathan was patient, but later he explained to me that these people were just so much dead weight to be carried.

The picture was far more encouraging farther on. After we had crossed the lower branch of the river we found ourselves in a richer land and one that seemed more homogeneous and united. For one thing the villages were considerably larger and had more of the air of permanency. This was the heartland, Visvanathan explained, and the real center of the Kisans' strength.

We stopped in one village for an early lunch. We were greeted immediately by all of the inhabitants who came flocking to the house where they heard we were stopping, chanting, singing, and shouting slogans. They brought us food from their meager stores and though Visvanathan and I had brought our own, they refused to allow us to eat it here. We were their guests, be they rich or poor. Their whole temperament and mood seemed different, not only from the suspicious outlanders we had met some while earlier, but from all of the Tamils I had met before; there was a certain casual friendliness that seemed new. I commented on this later and Visvanathan insisted that underneath the majority of Tamils were like this but that in most cases they could show it only in their own families since there was always the menace of the zemindars and upper castes. He explained, "You don't realize it, but if a villager goes about laughing and joking the landlord will decide that he must have stolen a share of grain or must have had an extraordinary yield. Taxes increase, crop shares decrease, until his attitude is more becoming to a Sudra. It is only natural that even in good times the cultivators complain and rub their bellies."

We tried to leave just a few minutes after eating, but the villagers would not let us; they demanded a speech. Visvanathan asked them what they wanted to hear and they replied that they wanted a report on the strike. There was nothing much to tell, but Visvanathan managed to piece together odds and ends of gossip and to conclude from these, however speciously, that the zemindars would soon be yielding. It was enough for the villagers. They hoisted him on their shoulders and marched him around the bazaar for many minutes. Probably they did not really believe what he told them but this was as good an occasion as any for a demonstration.

That afternoon I had a chance to talk with the local cell leader of the Kisans in this village. He was a simple farmer but he knew some English and where we had trouble communicating Visvanathan helped out. The old man was eager to talk to me; he had got the notion and he would not be rid of it that I was in a position to influence the zemindars, perhaps even to decide the strike by myself.

I asked him how long he had been living in this village. He had been born here, he replied, and he expected to die here. For two years he had worked in the mills of Madura but aside from that period he had never lived elsewhere. I asked whether the conditions of the villagers had improved since he was a boy. He said no; they were just about the same. "We have just enough to keep working," he explained. "The zemindars keep it at this level."

I wondered whether, before the Kisans came along, there had been any attempts at organized protest. There had been two attempts in his childhood, he said. In one of them his father, an organizer of the ryot, was dragged from his house and beaten to death by the hired goondas of the local zemindar. Visvanathan added a few details; the old man had been something of a local hero and one reason this section was so strongly Kisan was because of the influence that his son had wielded.

I asked the old man whether such things still happened. "No," he replied, "not since we have organized. About twenty years ago there was a big riot and the zemindars have been more cautious since then."

I was curious how much power the zemindars still wielded. This time I asked Visvanathan. He told me that their power was still enormous and he cited the case of a nearby village that had been evacuated and burned by the order of the zemindars because its people had been felt to be neglecting their fields. "You see," he explained, "the zemindars own the villages and houses as well as the fields themselves. It amounts to owning the villagers too, since to be driven off the land is like a sentence of death."

But how did they acquire these holdings, I wondered. "Acquire? They have always had them," said the old man. "For a hundred generations their people have been landlords and for a hundred generations my people have labored for them."

Visvanathan added, "In some cases this is true. More often, however, the zemindars have expanded by lending money to the independent farmers and then dropping the prices to destroy their markets. Sometimes, too, they lend money to their own villagers so that they are not free to leave even if they can. One of the things that the Kisans have tried to do is pay off these debts which the cultivators have contracted."

The old man touched his forehead as a gesture of thanks. "The Kisans have done that for me," he explained. "When I was young I borrowed quite a large amount before I left to work in Madura at the encouragement of the zemindar, who was anxious to have some control over the man who was a son of my father."

At this point a number of other villagers who had been gathered quietly around us broke into conversation. Each of them, it seemed, had some story to tell that demonstrated how much the Kisans had done. One after the other they spoke of the grievances about which they had scarcely been able to complain for fear the spies of the landlords would hear and have them thrown into jail or beaten.

"Five years ago," one villager told me, "my youngest daughter starved to death because I had complained to the zemindar that his measure was not right; as a punishment he

281

seized my entire crop. I've two daughters and one son left to me now, and we've barely enough food for another three weeks, but if the Kisans want to strike till all of us are dead, I'll do it and I won't regret it this time."

"It's been slow starvation for us anyway," said another. "For five years I've been working three acres of land and taking only a fourth of the crop for myself. It's less painful, I think, to die in a hurry."

"But it's not a matter of dying," said a third. "The zemindars need us more than we need them. If they're convinced that their crops will rot in the fields then they've got to meet our demands."

But it was still another who summed up the whole thing. "What have we got to lose?" he asked bluntly. "None of us has any illusions about this strike; we know that at best it is only a beginning, but all our lives we have been beaten and starved, frightened and theatened and told what to do. Well, now the zemindars can no longer control us. We are like the bullock whose mouth becomes hard to the bit! This strike! Whether we win or lose is not important. What is important is that we have struck in the first place. If for each thousand who die one zemindar is destroyed, it will still be the best bargain we ever got from them!"

It was a bitter philosophy, yet the others nodded. The price apparently seemed reasonable to them. The conversation continued in this strange vein of bitter, cynical optimism.

Yet I wondered whether the villagers really believed what they said. It was one thing to face hunger as an abstract possibility, another to feel the gnawing in your belly and watch your children growing sick and thin. It was encouraging in a way to hear such talk, for it demonstrated a certain basic strength in the cultivators, yet it was pitiful too, for I am sure that all of us knew just how much fear lay behind these boasts.

It was not that I feared that the Kisans' was a lost cause; far from it, for it was inconceivable to me that once begun this village revolution could be stopped anywhere short of absolute victory. But that was just the point. A battle like this is seldom fought on such rational grounds and I wondered how long the cultivators would be willing to work within the legal limits. Already some villages were running short of food. It seemed senseless to expect them to go without when the zemindars' fields were ripe with grain that, but for some obstruse legal ruling, was theirs for the taking.

There was something unreal about the Kisans' whole program. For one thing, it fought with the poorest weapons and in the name of a diverse undisciplined mass it sought to employ the most sophisticated means. How naïve to suppose that the Tamil ryot would have the patience to deal with the old, slow corruptions, that a hundred million people would beg for what they could take just by flexing a muscle.

In the abstract the program of the Kisans was excellent. It was according to the best parliamentary tradition, yet it made precisely the same error as the central government, it used twentieth-century means for twelfth-century ends. The real problem of the villages was the destruction of feudalism, and it was just a belated continuation of that struggle in Europe. Yet the Kisans were trying to wield their mass as if it were a highly organized and educated faction.

Visvanathan had promised me that in my tour of Tanjore we would stop off in at least one of the Communist strongholds. The idea particularly appealed to me now for all the signs of the times seemed to point in their direction. I was anxious to see how much success they had had in organizing on a more activist platform and to learn whether I was right in suspecting that the ryot was just about ready for full-scale revolt. I asked Visvanathan when we would reach one of these pockets. He said there was a large one about thirty miles north. If we traveled all night we ought to be able to reach it by the early part of the next afternoon.

[46]

THE borders of the Communist state were held by a cordon of well-trained peasant militia. After journeying through the night and most of the day, over a land uniformly quiet and fertile, we made contact with the outlying red sentries near the outskirts of a village some forty miles from Tanjore.

We had been traveling east for two days now and the land had not changed appreciably; yet we had noticed that the villages were progressively poorer, the people thinner and more miserably housed. Visvanathan explained that in this strip between the rivers the zemindars had always been particularly powerful and that for some time the political tension had been increasing as a result of the poverty of the cultivators. Some five years ago the Communists had moved in, infiltrating just a few trained leaders at first, but since then the whole district had swung to their cause so that now it was an independent soviet regime. Even the government had no practical power here. The party had been wise enough not to challenge it openly, but there were easier ways of achieving its ends than by expelling the police as they had done in some districts. Near Tanjore the Communists were consolidating whole areas; and the place we were visiting was just one of a large number where they were exerting the power of the ryot as a lever upon the petty officials and the corrupt lower functionaries. It was apparently advantageous to both the government and the party to preserve the fiction of law and order temporarily, yet the quiet grappling was going on throughout Tamilnad, flaring out only occasionally in all its potential violence.

The Communist leader in this area, I discovered, was a blind man named Arunapillai. After passing through the check point on the border of his territory we were taken to his headquarters to see him. Visvanathan explained the purpose of our visit and pleaded my good faith in having come to Tanjore. I was surprised that Arunapillai was as friendly as he was, for I had supposed that I would certainly be met with suspicion, yet his whole manner was the manner of an entertaining prince rather than that of a political intriguer. As a matter of fact, before he had finished Visvanathan found his explanations waved aside. "We have no reason for secrecy in this district!" said Arunapillai. "We will do all that we can to help your friend."

I asked if I could visit some of the nearby villages. Arunapillai assured me he would be delighted if I would do so; apparently he was aware of my initial prejudice and was anxious to dispel it as quickly as possible.

On the surface at least, the villages seemed quite peaceful. There was no strike in this district, for the previous year the Communists had forced down the throats of the zemindars a land-rent system that replaced the share cropping. According to the prevailing terms, the zemindars were awarded a fourth of the cash value of the crop, an arrangement which they accepted, according to Visvanathan, because they realized it was an alternative to receiving nothing. Any time that they wished, the Communist leadership could have requisitioned and collectivized all of the land, but since this would have necessitated an overt revolt they chose to pay off the zemindars and preserve appearances.

The villagers themselves seemed happy and satisfied almost without exception. This was perhaps suspicious in itself, for I doubt that in the program of the Tamil Communists there was much room for honest individual dissent. However, since there had never been any tradition of freedom the cultivators probably did not miss it now. It was a matter of the dictatorship of the proletariat having replaced a dictatorship of a smaller minority.

The Communist organization in the villages was quite extensive. Within limits, the pattern of the zemindar estate was quite adaptable to their own collectivist ends, providing for large-scale operations as it did. Moreover, schooled in the zemindar tradition, these cultivators were accustomed to working as a unit, little room being left for individual initiative and little recognition given for the exceptional individual. To them the whole change seemed advantageous; this system provided them a far better living. And if they still were expected to take orders without question? Well, that was nothing that they had not done before.

In one village I talked to a young farmer who had migrated to the Communist area from the adjoining district. He had been here for only two weeks, he told me, but already he had sent back for his wife and children. His reasons were simple for preferring life here. "In the first place," he said, "there is enough to eat. Our leaders make sure there is plenty of food before they give the zemindars their share. Where I was we were hungry half of the time; there was never enough so that we could save for bad years, but now we always have plenty to eat and sometimes even enough to sell for cash."

I asked whether he hadn't given up some of his freedom, but I sensed the weakness of the question as I was saying it. There was no freedom to lose for the cultivator, he replied, and of course in the largest sense that was true.

Some time during that day I asked Visvanathan how he felt about this soviet experiment. It was obvious that he was much impressed by it, for all his protests that he was a Kisan, and not a Communist. "But you see," he argued weakly, "this is only a beginning. I believe in what the party is doing here but I think that the condition of the cultivator can be improved without the revolution at which all this is aimed."

"Visvanathan," I said, "you'd have a hard time, I'm afraid, talking to the ryot about your *ends* and *means*. If most of them ever thought that they could come this far in so short a time they would not care about the rest."

"Perhaps," he said, "but I can't help feeling that improvements achieved our way would be more permanent and less costly."

I agreed, but I couldn't help wondering how far Visvanathan's argument would carry the villager.

[47]

THE last day of my stay in the Tanjore district found us, once again, at Arunapillai's headquarters. We had traveled almost all of the previous night, for I was anxious for this one last chat with the old man. Having seen the physical circumstances of the area and having got from Visvanathan some conception of its history, I hoped to supplement this practical knowledge with some idea of the psychology of Tamil communism.

Arunapillai was more than willing to talk. He had been working with the Communists for about twenty-five years and he enjoyed relating his experiences during that time and telling me how much conditions had changed. During World War I he had been a Socialist organizer until he was jailed for two years without trial by the British. In that time he had grown sufficiently bitter to join the Communists immediately upon release. It was an accident, he said, but a fortunate one for like the Kisans, the Socialists were not a force to be reckoned with. Both of them, according to Arunapillai's dogma, lacked the courage to face the major issues.

Visvanathan took good-natured objection to this, saying the Kisans had a separate aim. Arunapillai snapped back that their aims were the same but that the Kisans were simply not facing the facts. "The trouble with you," he told Visvanathan, "is that you are afraid to admit the strength that you wield. Why, if you wished, and had the courage, you could settle your strike tomorrow just by seizing a few of the landlords."

"Ayi, but that solves nothing permanently," said Visvanathan.

"It is the only permanent solution," replied Arunapillai. "Your bargains and contracts ignore the fact that the land should really be yours in the first place. Like so many pye-dogs begging for scraps—you Kisans who starve while rice rots in the field! For two years we have been governing ourselves up here. You say we do not have the permanent solution?"

I asked Arunapillai where this local communism fitted into the party plan for all India. "It is no secret," he said. "This is only the beginning. We are erupting all over the south already." He confirmed what Visvanathan had already told me, that these local colonies would continue to grow till at last they were too many for the government to handle. Then they would "assert their control" he said.

I wondered whether the colonies all followed the same pattern. "With minor exceptions," my host replied. "It depends, of course, on the strength in each area but at least the basic strategy is the same. Here in Tanjore where we are especially well organized, we can maintain an almost total control of the land, but in other places we can sometimes manage to assert ourselves only for short periods of time." Southeast of Tanjore there was a group of villages that had been organized by the Communists on more transient lines. For a year they had been able to hold out against the government but just a few months ago their hold had relaxed. "We could see that the issue was coming to a head and we were not prepared for that," Arunapillai said. "But next year when things have been quiet a while longer we will be able to seize control again."

The mechanism of this bloodless revolution interested me. "Just how do you manage to do this?" I asked. Arunapillai explained that they worked through the government, exploiting its very corruption and opportunism, applying pressure on the local officers and making them follow the party line.

"But I thought that the police were with the zemindars," I objected.

"They are not *with* anyone," Arunapillai corrected me. "They are anxious only to keep their jobs and preserve the appearance of order at the least cost to themselves. Well, where we are most powerful they do as we say or we contrive to make their jobs impossible. If I say to the government police in this village, 'Officers, arrest this zemindar for stealing,' they know they must do it just as everywhere else they know they must take the orders of the zemindar. In its weakness the government works for anyone who can make its simple police function most easy, who can promise enough force to give it at least some appearance of authority and strength."

Still I wondered why, if the Communists were so strong, they even bothered to work through legal channels. I knew that it was certainly not their innate propensity for doing things in the accepted fashion. "Temporarily it is most expedient," Arunapillai explained. In previous years the Communists had worked for some vaguely planned general uprising of the masses, but they had discovered that this was an impossible goal. "Even now," he said, "where we are working in small groups, it is easy for the government to pick us up. But here—" he laughed—"we can wait in safety till other areas have been educated to their needs."

But I still could not see why in Tanjore itself the Communists paid lip service to the government power. But Arunapillai insisted that though they were strong in this district, there was still a practical reason for caution. "This way," he said, "they cannot strike against us. They can march troops through the district without breaking our hold. Our strength is scattered all over the countryside; there is no army, no government that can be met head on!"

"But what is the end of all this then?" I asked. "An eventual revolution all over India?" No, Arunapillai replied that this depended entirely on what I meant by revolution.

"If you're thinking of war and bloodshed, then no, for there can be wars only between equal factions. By the time that we are ready to take a stand our power in the villages will be unchallenged," he said. He went on to explain that this was basic to communism, the theory that the old forms gradually destroy themselves, and he suggested, perhaps ingenuously, that the party was not really seizing power so much as falling heir to it.

"Actually there is no government now," he said. "We are in the process of establishing a government here. The babus in Delhi all take themselves seriously but they don't govern India any more than I do; India is governed from the villages and by the villages. Delhi is no more than a reflection, a shadow." He asked, "Where did you find the police in Tanjore? They hide as soon as any trouble starts. The government can't help us or hurt us. The Brahmins and zemindars are the real forces to be reckoned with." He laughed. "It is always like this. While things are peaceful the government is everywhere in evidence, brass buttons and swagger sticks on every corner, ordering us to be doing what we are doing anyway. As long as the government rides along with tradition it can preserve some illusion of its own importance, but when an issue arises? It goes underground. It closes up shop and takes down its sign."

I was amused at this way of putting the thing. On the surface it seemed to be fairly accurate, yet I suspected it was possible that Arunapillai was intentionally oversimplifying a little. I told him I had heard that the government was even now making some effort to settle the Tanjore strike. It was, he granted, but as usual its terms were precisely those of the zemindars themselves. "This strike has proved embarrassing," he explained. "It has come at a bad time from the government's point of view, for the legislators have been trying to bury a bill calling for the distribution of the larger estates. It is one of those things that Congress was promising years before we got independence, and now they're having a rather difficult time in keeping it out of their minds and consciences."

Wasn't it true, though, I wondered, that the Madras Presidency itself had already passed a bill abolishing the zemindars? Arunapillai said that it was, but he felt that it only strengthened his own case. "They have passed a bill but they do nothing," he laughed. "It is not their fault; there is nothing they can do till the issue has been thrashed out and decided in the villages. And then, of course, no bill will be needed.

"Understand," he continued, "I have no quarrel with the government if you want to insist that such a thing exists. Delhi and Madras do their pitiful best to keep peace on the terms that are dictated from the villages. But I am trying to tell you why it never will be necessary for the Communists to launch large-scale revolution in India. When the decision is made on the village level, Delhi will follow like the tail of a dog. And even on the village level, I doubt that it will ever be necessary to wage much of a fight. The whole program is one of education really. You can laugh if you want, but there it is."

But I didn't laugh. In the first place, while I was able to see the vital weakness of the Communist position, I knew very well that for the average villager this smooth dialectic would be almost irresistible. I didn't laugh because, while I distrusted Arunapillai, I knew there were millions of cultivators who did not.

Actually there was even more involved than Tamilnad. The south was advanced politically, perhaps, but its problems were the problems of every village area and if this section should go Communist the whole country would follow.

If this section should go Communist . . . I wondered whether there was really much chance that it would not. Certainly there was no other party or program that was able to offer the ryot half so much. Nor was it at all to the point to list the good reasons why the villagers ought to be wary of communism. All of the evils of a collective government were evils to which the cultivator was inured.

If I were to argue myself I wondered what I would say. Could I threaten the villagers with a loss of freedom? They would laugh in my face, they who have lived for generations in a society where the concept is unknown. Could I point out that communism ignores the individual? They would scarcely choose to be treated as individuals if only as a mass their conditions could be improved, if as a group they could secure enough to eat.

Perhaps, I decided, I really had no business deciding what was best for the villagers anyway. It was far too easy for me, well fed and comfortable, to dispose of what to them were life and death problems. Perhaps, I decided, if I were a villager I would not be so concerned with intangible virtues. The desire for freedom and for self-expression is probably much less basic than sheer physical hunger.

Visvanathan was apparently as disturbed as I was. When we rode off in the direction of Tanjore that evening he was reluctant to talk about Arunapillai's arguments except to dismiss them with the most general criticisms. "He is a clever talker," he admitted grudgingly, "but all of us know what communism has done elsewhere." And later he reflected, "Perhaps the Kisans are making a mistake in working closely with these people."

But I knew perfectly well what was bothering Visvanathan. It was the same thing that was bothering me. I think both of us realized, fearfully and yet finally, that the time, the place, and the party had met.

Concluding

Concluding

[48]

THE monsoons were almost upon us. As I said good-by to Visvanathan and rode out of Tanjore the wind was blowing from the southwest quarter, swirling the dust of the road into my eyes and my mouth.

It was a gray, quiet day when I left Tanjore, the sky overcast with a stratified haze that hung sulkily over the entire landscape draining the scene of its accustomed colors. The roads were gray under the dull, dry dust and spinning it in little whirlpools as I turned my tired bullocks toward the north.

Perhaps I only remember it that way, but it seems that my spirits were a dull gray too; I was not depressed but I was very tired, exhausted by too many strange, new experiences. In some vague sense I was headed toward Koornool on the border of Hyderabad and the Indian Dominion, where the central government was massing its troops for an assault on the Moslem government of that state. Perhaps I only remember it that way, but I don't think that I really expected to reach there. In a subjective sense my trip was complete and I felt as if anything else would be an anticlimax.

It was about two weeks out of Tanjore that it happened. The sky had cleared, the calm before the storm, and once again the sun was lashing down with an animate, passionate, sensual malevolence. I had sold my cart and I was traveling on foot over the country just west of the eastern ghats, in a burst of ridiculous overconfidence, trying to cover thirty miles in a single day. About noon I began to feel a little bit queer but I had been on short-water rations and I ascribed it to that, so I stopped in a village to fill my canteen with water, which the villagers freshly boiled for me. It was still hot when I left the village but I drank the water, sweating it out as fast as it went down, and for a while at least it answered the purpose, for the weakness that I had felt some time earlier disappeared.

My first signs that something was seriously wrong came just an hour or so later near another village. Suddenly I stopped perspiring entirely and my skin became peculiarly dry and cool. Other than that I felt perfectly all right, but it frightened me terribly for I had often before seen cases of heat exhaustion among the villagers and I knew that it frequently began with just these symptoms. I still might have been all right if I had kept calm, but I was afraid of collapsing before I could reach some shade and, my nerve gone completely, I began to run for a covered well about a quarter of a mile away. There was a farmer nearby, irrigating his field, and I began to shout to attract his attention, but his back was toward me and I remember hoping that when he plowed the next furrow he would see me if I fell.

I did fall. All at once my knees gave way and red spots began to swim before my eyes. The next thing I knew I was stretched out in the sand trying to raise my head to look at the farmer.

I was taken to the village. It was like a nightmare sleep, for I never completely lost consciousness and I remember that even in spite of the sharp pain that flickered back and forth behind my eyes I kept asking to be taken to the nearest railway and put on a train for Madras or Cuddapah. I was put on a train, but one of the villagers went with me as far as the closest railway hospital. And it was there some two days later that I awoke to a reasonable degree of sanity and confidence.

[49]

MY TRIP was over. I did not have to be told by the friendly Anglo-Indian doctor in charge that I had suffered a rather serious attack of heat exhaustion and that it would be necessary for me to rest for a few weeks. One look at the clean sheets on the bed where I lay, one drink of cool water from a covered pitcher, one meal of boiled liver served from plates was enough to rob me of any resistance.

By the third day of my stay I was feeling quite well. Before that I had a rather miserable time, for I had to stay in a darkened room and every stray ray of light was like a stab in my eyes. Each evening I was violently sick to my stomach and I was able to keep down only light foods, but when this passed I began to enjoy myself and revel in the unaccustomed animal comforts.

It was a startling change and for a while it was almost as if I were suffering from a state of temporary amnesia, for my normal life seemed to join together leaving just a seam representing the last six months. Once again I was getting a paper every day and hearing the news broadcasts over All India Radio, and so flexible is the mind of man in its deceptions, I was convinced that I had returned to "the real world."

A great deal had happened since I had left that world. I had kept track of the major developments, of course, but in the last six months I had been busy myself and the details at least were hazy in my mind. Dr. Shanmugam Chetti, I learned from the headlines, was drawing up a new budget for the Madras Presidency and a yogi in Bombay had been buried for ten days in a state of suspended animation. A farmer in Iowa had married his niece, who was twelve years old to his seventy-five, and in all respects the world was proceeding just about as usual.

It was nearly a week before the memory of my trip had

healed enough so that I dared to touch it. Even then, I preferred my newspapers and novels and a radio program called "America Calling." My real world was composed of such things as this and my real world had delicate walls, so delicate that even a thought could destroy them and reveal the sordid view outside. Yet I couldn't actually forget, of course. India . . . the villages . . . it was all too close. It was my ragged tooth, my Moby Dick, everything there is that repelling attracts. Yet I could hardly separate the memory of the trip from the memory of the stroke that brought it to a close, so that thinking of Kathiawar, Maharashtra, Tamilnad was almost like having a physical relapse.

And yet there it was, sprawling and dirty. There they were. Four hundred million people. The smells and the crying and the births and the dying were all around me and there was no escaping. I would think it through just once, I decided, relive the whole memory in order to be rid of it, arrange six months and twenty-three hundred miles into some sort of rational order if I could.

And yet the first fact loomed so large I could hardly see around it. It was the fact of the atrocious poverty of village India; even starvation and famine could not measure its depths, for it was like something malignant with a life of its own. This memory I could no longer differentiate; it was a mass of hoarse cries and protruding bones, the smell of disease in a thousand villages, the smoke of a hundred burning ghats. It was a deep, visceral memory that cut through all the mythology of the splendor and glory of ancient India, but it was like a two-edged sword for it cut as well against the mythology of a simple but happy people. India was neither simple nor happy but complex and miserable, involved and squalid, the breath of its people coming labored and uneven through the weight and mass of superstition and ignorance.

One was tempted, of course, to blame the government; its very ineffectuality was maddening in itself. Its whole policy since independence had been one of dazed acceptance of the old regime. At the beginning there had been talk of sweeping reforms, but when the leaders saw what these reforms would mean they decided that they would have to be put off temporarily, at least till the new government had found itself. Yet what Nehru and all of the others had forgotten was that the first actions of a new government are all important and that they inevitably lead to further commitments so that the whole direction of a regime can be decided in the first months. They had forgotten, or ignored the fact, that once the power is delivered into the hands of one group it is there to stay till it is wrested from them, regardless of the nature of the original understanding. Already the liberals of the Congress regime were discovering the extent to which they were committed by positions that they had branded temporary and expedient to policies that they now discovered were neither.

Actually the choice had been a simple one, whether to begin with a sweeping rebuilding of the government or to accept the forms that the British had left and allow themselves to be committed to them. And the basis for deciding was likewise simple. It was a question of whether you wanted reform or order. The whole organization of India was so rotten that it would have been impossible ever to reconcile the two.

The government had apparently chosen to preserve order. At any rate it had established its whole contact with the nation through the medium of an involved and corrupt bureaucracy that was interested only in preserving its great self. Nehru spoke of the freedom of the people, yet I had talked with three editors who had been jailed for criticizing him. Mrs. Pandit talked roundly of the rights of the cultivators while the provisional legislature tabled the reform bills. And the tragedy was, these people were sincere. But they had made the mistake of starting on the wrong foot. Now, try as they might, they were forever out of step with the people of India and the real good of the country.

Even the murder of Gandhi had been virtually white-washed at the insidious demand of the rightist congressmen. The whole issue had been dismissed as if it were a matter for police action when actually it raised important political questions. The Mahasabha and the R.S.S. were outlawed and a few of their less important leaders were jailed. But what of the pro-Mahasabha wing of Congress? At last reports it was thriving.

The essential error that the liberals had made was accepting the heretical and cowardly doctrine that the first job of a government is to preserve the peace, by any means possible. Actually, of course, the first duty of Congress was to assist and legalize the necessary revolution that would unseat the privileged castes from power and lead to economic if not political democracy. But instead the congressmen had transformed almost unrecognizably from courageous rebels who had gone to prison for their beliefs, to the all-too-respectable representatives of the State who wanted above all else to keep their newly won powers. Compromise, temporize, pacify had been their slogans and on these pillars they had built their nation. The only thing wrong was that the new "Free India" was almost indistinguishable from the vassal of Britain. The Congress machinery was so afraid of justifying the dire predictions of its erstwhile masters that in its frantic effort to do as well it compromised on doing the same things. What India needed was a revolutionary leadership that would tear down the rotting props of the old order; what it got was a change of leadership at the top and a polite note stating that the claims would be considered.

Yes, it was easy to blame the central government. It had been weak and stupid and jealous of its new power. Yet it was not entirely just to blame the government for the situation that existed in the first place.

Every scholar of Indian history will agree that properly

speaking the British never conquered India. They appeared on the scene amidst a natural dissolution and provided a synthetic and temporary catalyst. Their "control" of the country was a tenuous balancing of the interests of one group against the interests of another and what "power" it wielded it wielded by virtue of the incredible weakness of the country itself. It had been all too easy for Congress to continue this. Perhaps in the end, it would be asking too much to expect any legally constituted government to begin by destroying the basis of its power. The problem went back to the villages really, and to the decline, the corruption of their way of life, back to the pavilion, back to the palace, back, especially, to the temple.

It was necessary, I knew, to make the distinction between the literary, the idealized Hinduism and the real, between the welter of bad poetry and mediocre sophistry which myopic western mystics and retired Methodist ministers unearth by dint of long study in the Vedas, and the sordid reality of tribalism and superstition which it so often amounts to in its degenerate practice. In Hinduism a villager's death by starvation is not a sign of some social maladjustment. According to the present corruptions it is the right and proper workings of the law of Karma. The refugees from the Tinnevelly famine—they were not symptoms of some deficiency in the economic order. They were not even to be pitied, for in previous incarnations they had earned whatever humiliation they suffered. Misery, squalor, death, and disease—all were accepted, not as necessary evils, but as the laudable instruments of the gods' retribution and therefore beyond all mortal criticism.

I could never help feeling that these vast distortions were not really disinterested on the part of the Brahmins; as keepers of the religious law and doctrine it had been easy for them to manipulate it to serve their own ends. It was altogether too convenient that though they had originally been constituted as a band of scholars, leaders of the spirit, they

301

had lately turned into a sort of landed aristocracy in spite of the laws enjoining them to poverty. Corruption was perhaps too charitable a name to use for these gradual distortions of the scripture, for corruption suggests an irresistible process. This was nothing but simple conspiracy.

And yet even if one was able to trace the "blame" . . . Would that help in finding some solution to the problem? Probably it would not, but it might well suggest from what direction that solution eventually might come.

I was sick to death of those who prate of "the glorious traditions of India." Certainly the villagers could derive no hope from the idea of return to some earlier period. Actually the "glorious traditions of India" are traditions of slavery and continual despotism. Even in the so-called golden ages there was less political freedom than in Nazi Germany. Perhaps the architecture of these periods is glorious but those very temples are monuments to slave labor, built by workmen driven on by the whip and ornamented by craftsmen who died for their errors. If India looks backward it can see nothing but a tradition of misery and serfdom for her common people, yawning centuries of poverty and fear which no buildings or shrines or temples can change. "The glory that was India" is still to be seen, in Maharajas' palaces and among the ornate ruins. It was never in existence anywhere else. Certainly it was not something for the common man.

There were times in my long months of touring through the villages when I felt that perhaps there were no solutions, that perhaps Asia was already beginning to prove that the progress of the race is not inevitable. There were times during my first few days in the hospital when I wondered if this might not be the reversal of evolution, the first awful steps in that downward march that would lead again to the Silurian sea bottoms. If one thought of India in terms of her problems it was infinitely depressing, deeply discouraging, and it was possible to go on in an agony of doubt till the whole problem seemed philosophical more than political.

And yet it was at times like this that I would think of the people that I had come to know in the various villages. It was at times like this that the raucous laughter of the Halvad durbars would ring in my ears. It was at these depressing moments that I would think of some joke that had passed between my Kanarese guide and me or the good and happy times that I had spent with the rebellious men of Bursad.

When idea fails, one goes back to the fact, and the fact in India is life rather than death. It is violence and hunger and pain and fear, and yet with all this misery the fact is still life. In a sense it was a philosophic problem and perhaps it needed a philosophic answer. I decided that with India as with the rest of the world, the worst, and the best, are still ahead.

Glossary

OF THE VILLAGE IDIOM

anna   An Indian coin, formerly worth about two cents and now worth about one and one quarter cents.

Ayurveda   The Hindu system of naturopathic and homeopathic medicine, first enunciated and advocated in vedic scripture.

babu   An Indian bureaucrat or shopkeeper, generally assumed to be avaricious and unimaginative, often to be slavish and corrupt.

bajri   A tall cereal grass which provides one of the staples of diet in western India.

bania   A subdivision of the Vaisaya or tradesman-shopkeeper caste, now almost universally assumed to be selfish, avaricious, and corrupt.

betel   The nutlike seed of a variety of palm tree, chewed throughout India for its medicinal and slightly narcotic effects.

Bhagavad-Gita   A section of the Mahabharata containing an extended dialogue between Krishna and Arjuna; now the Bible of Hinduism.

Brahmin   The highest caste in the Hindu social structure, traditionally enjoying numerous prerogatives and theoretically dedicated to poverty, piety, and learning.

chapatty   In north and central India, a thin fried cake of unleavened bread.

charpoy The rude bed used by some Indian villagers, constructed of tapes or rope stretched over a square frame.

dacoit A professional thief and killer, usually a member of a well-organized band.

dal A coarse Indian pea.

dewan The chief administrative officer of a native state.

dharma Literally, duty, but indicative of the whole Hindu conception of virtue and conformity.

dharmsala A shelter or porch maintained by most villagers for the use of official or privileged visitors.

dhoti A short, skirtlike garment worn in any of several modes by the men of most sections of India.

durbar (1) In western India, a petty baron or local representative of the ruling rajah. (2) A gathering where the vassals of a rajah or chief appear to acknowledge their fealty; now loosely used to refer to any testimonial gathering.

Ganesh One incarnation of the Hindu godhead, the symbol of wisdom and prudence; the "elephant god."

ghats Hills or mountains; sometimes the small elevations built for cremation of the dead.

goonda A professional thug or terrorist.

guru Teacher, generally on subjects of religion and the spirit.

harijan Literally, "child of god"; Gandhi's name for the untouchable class.

Jain A member of a religious sect which has roots in Brahminism, Buddhism, and Hinduism, its members being distinguished by their ritual reverence for all life forms.

jowar   A dark coarse grain used to make bread for general cookery in western India.

khaddar   A rough-textured cloth, spun and woven by the wearer as a testament of loyalty to Gandhi's principle of economic self-sufficiency.

karma   A word referring generally to the system of duty, causality, and retribution elaborated in Hindu scripture.

koli   In western India, a subdivision of the Sudra or laboring caste; a "criminal caste," one discriminated against by law because of a general notion of the dishonesty of its members.

Kshatriya   A member of the second highest, or warrior, caste

lakh   A unit of one hundred thousand.

lathi   A heavy staff carried by police and military officials and employed as a club in dispersing riots, demonstrations, etc.

Mahabharata   The last of the epic poems which comprise the historical scripture of Hinduism.

Mahasabha   The militantly rightist organization dedicated to the preservation of the Hindu way of life, particularly to the economic and social traditionalism which Hinduism represents.

maidan   A park or field used for public meetings and assemblies.

Manipuri   Native to Manipur, the easternmost section of India.

naik   A subordinate officer in the Indian Army.

neem   A tree, common to most of India, whose twigs have a medicinal property and are shredded for the cleaning of teeth, etc.

paddy Rice, in its refined or unrefined state.

panchayat Literally, "council of five," and in practice, the body of elders chosen in many village areas to decide civil and administrative questions.

Parsi A descendant of the Zoroastrian fire worshipers who came to India from Persia under the pressure of Mohammedan persecutions in the seventh and eighth centuries.

peepul A large tree growing over most of India and given a certain religious veneration by most Hindus for the shelter it traditionally affords the traveler, senayasi, sadhu, and pilgrim.

pye-dog A stray dog attached to, and tolerated by, one village or a particular area; ordinarily diseased, malnourished, and evil tempered toward strangers.

Rani The wife of a rajah or the feminine ruler of an Indian state.

Raj The common referent term for the force and instruments of the British Empire in India.

Rajput A native of Rajputana in western India, a member of the Kshatraya or warrior caste, descended from the one-time rulers of central India.

Rashtraya Swayamsevak Sangh The violently reactionary activist organization which planned and executed the murder of Gandhi; literally, "Society for the Preservation of Hindu Culture."

rupee The largest unit of Indian currency, formerly worth about thirty-three cents, now worth about twenty cents.

ryot The Indian peasantry; the body of cultivators and small landowners.

sadhu An ascetic or penitent Hindu holy man, often dedicated to vows of poverty, homelessness, and fasting.

sahib The respectful term employed by servants to their masters and by most lower-caste Indians to Europeans generally.

sangh Society or organization.

senyasi An elderly Hindu who has retired to a life of contemplation and penitence.

Sikh A member of a latter-day religious offshoot of Hinduism which is notable for its contribution of manpower to the British forces in India.

Siva One of the supreme Hindu deities, nominal patron of the Sivite sect of Hinduism, the most strict and authoritarian.

Sudra A member of the lowest, or laboring, caste, in the Hindu social structure, including cultivators, seepers, pariahs, etc.

swaraj Literally, "freedom," and the slogan of the Indian independence movement.

taluk An administrative subdivision comparable in size and importance to a township in America.

todi The fermented sap of one variety of palm tree, and the common intoxicant of the Indian villager.

untouchables The large body of casteless Hindus, avoided and ignored because religious and social doctrine does not acknowledge their existence and hence does not provide any laws or regulations governing their place in the Hindu hierarchy.

Upanishad One of the later philosophic treatises from the vedic literature.

Vaisya A member of the third, or tradesman, caste of the Hindu social structure, including shopkeepers, artisans, moneylenders, etc.

Vedas The body of hymns, charms, verses, chants, prayers, etc. which comprise the earliest Hindu liturgy and scripture.

zemindar A large landowner or proprietor, in some sections exercising broad feudal and quasi-governmental powers over the villages located on his lands.